WITHDRAWN

POETS OF OHIO

POETS OF OHIO

SELECTIONS REPRESENTING THE POETICAL WORK
OF OHIO AUTHORS FROM THE PIONEER
PERIOD TO THE PRESENT DAY, WITH
BIOGRAPHICAL SKETCHES
AND NOTES

EDITED BY
EMERSON VENABLE

CINCINNATI
THE ROBERT CLARKE COMPANY
MDCCCCIX

Republished by Gale Research Company, Book Tower, Detroit, 1974

Library of Congress Cataloging in Publication Data

Venable, Emerson, 1875-   ed.
  Poets of Ohio.

  Includes bibliographical references.
  1. American poetry--Ohio. 2. Poets,
American--Ohio--Biography. I. Title.
[PS571.O3V4   1974]   811'.008   73-18459
ISBN 0-8103-3622-7

PREFACE

THIS volume was compiled for the purpose of supplying libraries, reading circles, public schools, and colleges, with a convenient anthology fairly representing the rich and diversified poetical achievement of Ohio authors, from the pioneer period to the present day.

The student wishing further to extend his knowledge of the poetry of the Buckeye State, is referred to the bibliographic lists given in the Appendix.

To Dr. F. B. Dyer, Superintendent of Public Schools of Cincinnati, at whose suggestion the volume was prepared with special reference to educational demands, the editor gratefully records his obligation for many helpful criticisms, and for encouragement received from commendatory words endorsing the book as a desirable repository of select verse comprising abundant and varied material for reading supplementary to the prevailing intermediate and high-school courses in American literature.

Special acknowledgment is rendered to Mr. I. Benjamin, for his courtesy in furnishing original photographs of several of the writers whose portraits appear in the frontispiece; to the Historical and Philosophical Society of Ohio, which loaned for reproduction the rare silver-print cabinet-picture of Phoebe Cary; and to Mr. Anthony Bill, (with Mr. Benjamin,) for preparing the group of likenesses from which the half-tone was made.

Thanks are due to the Houghton Mifflin Co. for the privilege of reprinting poems by W. D. Howells, Edith M. Thomas, and Alice and Phoebe Cary; to Harper & Brothers, for poems by W. D. Howells and Alice Archer S. James; to Rand, McNally & Co., for poems by Coates Kinney; to Dodd, Mead & Co., for poems by W. H. Venable; to The Century Co., for poems by Alice

PREFACE

Archer S. James, John Bennett, Henry H. Bennett, and Alice Williams Brotherton; to the J. B. Lippincott Co., for poems by Thomas Buchanan Read; to Little, Brown & Co., for poems by Sarah C. Woolsey; to The Robert Clarke Co., for poems by William D. Gallagher and William H. Lytle; to Richard G. Badger, for poems by Edith M. Thomas and W. H. Venable; to the Atlantic Monthly, for poems by Alice W. Brotherton; to the Youth's Companion, for a poem by H. H. Bennett; and to Dodd, Mead & Co., for poems by Paul Laurence Dunbar.

In the preparation of this anthology some two hundred volumes, comprising the published verse of more than one hundred Ohio writers, were examined. The editor had frequent occasion to consult the pages of various standard works of reference, among which he would specially mention: Coggeshall's The Poets and Poetry of the West (1860); Stedman's An American Anthology (1901); Venable's Beginnings of Literary Culture in the Ohio Valley (1891); Venable's Literary Men and Women of Ohio (1904); Gallagher's Selections from the Poetical Literature of the West (1841); Thomson's Bibliography of Ohio (1880); Biographical Cyclopædia of Ohio (1887); Adams's A Dictionary of American Authors (1902); and Who's Who in America (1908-9).

Thanks are returned to Mr. N. D. C. Hodges, of the Public Library of Cincinnati; to Mr. C. B. Galbreath, of the Ohio State Library, Columbus; to Mr. W. H. Brett, of the Public Library of Cleveland; and to Mr. Herbert Putnam, of the Library of Congress, Washington, D. C.,— for the loan of numerous publications now out of print. E. V.

Cincinnati, Ohio,
September, 1909.

CONTENTS

WILLIAM DAVIS GALLAGHER (1808-1894) PAGE
   Biographical Sketch 15
   Extracts from "Miami Woods:"
      The Primeval Forest... 17
      Glimpses of June... 18
      Autumn 19
      Indian Summer 19
      The Coming of Winter... 22
      In Memoriam 22
   The Song of the Pioneers... 26
   The Spotted Fawn... 29
   "Ah! Well-a-way!" 30
   May 31
   August 31
   Truth and Freedom... 33
   Conservatism 33

JULIA A. DUMONT (1794-1857)
   Biographical Sketch 34
   The Future Life.. 35

EDWARD A. McLAUGHLIN (1798-?)
   Biographical Sketch 37
   The Seminole 38
   Extract from "The Lovers of the Deep:"
      "Poor Have I Lived"... 41

HARVEY D. LITTLE (1803-1833)
   Biographical Sketch 42
   On Judah's Hill.. 43

OTWAY CURRY (1804-1855)
   Biographical Sketch 44
   The Lost Pleiad.. 46
   The Goings Forth of God... 47
   To a Midnight Phantom... 48
   Buckeye Cabin 49

POETS OF OHIO

FREDERICK WILLIAM THOMAS (1811-1866)   PAGE
  Biographical Sketch 51
  Extracts from "The Emigrant:"
    Daniel Boone 52
    The Indian 53
  'Tis Said that Absence Conquers Love........................ 54

LEWIS FOULKE THOMAS (1815-1868)
  Biographical Sketch 56
  Love's Argument 56

CHARLES A. JONES (1815-1851)
  Biographical Sketch 58
  Tecumseh 59
  The Old Mound.. 61

DANIEL DECATUR EMMETT (1815-1904)
  Biographical Sketch 63
  Dixie 64

ALICE CARY (1820-1870)
  Biographical Sketch 66
  Balder's Wife 68
  Pictures of Memory.. 69
  Now, and Then.. 71
  Tricksey's Ring 72
  The Gray Swan.. 77
  Idle 79
  Nobility 80
  An Order for a Picture... 81
  "Thy works, O Lord, interpret Thee"...................... 82
  My Dream of Dreams... 82

PHOEBE CARY (1824-1871)
  Biographical Sketch 83
  Our Homestead 84
  The Only Ornament.. 85
  True Love 87
  Song 88
  Vain Repentance 88
  A Weary Heart.. 88

THOMAS BUCHANAN READ (1822-1872)
  Biographical Sketch 90
  Sheridan's Ride 91

CONTENTS

THOMAS BUCHANAN READ (1822-1872)— *Con.*   PAGE
  Drifting 93
  The Closing Scene 96

WILLIAM JAMES SPERRY (1823-1856)
  Biographical Sketch 99
  A Lament for the Ancient People 100

WILLIAM PENN BRANNAN (1825-1866)
  Biographical Sketch 102
  Extracts from "Saint Mary's Hospital:"
    "The east is red with beacon-fires" 102
    "The sunshine flashes down the walls" 103
    "And where is he that died today?" 103
    "I will not bow with patient knees" 104
    "I envy every bird that flies" 105

HELEN LOUISA BOSTWICK BIRD (1826-1907)
  Biographical Sketch 106
  Drafted 107
  My Mountain 109
  My Island 109
  My River 110
  My Lake 111
  So Many Times 111
  How the Gates Came Ajar 112
  The Lost Image 113
  The Little Coffin 114
  In the Fisher's Hut 115
  Too Fine for Mortal Ear 116

WILLIAM HAINES LYTLE (1826-1863)
  Biographical Sketch 117
  Antony and Cleopatra 119
  Popocatapetl 120
  Macdonald's Drummer 122
  Brigand's Song 124
  Anacreontic 126
  In Camp 127
  "When the Long Shadows" 128

COATES KINNEY (1826-1904)
  Biographical Sketch 129
  Extracts from "Mists of Fire:"
    Oneirode 134
    Antoneirode 137

COATES KINNEY — Con.

	PAGE
To an Old Appletree	139
Miscellaneous Extracts	141
Consummation	145
"Did I Not Realize?"	146
Ships Coming In	146
Child Lost	148
Egypt	149
Rain on the Roof	151

FLORUS BEARDSLEY PLIMPTON (1830-1886)

Biographical Sketch	153
Summer Days	156
The Reformer	157
Pittsburg	159
In Remembrance	159
Return	160
Springtime	161
Waiting to Die	161

BENJAMIN RUSSEL HANBY (1833-1867)

Biographical Sketch	163
Darling Nelly Gray	163

JOHN JAMES PIATT (1835—)

Biographical Sketch	165
King's Tavern	169
Honors of War	170
Sonnet — in 1862	171
The Golden Hand	172
The Morning Street	173
The Open Slave-Pen	175
A Lost Kingdom of Gods	176
Farther	177
The Book of Gold	177
Sundown	178
A Voice in Ohio	178
Taking the Night-Train	179
Reading the Milestone	180
The Three Work-Days	181
Use and Beauty	181
Torch-Light in Fall-Time	182

CONTENTS

JOHN JAMES PIATT — *Con.*   PAGE
   At Home 182
   The Guerdon 182

SARAH MORGAN BRYAN PIATT (1836—)
   Biographical Sketch 183
   Leaving Love 185
   A Doubt 186
   Transfigured 187
   The Thought of Astyanax before Iulus........................ 188
   No Help 189
   Calling the Dead... 190
   A Pique at Parting... 191
   Caprice at Home... 192
   The House below the Hill.................................... 194
   Sad Wisdom — Four Years Old............................... 196
   To be Dead.. 196
   A Look into the Grave....................................... 197
   The Highest Mountain....................................... 197
   Life and Death... 198
   "I Want It Yesterday".. 198
   In Doubt 199
   Say the Sweet Words.. 199
   For Another's Sake... 199
   Little Christian's Trouble..................................... 200
   My Wedding Ring... 200
   To — 201

WILLIAM HENRY VENABLE (1836—)
   Biographical Sketch 202
   My Catbird: a Capriccio...................................... 205
   The Founders of Ohio.. 207
   The Teacher's Dream... 207
   National Song 210
   An Old Spanish Bugle.. 211
   Immortal Birdsong 213
   Summer Love 213
   Coffea Arabica 214
   A Welcome to Boz... 216
   The Poet of Clovernook...................................... 218
   A Gentle Man... 219
   Inviolate 220
   A Diamond 220

WILLIAM HENRY VENABLE — *Con.*   PAGE
From "Floridian Sonnets:"
- "The Golden Treasury" 221
- Milton 221
- Wordsworth 222
- Sursum Corda 222
- Mutation 223
- To Coates Kinney 223

WILLIAM DEAN HOWELLS (1837—)
- Biographical Sketch 224
- The Movers 225
- Forlorn 228
- In Earliest Spring 231
- Dead 232
- Society 233
- Respite 234

DENTON JAQUES SNIDER (1841—)
- Biographical Sketch 235
Extracts from "Delphic Days:"
- Elpinike 236

SARAH CHAUNCEY WOOLSEY (1845-1905)
- Biographical Sketch 242
- Gulf-Stream 242
- Good-bye 243
- Bereaved 245
- Ashes 246
- Thorns 247

ALICE WILLIAMS BROTHERTON
- Biographical Sketch 249
- The Blazing Heart 250
- Rosenlied I 251
- Rosenlied II 252
- The Poison Flask 252
- My Enemy 254
- The Living Past 256
- A Persian Fable 257
- Campion 257
- The Spinner 258
- Shakespeare 259
- Woman and Artist 259

CONTENTS

EDITH MATILDA THOMAS (1854—)   PAGE
  Biographical Sketch 261
  Dead Low Tide... 262
  Thefts of the Morning... 263
  Wild Honey 265
  Syrinx 266
  Avalon — Fair Avalon... 267
  At Lethe's Brink 268
  Vertumnus 270
  A Rainbow 271
  Migration 271
  "Oft Have I Wakened".. 272

THOMAS EMMETT MOORE (1861—)
  Biographical Sketch 273
  Soul Song 274
  Light 275
  The Palmer 275

HENRY HOLCOMB BENNETT (1863—)
  Biographical Sketch 276
  The Flag Goes By... 277
  The Redbird's Matins 278

JOHN BENNETT (1865—)
  Biographical Sketch 280
  The Merry Springtime 281
  Song of the Hunt.. 282
  Song of the Dutch Cannoneers................................ 282
  To the Robin That Sings at My Window...................... 283
  The Hills of Ross.. 284
  Obstinacy 285

FRANCES NEWTON SYMMES (1865—)
  Biographical Sketch 286
  Heart Stirrings 287
  Repression 287
  Listening 288
  Fate 288
  Revival 289
  Forebodings 289
  Afterwards 289
  Twilight 290
  Dawn 290

WILLIAM NORMAN GUTHRIE (1868—)
	PAGE
Biographical Sketch	291
The Lion	292
Evocation	296
An Old Nest	297
A Respite	297
In Vain	298
Higher Mathematics	299
Whence? Whither?	299

ALICE ARCHER SEWALL JAMES (1870—)
Biographical Sketch	300
The Passing of the Wild	301
Youth	303
To A New-Born Baby	304
Say Not Farewell	307

PAUL LAURENCE DUNBAR (1872-1906)
Biographical Sketch	309
Harriet Beecher Stowe	312
Weltschmertz	313
Angelina	314
Little Brown Baby	315
Parted	316
Hymn	317

OHIO COMMEMORATION ODES.
Ohio Centennial Ode....by Coates Kinney	321
Cleveland Centennial Ode....by John James Piatt	326
Cincinnati: A Civic Ode....by William Henry Venable	335

APPENDIX — REFERENCE-LISTS, BIBLIOGRAPHIC AND CRITICAL...... 345

WILLIAM DAVIS GALLAGHER

WILLIAM DAVIS GALLAGHER, son of Bernard and Abigail (Davis) Gallagher, was born in Philadelphia, Pa., August 21, 1808. His father, an Irish refugee and a former compatriot of Robert Emmet, died in the year 1814, two years after which event the widowed mother and her four young sons, Edward, John, William, and Francis, removed to Cincinnati. William received his first rudimentary knowledge of books in a log schoolhouse near Mount Healthy, Ohio, and later he attended for a time the Lancaster Academy, an institution which in 1819 was reorganized and chartered as the Cincinnati College. Young Gallagher learned the printer's trade, working successively on several Cincinnati newspapers, and while yet in his nonage, collaborating with his brother Francis, he conducted a short-lived sheet called the Western Minerva. In 1830 he went to Xenia, where for nine months he edited the Backwoodsman, a campaign organ favoring Henry Clay, the Whig candidate for President, and where, in the summer of 1831, he married Miss Emma Adamson, of Cincinnati. Returning with his wife to the Queen City, in the following autumn, he entered upon his first important literary undertaking, the editorship of the Cincinnati Mirror and Ladies' Parterre, a family journal of wide influence. In 1835 Mr. Gallagher removed to Columbus, where, besides writing leading editorials for the Ohio State Journal, he established a vigorous monthly magazine, the Hesperian. In 1839 he was invited by the distinguished journalist, Charles Hammond, to become assistant editor of the Cincinnati Daily Gazette, a position which he accepted and which he held until 1840, when, upon the death of Hammond, he was chosen editor-in-chief. In 1850 he was appointed private secretary to Thomas Corwin, after whose retirement from Fillmore's Cabinet he went to Louisville, where, as one of the proprietors of the Daily Courier, he championed the presidential candidacy of Corwin. On severing his relations with the Courier in 1854, he withdrew to a rural estate which he had purchased near Pewee Valley, where the family thereafter resided for thirty years.

He was a delegate to the National Convention which nominated Abraham Lincoln, and at the outbreak of the Civil War he became private secretary to Salmon P. Chase. He was later appointed, by Lincoln, Special Commercial Agent for the Upper Mississippi Valley, and in 1863, Surveyor of Customs for Louisville.

In the year 1867 Mr. Gallagher was bereft of his wife, who died of heart-failure, at Fern Rock Cottage, Pewee Valley. Of the nine children she bore to him, two are yet living, Mrs. Jane Cotton and Miss Frances Gallagher.

The venerable poet died at his home in Louisville, June 27, 1894. He was buried in Spring Grove Cemetery, Cincinnati, beneath the shade of native forest trees, within a few paces of the spot marked by the monument to his old friend Rufus King.

Preëminent among the early poets of Ohio, Gallagher, in his day, exerted in the West a persistent and formative influence comparable to that exerted in a wider field by his more distinguished New England contemporaries, to several of whom he bears a certain intellectual and moral kinship. His rugged and energetic "Ballads of the Border," no less than his spirited songs of freedom, are resonant with the same bold and manly note as that which rings clear in the stirring verse of Whittier; and in his calmer and more exalted moods our Western pioneer bard brings to the temple of Nature the same devout and unquestioning faith as that which finds solemn utterance in "Thanatopsis" and "Forest Hymn." What Bryant did for the ancient woodlands of the East, and Longfellow for the live-oak and cypress groves of Louisiana, Gallagher, in the stately and melodious verse of his Western pastoral, "Miami Woods," has done for the majestic primeval forests of southern Ohio.

WILLIAM DAVIS GALLAGHER

No other American poet brings the reader into more vital contact with Nature,— into closer communion with birds and breezes, hills, streams, trees, and flowers,— than does the author of "Miami Woods;" and no other American writer has depicted with a more delicate and absolute realism,— with truer eye to color, form, and motion,— the varying aspects of the changing year.

MIAMI WOODS
(Extracts)

> *"I know each lane, and every alley green,*
> *Dingle or bushy dell of this wild wood,*
> *And every bosky bourn from side to side,*
> *My daily walks and ancient neighborhood."*
> — Milton.

Sage monitors of youth are wont to say
The eye grows early dim to nature's charms,
And commerce with the world soon dulls the ear
To heavenliest sounds. It may be so; but I,
Whose feet were on the hills from earliest life,
And in the vales, and by the flashing brooks,
Have not so found it :— deeper in my heart,
Deeper and deeper year by year, has sunk
The love of nature, in my close, and long,
And fond companionship with woods and waves,
With birds and breezes, with the starry sky,
The mountain-height, the rocky gorge, the slope
Mantled with flow'rs, and the far-reaching plain
That mingles with the heavens.

THE PRIMEVAL FOREST [1]

Around me here rise up majestic trees
That centuries have nurtured: graceful elms,
Which interlock their limbs among the clouds;

---
[1] Topic-headings here employed do not, of course, appear in the original text.

Dark-columned walnuts, from whose liberal store
The nut-brown Indian maids their baskets fill'd
Ere the first pilgrims knelt on Plymouth Rock;
Gigantic sycamores, whose mighty arms
Sheltered the Redman in his wigwam prone,
What time the Norsemen roamed our chartless seas;
And towering oaks, that from the subject plain
Sprang when the builders of the tumuli
First disappeared, and to the conquering hordes
Left these, the dim traditions of their race
That rise around, in many a form of earth
Tracing the plain, but shrouded in the gloom
Of dark, impenetrable shades, that fall
From the far centuries.

GLIMPSES OF JUNE

How beautifully glimmer on my sight
The fresh green fields afar! How grandly rise
The groves that gloom around me! What a hush
Broods o'er this dell! And how yon hillside basks
In the full blaze of this unspotted day!
* * * * A statlier growth is now
Giving green glory to the forest-aisles,
And beauty to the meadows. Far away
The elder-thicket, robed in brightest bloom,
Is shining like a sunlit cloud at rest;
Nearer, the briar-roses load the air
With sweetness; and where yon half-hidden fence
And toppling cabin mark the Pioneer's
First habitation in the wilderness,
The gay bignonia to the ridge-pole climbs,
The yellow willow spreads its generous shade
Around the cool spring's margin, and the old
And bent catalpa waves its fan-like leaves
And lifts its milk-white blossoms. Beautiful!

WILLIAM DAVIS GALLAGHER

AUTUMN

The autumn time is with us!— Its approach
Was heralded, not many days ago,
By hazy skies that veiled the brazen sun,
And sea-like murmurs from the rustling corn,
And low-voiced brooks that wandered drowsily
By pendent clusters of empurpling grapes
Swinging upon the vine. And now, 'tis here!
And what a change hath pass'd upon the face
Of nature, where the waving forest spreads,
Then robed in deepest green! All through the night
The subtle frost has plied its magic art;
And in the day the golden sun hath wrought
True wonders; and the winds of morn and even
Have touch'd with magic breath the changing leaves.
And now, as wanders the dilating eye
Athwart the varied landscape, circling far,
What gorgeousness, what blazonry, what pomp
Of colors, bursts upon the ravished sight!
Here, where the poplar rears its yellow crest,
A golden glory; yonder, where the oak
Stands monarch of the forest, and the ash
Is girt with flame-like parasite, and broad
The dogwood spreads beneath, and, fringing all,
The sumac blushes to the ground, a flood
Of deepest crimson; and afar, where looms
The gnarlèd gum, a cloud of bloodiest red.

INDIAN SUMMER

— The weary gales
Come sighing from the meadows up the slope,
And die in plaintive murmurs: in the elm
The jay screams hoarsely, and the squirrel barks
Where the old oak stands naked: from the leaves,
That rustle to my tread, an odor comes

As of mortality. It is the sad,
Sweet period of the year our calends call
The "Indian Summer." Beautifully pass
The seasons into this. The harvest done,
The summer days round slowly with a hush
Into the quiet of the August noons.
Fields then lie bare; the skies grow milky-blue;
The streams run lazily; the tiniest child
Can jump the brooks, or wade them dry at knee;
One far retired in this wide Wood, can hear
Its deep heart throb, so still is every thing:
Out o'er the meadows, where from earliest morn
The grazing herds have fed, they quit the dry,
Hot grasses, and seek out the shadiest pools,
Where, plunging belly-deep, they thus await
The cooler eve's approach so quietly,
They look like statues from red granite hewn,
Or cast in bronze, or cut in ivory;
The restless sheep are scattered, each with nose
Thrust in protecting grasses; by the bars,
Beneath the walnut shade, the horses doze
The mid-day hours away; around the fields,
The groves are silent; dotting here and there
The faded landscape, like gray clouds at rest,
The old farm-houses lie; the lolling dog,
That ever claims the shadow of the porch,
Frets the hot noon through; all is still beside.

   The quivering flame of August noons, at length,
Burns out; and with September's equinox
The earth grows cooler, and the quicken'd airs
More freshly touch the cheek: but summer's breath
Yet lingers, till the still October comes
With frosty nights, and slumberous, sunny days:
Then falls the leaf; then fades along the fence
The golden-rod; then turns the aster pale;

WILLIAM DAVIS GALLAGHER

Then fly the song-birds, by the robin led,
Whose voices through the summer months have fill'd
The woods with music, far to southern haunts,
In orange thickets by Suwanee's shore,
And Mississippi's broad magnolia groves.

   A sweet, voluptuous languor fills the air:
The sun is shorn of his bright beams, and looks
Redly and dimly down upon the earth:
The moon glows like a buckler, as she mounts
In quiet from the misty depths, which now
No marked horizon separates from the dome
That spreads above: the starry hosts are lost,
All but the larger lights, which dimly walk
The heavens alone. * * * * The warm
And wanton airs that through the slumberous day
Steal gently up from southern climes, caress
The willing cheek, and fold the languid frame
In long embraces, and on couches spread
In sunny spots of silence, thickly strewn
With sweetest smelling leaves, lie down with it
In panting ecstacies of soft delights.

   Now all the woodlands round, and these fair vales,
And the broad plains that from their borders stretch
Away to the blue Unica, and run
Along the Ozark range, and far beyond
Find the still groves that shut Itasca in,
But, more than all, these old Miami Woods,
Are robed in golden exhalations, dim
As half-remembered dreams, and beautiful
As aught of Valambrosa, or the plains
Of Arcady, by fabling poets sung.
The night is fill'd with murmurs, and the day
Distils a subtle atmosphere, that lulls

The senses to a half repose, and hangs
A rosy twilight over nature, like
The night of Norway summers, when the sun
Skims the horizon through the tedious months.

THE COMING OF WINTER

— Now, from the stormy Huron's broad expanse,
From Mackinaw and from the Michigan,
Whose billows beat upon the sounding shores
And lash the surging pines, come sweeping down
Ice-making blasts, and raging sheets of snow:
The heavens grow darker daily; bleakest winds
Shriek through the naked woods; the robber owl
Hoots from his rocking citadel all night;
And all the day unhousèd cattle stand
Shivering and pinch'd. By many a potent sign
The dark and dreary days of winter thus
Inaugurate their king. A summer bird,
I fly before his breath.— Loved haunts, farewell!

IN MEMORIAM

*"A solitary sorrow, antheming
A lonely grief."* — Keats.

I see her now, through shadows and through tears,
In all her beauty wandering by my side,[1]
And hear her voice, with snatches of old song,
Swell up, and die away, and wake again.
— Vain apparition! memories vainer still!
Ye make me feel how much alone I am,
More than I felt before: ye bend the bow,
And barb the arrows that transfix my heart.

---

[1] The reference in these beautiful and tender lines is to the poet's daughter Mary, who died in girlhood.

Oh, from this scene the bloom hath faded now;
And that which was the soul of it to me,
The glory and the grace, sits far away,
Beneath the shadow of a sorrow big
With all that can affright, or overwhelm.

   . . . My heart would break — my stricken
            heart would break,
Could I not pour upon the murmuring winds,
When thus it swells, the burden of its woe,
In words that soothe, how sad soe'er they be.

1
Sweet bird that, deep in beechen shades embower'd,
Sittest and pour'st the sorrow of thy heart,
   Till all the woods around
   Throb as in heavy grief —
Mourn now with me: in deepest shades of sorrow
Sits my lone heart, and pours its plaint of woe,
   Till in sad unison
   Throbs every heart around.

2
Sweet brook, that over shining pebbles glidest
In quiet, with a low and plaintive moan,
   Made to the listening woods
   And to the leaning flowers —
Mourn now with me: like thine my life in quiet
Glides on and on, with songs of flowers and woods;
   Nor asks a gayer scene,
   Or other auditors.

3
Sweet summer wind, that, high among the branches
Of elm, and poplar, and of towering oak,
   Sighest the morning out,
   Sighest the evening in —

Mourn now with me: in and from early boyhood,
I've loved with you these lone and sinless haunts,
    Nor asked to pour my song
    Where the proud world might hear.

4

Sweet bird, sweet brook, sweet summer wind, oh listen!
Come to me from the throbbing beechen shade,
    From moaning hollows come,
    And from the sighing trees —
Mourn now with me: mourn for the dear one absent,
Who loved you with a love as strong as mine:
    Mourn for the mind's eclipse —
    Unutterable woe!

I had a little sprite whose name was Hope —
It sang glad songs into my eager ear;
But when most loved its notes died all away,
And now its songs are still'd forevermore —
    Forevermore.

I heard a voice, born of my human love,
Speak to my human weakness words of joy;
Each was as sweet as sounds of dulcimers,
But all are silent now forevermore —
    Forevermore.

I held within my own a little hand,
White as the moon, and it became as cold;
I pressed it to my lips in agony;
'T was then withdrawn — withdrawn forevermore —
    Forevermore.

I've worn a faded lily on my breast
These many days, these many weary days;
But now, by unseen fingers touch'd, it falls,
It falls away, and falls forevermore —
    Forevermore.

WILLIAM DAVIS GALLAGHER

Oh, many are the sweet and gentle flowers,
Caught by untimely frosts, that droop and die
Ere half their beauty has disclosed itself:
The dews of evening and the stars of night
Watch o'er and weep for them, and kindly airs
Bear them to earth, and lay them in repose.
And many are the pure and gentle hearts,
Untimely touched by Death, that render up
The hopes and promises of opening life
Without a murmur, and go calmly down,
Along the way of shadows, to the grave.
And such an one has just been laid to rest,
Here, where the hectic leaf of autumn falls
And strews the fresh-heap'd earth, and where the pale
And perishing blossoms of the year lie low.

1

Birds of the greenwood groves and sunny meads!
Whose voices ever fill'd her with delight,
Come from the mirror of the glassy pool,
Come from the thicket's edge where berries hang,
Come from each airy perch and favorite haunt,
And from your sweet and ever-plaintive throats
Pour forth, in soft and melancholy staves,
A dirge above the loved and early lost!

2

Winds of the spring-time! ye that bear the sounds
Of far-off murmurs on your dewy wings,
And steal a cadence from the running brook,
That rob the insect of its hum, and catch
The harp's last note, still trembling on the strings,
Pause here a little while, above this grave,
And in the tenderest tones of all, breathe out
A requiem for the loved and early lost.

3

Light breezes of the summer! wandering far,
Combine in one the many sounds of grief
Ye gather in your long and lonely way,
And wed with them all sounds of earth and air
Too sorrowful for other company,
And murmur them at morn and eventide,
And in the hush of noon, above the spot
Where sleeps in death the loved and early lost!

4

Soft, sighing gales of autumn! from the brown
And melancholy meadows, from the gloom
Of rocky caverns, from the plaining woods,
That mourn the hectic leaf and fading flower,
From deepest hollows and from highest hills,
Bring all the soft, sweet voices that are born,
And pour the saddest plaint that ever yet
Was uttered, for the loved and early lost!

THE SONG OF THE PIONEERS [1]

1

A song for the Early Times Out West,
    And our green old forest-home,
Whose pleasant memories freshly yet
    Across the bosom come:
A song for the free and gladsome life
    In those early days we led,
With a teeming soil beneath our feet,
    And a smiling Heav'n o'erhead!
Oh, the waves of life danced merrily,
    And had a joyous flow,
In the days when we were Pioneers,
    Fifty years ago!

---

[1] Written early in the eighteen forties.

2

The hunt, the shot, the glorious chase,
    The captured elk, or deer;
The camp, the big bright fire, and then
    The rich and wholesome cheer:—
The sweet sound sleep at dead of night,
    By our camp-fires blazing high —
Unbroken by the wolf's long howl,
    And the panther springing by.
Oh, merrily pass'd the time, despite
    Our wily Indian foe,
In the days when we were Pioneers,
    Fifty years ago!

3

We shunn'd not labor: when 't was due
    We wrought with right good will;
And for the homes we won for them,
    Our children bless us still.
We lived not hermit lives, but oft
    In social converse met;
And fires of love were kindled then,
    That burn on warmly yet.
Oh, pleasantly the stream of life
    Pursued its constant flow,
In the days when we were Pioneers,
    Fifty years ago!

4

We felt that we were fellow men;
    We felt we were a band
Sustain'd here in the wilderness
    By Heaven's upholding hand.
And when the solemn Sabbath came,
    Assembling in the wood,
We lifted up our hearts in prayer
    To God the only Good.

Our temples then were earth and sky;
  None others did we know,
In the days when we were Pioneers,
  Fifty years ago!

5

Our forest-life was rough and rude,
  And dangers closed us round;
But here, amid the green old trees,
  Freedom was sought and found.
Oft through our dwellings wintry blasts
  Would rush, with shriek and moan;
We cared not — though they were but frail,
  We felt they were our own!
Oh, free and manly lives we led,
  Mid verdure, or mid snow,
In the days when we were Pioneers,
  Fifty years ago!

6

But now our course of life is short;
  And as, from day to day,
We're walking on with weakening step,
  And halting by the way,
Another Land more bright than this,
  To our dim sight appears,
And on our way to it we all
  Are moving with the years.
Yet while we linger, we may still
  Our backward glances throw,
To the days when we were Pioneers,
  Fifty years ago!

WILLIAM DAVIS GALLAGHER

THE SPOTTED FAWN [1]

On Mahketewa's flowery marge
    The Red Chief's wigwam stood,
When first the white man's rifle rang
    Loud through the echoing wood,
The tomahawk and scalping-knife
    Together lay at rest;
For peace was in the forest shades,
    And in the red man's breast.

    Oh, the Spotted Fawn!
    Oh, the Spotted Fawn!
The light and life of the forest shades
With the Red Chief's child is gone.

By Mahketewa's flowery marge,
    The Spotted Fawn had birth,
And grew, as fair an Indian girl
    As ever blest the earth.
She was the Red Chief's only child,
    And sought by many a brave;
But to the gallant young White Cloud,
    Her plighted troth she gave.

From Mahketewa's flowery marge
    Her bridal song arose —
None dreaming, in that festal night,
    Of near encircling foes;
But through the forest, stealthily,
    The white men came in wrath;
And fiery deaths before them sped,
    And blood was in their path.

---

[1] "The Spotted Fawn was the beautiful daughter of an Indian chief, who dwelt in the valley of the Mahketewa, who, with her bridegroom, White Cloud, was slain on her bridal night by the cruel white man who in time of peace stole in upon them in their slumbering hours. The Mahketewa is the Indian name for a stream that empties into the Ohio at Cincinnati, commonly called Mill Creek."—Howe's *Historical Collections of Ohio.*

On Mahketewa's flowery marge,
   Next morn, no strife was seen;
But a wail went up, where the young Fawn's blood
   And White Cloud's, dyed the green;
And burial in their own rude way,
   The Indians gave them there,
While a low and sweet-toned requiem
   The brook sang and the air.

    Oh, the Spotted Fawn!
    Oh, the Spotted Fawn!
The light and life of the forest shades
With the Red Chief's child is gone.

"AH! WELL-A-WAY!"

    Ah! well-a-way!
The cloud will come; but after comes the sun.
Youth lies within the heart, and youth and sorrow
Were never strangers since the Eden-fall.
Sorrow descends upon the flower of youth,
As snow upon the crimson April-bloom,
Not with a blighting chill, but with a soft
And kindly pressure, that to youth gives strength,
Warmth to the crimson blossom, and to both
    The panoply that shields
    From after-coming storms.

    Ah! well-a-way!
Sin was begot in Hell, and sorrow born
In Eden, but the two are ever twinn'd.
Without the sin the sorrow might not come:
But with the sin, the sorrow is a bright,
Redeeming angel, pointing to a time
When sin was not; to an eternity

When sin shall be no more; and to a God
Who in his mercy gave the sorrow birth,
    That thus the sin might die,
    And man again be pure.

MAY
(Extract)

Would that thou couldst last for aye,
Merry, ever-merry May!
Made of sun-gleams, shade and showers,
Bursting buds, and breathing flowers!
Dripping-lock'd, and rosy-vested,
Violet-slipper'd, rainbow-crested;
Girdled with the eglantine,
Festoon'd with the dewy vine:
Merry, ever-merry May!
Would that thou couldst last for aye!

AUGUST

    Dust on thy mantle! dust,
Bright summer, on thy livery of green!
    A tarnish, as of rust,
    Dims thy late-brilliant sheen:
And thy young glories — leaf, and bud, and flower —
Change cometh over them with every hour.

    Thee hath the August sun
Look'd on with hot, and fierce, and brassy face;
    And still and lazily run,
    Scarce whispering in their pace,
The half-dried rivulets, that lately sent
A shout of gladness up, as on they went.

Flame-like, the long mid-day,
With not so much of sweet air as hath stirr'd
The down upon the spray,
Where rests the panting bird,
Dozing away the hot and tedious noon,
With fitful twitter, sadly out of tune.

Seeds in the sultry air,
And gossamer web-work on the sleeping trees;
E'en the tall pines, that rear
Their plumes to catch the breeze,
The slightest breeze from the unfreshening west,
Partake the general languor and deep rest.

Happy as man may be,
Stretch'd on his back, in homely bean-vine bower,
While the voluptuous bee
Robs each surrounding flower,
And prattling childhood clambers o'er his breast,
The husbandman enjoys his noonday rest.

Against the hazy sky,
The thin and fleecy clouds unmoving rest:
Beneath them far, yet high
In the dim, distant west,
The vulture, scenting thence its carrion-fare,
Sails, slowly circling in the sultry air.

Soberly, in the shade,
Repose the patient cow, the toil-worn ox;
Or in the shoal stream wade,
Shelter'd by jutting rocks;
The fleecy flock, fly-scourged and restless, rush
Madly from fence to fence, from bush to bush.

Tediously pass the hours,
And vegetation wilts, with blister'd root —
And droop the thirsting flowers,

WILLIAM DAVIS GALLAGHER

Where the slant sun-beams shoot;
But of each tall old tree, the lengthening line,
Slow-creeping eastward, marks the day's decline.

Faster, along the plain,
Moves now the shade, and on the meadow's edge:
　　The kine are forth again,
　　'Birds flitter in the hedge.
Now in the molten west sinks the hot sun:
Welcome, mild eve! — the sultry day is done.

TRUTH AND FREEDOM
(Extract)

Be thou like the first apostles —
　　Be thou like heroic Paul:
If a free thought seek expression,
　　Speak it boldly!— speak it all!

Face thine enemies — accusers;
　　Scorn the prison, rack, or rod!
And, if thou hast Truth to utter,
　　Speak! and leave the rest to God.

CONSERVATISM
(Extract)

The Owl, he fareth well
　　In the shadows of the night;
And it puzzleth him to tell
　　Why the Eagle loves the light.

And he hooteth loud and long:—
　　But the Eagle greets the day,
And, on pinions bold and strong,
　　Like a roused Thought, sweeps away!

JULIA L. DUMONT

JULIA L. DUMONT, whom her biographer in William T. Coggeshall's The Poets and Poetry of the West,[1] distinguishes as "the earliest female writer in the West whose poems, tales, and sketches have been preserved," was the daughter of Ebenezer and Martha D. Covey, who in 1788 moved from Rhode Island to Ohio, being among the pioneers of Marietta, the first Settlement in the Buckeye State. She was born in Washington County, Ohio, at Waterford, on the Muskingum River, in October, 1794. While she was still in her infancy her parents returned to Rhode Island, where her father died. Soon thereafter the widowed mother removed to Greenfield, Saratoga County, N. Y., and here Julia received her elementary education. Later she attended the Milton Academy, at which institution she manifested unmistakable literary talent. She taught school, in 1811, at Greenfield, and, in 1812, at Cambridge, N. Y. In August, 1812, she was married, at Greenfield, to John Dumont, with whom in October of the following year she returned to Ohio, where the newly wedded couple lived for about a year and a half. In March, 1814, Mrs. Dumont accompanied her husband to Vevay, Indiana, in which picturesque village on the Ohio River she resided until her death, which occurred on January 2, 1857.

Mrs. Dumont was a frequent contributor to several Cincinnati periodicals, including the Cincinnati Literary Gazette, the Cincinnati Mirror, the Western Literary Journal, and the Ladies' Repository. No volume of verse from her pen has ever been published, although a collection of her stories and other prose writings was issued, in 1856, from the press of Appleton & Company, New York, under the title, "Life Sketches from Com-

---

[1] The Poets and Poetry of the West, by William T. Coggeshall. Follett, Foster & Co., Columbus, 1860; New York, 1864.

mon Paths." It is a fact of peculiar interest to the student of Western history that in 1835 she had gathered materials for a Life of Tecumseh, the famous Ohio Indian Chief.

Sincerity and moral earnestness are qualities never absent from Mrs. Dumont's verse, which, though too often lapsing into mediocrity, is characterized at times not less by originality of thought than by imaginative fervor and melodious charm.

THE FUTURE LIFE
(Extract)

Well, let me meet the thought — it hath no power
    To daunt the soul that knows its heavenly birth;
Pass, pass away! brief splendors of life's hour,
    The sights, the sounds, the gorgeous hues of earth.

All sights, all sounds, all thoughts and dreams of time,
    Of a pure joy that wake the passing thrill,
Are yet but tokens of that better clime,
    Where life no more conflicts with change or chill.

The flush, the odor of the summer rose,
    The breath of spring, the morning's robe of light,
The whole broad beauty o'er the earth that glows,
    Are of the land that knows no touch of blight.

The melodies that fill the purple skies,
    The tones of love that thrill life's wide domain,
Are all but notes of the deep harmonies
    Poured round the Eternal, in triumphant strain.

And I, while through this fading form of dust
    There burns the deathless spark, derived from Him,
May look on change with calm, though solemn trust,
    Bearing a life its shadows may not dim.

Oh bless'd assurance of exulting faith!
    Humble, and yet victorious in its might,
Through the dark mysteries of decay and death,
    Sustaining on,— a pillar still of light.

The life immortal! of a peace intense,
    Holy, unchanging, save to brighter day,
How fails the mind in upward flight immense,
    When, to conceive it, human thoughts essay!

How fade the glories of our fairest spheres,
    As faith's fixed eye pursues that heavenward flight!
The hopes and joys, the pain, the passionate tears,
    How shadowy all — phantasmas of the night!

What I am now, and what I once have been,
    E'en when each pulse with health's full bound was rife,
Melt as a dream — a strange and struggling scene,
    A dim and fitful consciousness of life.

Pass, pass away! things of a fondness vain,
    Fade on, frail vestments meant but for decay;
I wait the robes corruption may not stain,
    The bloom, the freshness of immortal day.

EDWARD A. McLAUGHLIN

EDWARD A. McLAUGHLIN, author of a discursive poem in four Byronic cantos,[1] entitled "The Lovers of the Deep," inspired by the adventures of a sea-faring life, was born at North Stamford, Conn., January 9, 1798. Being discharged from the naval service on account of impaired health, in 1829, he became a wanderer, a new-world troubadour, and, under the impulse of an imaginative spirit, he wrote with remarkable energy and correctness of form, considering his entire lack of school education and of literary training. His volume, much of which was composed in Cincinnati, was published in that city in 1841, by Edward Lucas, and is dedicated to Nicholas Longworth. Among its miscellaneous contents are poems inscribed to Stephen S. L'Hommedieu, Peyton S. Symmes, Bellamy Storer, and Jacob Burnet. We have not been able to ascertain the date or the place of McLaughlin's death.

In the autobiographical preface to his poems the author naïvely relates: "I am a native of the State of Connecticut, and from my youth have been rather of a lively and roving disposition. At an early age I absconded from home, with an intention of joining the army; but was reclaimed, and shortly afterward bound an apprentice to the printing business. At the age of twenty-one, I indulged my military enthusiasm, and joined the Missouri expedition. At the reduction of the army in 1821, I received my discharge at Belle Fontaine, and, descending the Mississippi, commenced a new career on the ocean. I liked this

---

[1]The author of "Childe Harold" noted with pride his growing popularity in the freedom-loving West. "These are the first tidings that have sounded like fame to my ears,—to be redde on the banks of the Ohio," he recorded in his diary, December 5, 1813.—Nowhere in the world, perhaps, was Byron hailed with more enthusiasm than in the Ohio Valley, where he had many admiring readers, and where the influence of his genius is discernible in both the form and the spirit of the verse of several of the pioneer bards.

element better than the land; and the desire of seeing foreign countries induced me to follow, for some years, the life of a sailor. Being discharged at one time from the La Plata frigate, in Carthagena, Colombia, I was forcibly impressed into the Patriot service. After many vicissitudes of fortune, I was enabled, through the generous assistance of George Watts, British Consul for that Republic, to return home. I subsequently entered the American Navy, in which I served about three years and a half. My last voyage was in the Hudson frigate, on the Brazil station, from which ship I was sent home an invalid, to Washington, where I was finally discharged from the service in 1829.—I have written under many and great disadvantages. With a mind not characterized by any great natural force; stored with but little reading, and that mostly of a local and superficial character; without books of any kind — not even a dictionary — I was thrown altogether upon my own slender resources. The leading poem was begun and concluded under circumstances never above want: though a regard for truth constrains me to acknowledge that these circumstances were not unfrequently the consequence of a lack of moral firmness and stability on my own part — to say the least of it — induced by the sudden and unlooked-for overthrow of cherished hopes and desires."

THE SEMINOLE

Inscribed to Stephen S. L'Hommedieu, Esq.

(Extract)

Muse of the wild, unlettered birth of Time,
In native grace and purity arrayed;
Simple, yet powerful; artless, yet sublime —
Whose dwelling is the wilderness of shade,
Or deep romantic glen — or vale embayed
Between the green-bound hills, where Nature smiles
In her prolific joy, and sits displayed
The blooming Queen of continents and isles:
Low lies thy freeborn Son — victim of treacherous wiles.

EDWARD A. M'LAUGHLIN

Inspire the heart, and guide the hand of him,
Who sings the requiem of the Seminole!
Nerveless his arm — his eagle eye is dim,
And in the Land of Spirits wakes his soul:
There mourns the tempest he could not control —
That, like the whirlwind, oaks nor rocks withstand,
Launched from the Andes, or the stormy pole —
Hurled ruin on his tribe — scattered his band,
And drenched in their best blood the Indian Hunters' land!

Famine and war pursue the hapless race,
The unsheathed sword is gory with their blood —
In dismal swamps they seek a resting place,
And waste their feeble strength against the flood;
Or, driven far within the marshy wood,
Where scattered hammocks heave their heads in sight,
Like oases on Sahara's bosom strewed;
The hunted Warriors rally all their might,
And, side by side, renew the stern but hopeless fight.

Shout! Seminoles, once more your battle cry,
And grapple, throat to throat, the tyrant foe!
Call up your wrongs, rouse all your chivalry,
And deal a deadly wound with every blow!
Remember sires', and wives', and children's woe —
Remember with your blood your land is red,
And that your fathers' ashes sleep below:
Strike for revenge — palsy their souls with dread —
Hurl them all down to earth, and pile it with their dead!

It may not be — their destiny is told —
The Master Spirit of his tribe is gone!
Wrapt in earth's bosom, rigid, wan, and cold,
The violated Warrior lies alone,
With none but strangers o'er his grave to moan:
No files of those he led to victory
Surround the Chief whom Freedom calls her own —

Whose barbèd shaft was winged for liberty —
Whose warwhoop rung the knell of pale-faced tyranny.

The noble Captive bears him unsubdued,
Albeit with manacles his limbs they bind:
His unquenched spirit towers in haughty mood,
And fiercer burns as feels its force confined —
They cannot chain the freedom of the mind,
Degrade him as they may: a Roman's part
The lofty Chief sustains, and bows resigned:
In silence, broods o'er his deep wrongs, apart,
Weeps for his country's woes, and sinks — a broken heart.

O Muse, whom I invoke within the deep
Recesses of the wood, in numbers wild;
Shall retribution — shall red vengeance sleep,
When cries from earth the blood of Nature's child;
Whose green retreats the murderer hath defiled,
And poured life's purple stream in every grove?
Thy blooming vales, where innocence beguiled
The hours, and woke the melody of love —
Are silent, tenantless, save where the demons rove.

I hear thy voice in tones of sad despair,
I mark thine eye, and vanished is its glow;
The notes of sorrow float upon the air,
The bitter tears of anguish overflow:
Hope sleeps in death on arid plains below,
Bleak as the fields that bind the Arctic wave:
And 'mid the broken arrow and the bow,
Bleach there the bones of Chief and Warrior brave,
The mist their winding sheet — a ruined land their grave.

Thy harp, unstrung, hangs on the cypress tree,
Mute as the stilly depths of solitude:
No ear remains to list the minstrelsy,
Save the gaunt wolf's, that prowls the dreary wood,
Or panther's, scenting o'er the fields of blood:—

Its wreath of flowers has faded from the view,
And all the magic of its strains subdued:
Thy harp dissolves away in tears of dew,
As the dirge-moaning winds the listless chords sweep through.

Peace, Warrior, to thy shade!— thy sun did set,
Or e'er thy morn had reached the zenith's height;
But Glory crowns thee with her coronet,
And Fame inscribes thy name on tablets bright:
No thirst for conquest lured thee to the fight,—
No blood of innocence lies on thy soul:
But, battling singly for thy country's right,
Thou fell — when at thy back the tyrants stole,
Who quailed beneath thy glance—THE MURDERED SEMINOLE!
CINCINNATI, February, 1838.

"POOR HAVE I LIVED"
(Extract from "The Lovers of the Deep")

Poor have I lived, the son of discontent,
In want and sorrow — better scarce can die;
But may no nabob rear a monument
To insult the dead, that, living, he passed by:
Wrapt in my humble fortune, let me lie
Within the green-bound wood, without a stone
To mark the spot where sleeps the wanderer's eye:
There would I rest in solitude, unknown,
While the sweet bird of spring chants my last dirge alone.

Nature, to whom my earliest song I gave,
Her verdant carpet o'er my couch shall spread,
Deck with wild flowers the sleeping poet's grave,
And her green canopy wave o'er my head:
The dewy tear shall to my memory shed,
And breathe her sighs upon the zephyr's wing,
While her plumed offspring, to the forest led,
In untaught strains my requiem shall sing,
And answering Echo back the varied music fling.

HARVEY D. LITTLE

HARVEY D. LITTLE was born in Weathersfield, Conn., in 1803. When but twelve or thirteen years old, he came with his parents to Franklin County, Ohio, where he spent the remainder of his life, residing first on a farm and afterward in the city of Columbus. Early in youth he learned the printer's trade, and later he became connected successively with several Ohio newspapers, as editor and co-publisher. He studied law, and was admitted to the bar at the age of twenty-five. Domestic considerations, however, induced him to abandon the practice of law and to resume his former vocation as an editor; and he was engaged in the management of a local periodical, the Eclectic and Medical Botanist, when his career was cut short by a sudden and fatal illness. He died of Asiatic cholera, in Columbus, Ohio, August 22, 1833, leaving behind him a wife and one child.

A sketch of Mr. Little's life, by W. D. Gallagher, and several of his poems, are preserved in Coggeshall's compilation of 1860. To quote the words of his biographer: "Mr. Little was a type of a class of young men who, though not altogether peculiar to the West, have marked this section of the Union more distinctly than any other. Harvard, Yale, West Point, and similar institutions in the Eastern States, have severally been the *Alma Mater* of men who have risen to distinction at the bar, in the army, in the pulpit, and in the halls of legislation. In the Western States, however, those places have been, and now are, to an extent which makes it worthy of remark, filled by men who, like Mr. Little, graduated in a printing-office instead of a college." Of the author's poetical attainment the same writer observes: "The tones of his harp were like the breathing of the 'sweet southwest,' and came upon the heart mildly and soothingly. The melody of his verse was perfect; its imagery rich; its language choice; its figures striking and appropriate."

HARVEY D. LITTLE

ON JUDAH'S HILL

On Judah's hill the towering palm
    Still spreads its branches to the sky,
The same, through years of storm and calm,
    As erst it was in days gone by,
When Israel's king poured forth his psalm
    In strains of sacred melody.

And Lebanon, thy forests green
    Are waving in the lonely wind,
To mark the solitary scene,
    Where wandering Israel's hopes are shrined:
But the famed Temple's ancient sheen
    The pilgrim seeks, in vain, to find.

And Kedron's brook, and Jordan's tide,
    Roll onward to the sluggish sea:
But where is Salem's swollen pride,
    Her chariots, and her chivalry,
Her Tyrian robes in purple dyed,
    Her warlike hosts, who scorned to flee?

Gone! all are gone! In sullen mood
    The cruel Arab wanders there,
In search of human spoils and blood,—
    The victims of his wily snare:
And where the holy prophets stood
    The wild beasts make their secret lair.

OTWAY CURRY

OTWAY CURRY, the eldest son of James Curry, a brave and patriotic officer in the Revolutionary army, was born March 26, 1804, on a farm which has since given place to the village of Greenfield, Highland County, Ohio. "He was a child of the wilderness," writes his biographer, Dr. Edward Thomson, "— a situation not unsuitable to awaken imagination, to cultivate taste, and to call forth the love of nature and the spirit of poesy." The scant and irregular instruction which the boy received in the back-woods log schoolhouse was both anticipated and supplemented by careful and sympathetic home training. We are told that he "heard his father relate the tale of the Revolution, the wrongs of the colonists, their determined rebellion, their bloody battles, and their final triumph;" and that he "heard him describe the characters of the leading statesmen and warriors of that period, the organization of the State and National Governments, the causes, and actors, and consequences of the war of 1812."—"Moreover," continues the narrative, "the pious mother had her pleasant legends and fairy tales, with which she kept down the rising sigh, and kept open the leaden eyelids of the little ones as she sat plying her spinning-wheel, and waiting for the return of her husband from the mill, when the driving snow-storm delayed him far into the hours of the night. She seems, indeed, to have been no ordinary woman. She was accustomed to relate over and over, at her fireside, the whole story of Paradise Lost, as well as of many other classic poems, so that young Otway was familiar with their scenes and characters long before he could read. She would often beguile the weary hours of summer nights as she sat in the cabin doorway with her young ones, watching for the return of the older from the perilous chase, by naming the constellations as they came up to the horizon, and explaining the ordinances of heaven."

OTWAY CURRY

Thrown upon his own resources at the age of nineteen, Curry, in the year 1823, went to Lebanon, Ohio, where he learned the carpenter's trade, at which he afterwards worked, first in Cincinnati, then in Detroit, and later in Port Gibson, Miss. It was within this period of unsettled employment as a "journeyman carpenter" that he contributed to the press, anonymously, his first successful experiments in lyric composition, including the once widely popular song of faith entitled "Kingdom Come." Returning to Cincinnati in 1826, he formed the intimate acquaintance of William D. Gallagher, by whose influence, at a later period, his poetic achievement was brought conspicuously to the attention of the reading public. On December 17, 1828, Mr. Curry was married, in Union County, to Miss Mary Noteman; and in the following year he again went South, and spent some months in Baton Rouge. Upon his return to Ohio he settled in Union County, where for a period of ten years he devoted himself to the pursuits of farm-life, without, however, wholly relinquishing his literary avocation. In 1836 he was elected a member of the Ohio Legislature, to which body he was re-elected in 1837, by unsolicited suffrages. After completing his second term of office as legislator, in 1838, he was for six months associated with Mr. Gallagher as one of the editors of the Hesperian, a monthly magazine published in Columbus. In 1839 he removed to Marysville, where he commenced the study of law. He was again elected to the Legislature in 1842, and in the following year he purchased the Greene County Torch-Light, a weekly paper issued in Xenia, Ohio, to which town he removed in the spring of 1843. Disposing of his interest in this paper in 1845, he returned to Marysville, and there engaged in the practice of law.

In 1850 Mr. Curry was a delegate to the second Ohio Constitutional Convention, which met at Cincinnati, and in January, 1854, he was President of the Ohio Editorial Convention, which also was held in the Queen City.

The poet died February 17, 1855, at Marysville, Ohio.

In the memoir from which we have already quoted occurs the following description of Otway Curry, and of his habits as a literary artist: "He had an open countenance, a broad and lofty brow, a noble form, tall and well proportioned, which might have borne with ease the armor of a knight of the middle ages. His spirit was that of Southern chivalry mingled with the Puritan. He was a man of fine taste. This he exhibited in his dress, his language, his reading,— in everything. . . . His words, whether written or spoken, were few and well chosen. This is the more remarkable, considering that his early education was so limited. He would allow no thought of his to go abroad in an unsuitable garment, however protracted might be the process of fitting it. When he wrote for the press his first drafts were scanned, laid aside, examined again, altered, and re-written, sometimes often, before they were published. Every word was scrutinized. Hence, his poems bear criticism, and will be best appreciated by those who most closely examine them."

THE LOST PLEIAD

. Millions of ages gone,
Didst thou survive, in thy enthronèd place,
Amidst the assemblies of the starry race,
    Still shining on — and on.

And even in earthly time
Thy parting beams their olden radiance wore,
And greeted, from the dim cerulean shore,
    The old Chaldean clime.

Sages and poets, strong
To rise and walk the waveless firmament,
Gladly to thee their richest offerings sent,
    Of eloquence and song.

But thy far-flowing light,
By time's mysterious shadows overcast,
Strangely and dimly faded at the last,
    Into a nameless night.

Along the expanse serene,
Of clust'ry arch and constellated zone,
With orbèd sands of tremulous gold o'erstrown,
No more canst thou be seen.

Say whither wand'rest thou?
Do unseen heavens thy distant path illume?
Or press the shades of everlasting gloom
Darkly upon thee now?

Around thee, far away,
The hazy ranks of multitudinous spheres,
Perchance, are gathering to prolong the years
Of thy unwilling stay.

Sadly our thoughts rehearse
The story of thy wild and wondrous flight
Thro' the deep deserts of the ancient night
And far-off universe.

We call — we call thee back,
And suns of many a constellation bright
Shall weave the waves of their illuming light
O'er thy returning track.

THE GOINGS FORTH OF GOD
(Extract)

God walketh on the earth. The purling rills
And mightier streams before Him glance away,
Rejoicing in His presence. On the plains,
And spangled fields, and in the mazy vales,
The living throngs of earth before Him fall
With thankful hymns, receiving from His hand
Immortal life and gladness. Clothed upon
With burning crowns the mountain-heralds stand,
Proclaiming to the blossoming wilderness
The brightness of His coming, and the power
Of Him who ever liveth, all in all!

God walketh on the ocean. Brilliantly
The glassy waters mirror back His smiles.
The surging billows and the gamboling storms
Come crouching to His feet. The hoary deep
And the green, gorgeous islands offer up
The tribute of their treasures — pearls, and shells,
And crown-like drapery of the dashing foam.
And solemnly the tesselated halls,
And coral domes of mansions in the depths,
And gardens of the golden-sanded sea,
Blend, with the anthems of the chiming waves,
Their alleluias unto Him who rules
The invisible armies of eternity.

God journeyeth in the sky. From sun to sun,
From star to star, the living lightnings flash;
And pealing thunders through all space proclaim
The goings forth of Him whose potent arm
Perpetuates existence, or destroys.

* * * * *

TO A MIDNIGHT PHANTOM
(Extract)

Pale, melancholy one,
  Why art thou lingering here,
Memorial of dark ages gone,
  Herald of darkness near?
Thou stand'st immortal, undefiled —
Even thou, the unknown, the strange, the wild,
  Spell-word of mortal fear.

Thou art a shadowy form,
  A dream-like thing of air;
My very sighs thy robes deform,
  So frail, so passing fair;

OTWAY CURRY

Thy crown is of the fabled gems,
The bright ephemeral diadems
    That unseen spirits wear.

Thou hast revealed to me
    The lore of phantom song,
With thy wild, fearful melody,
    Chiming the whole night long
Forebodings of untimely doom,
Of sorrowing years and dying gloom,
    And unrequited wrong.

BUCKEYE CABIN[1]

Oh, where, tell me where, was your Buckeye cabin made?
Oh, where, tell me where, was your Buckeye cabin made?
'Twas built among the merry boys that wield the plow and spade,
Where the long cabin stands, in the bonnie Buckeye shade.

Oh, what, tell me what, is to be your cabin's fate?
Oh, what, tell me what, is to be your cabin's fate?
We'll wheel it to the Capital, and place it there elate,
For a token and a sign of the bonnie Buckeye State!

Oh, why, tell me why, does your Buckeye cabin go?
Oh, why, tell me why, docs your Buckeye cabin go?
It goes against the spoilsmen, for well its builders know
It was Harrison that fought for the cabins long ago.

Oh, what, tell me what, then, will little Martin do?
Oh, what, tell me what, then, will little Martin do?
He'll "follow in the footsteps" of Price and Swarthout too,
While the long cabin rings again with old Tippecanoe.

---

[1] This campaign song was written for the memorable Whig convention of February 22, 1840, when twenty thousand people from all parts of the State met at Columbus, Ohio, to ratify the nomination of Harrison and Tyler. "In the procession," says Hon. C. B. Galbreath, in an article entitled "Song Writers of Ohio," "was a cabin on wheels, from Union County. It was made of buckeye logs, and in it was a band of singers discoursing, to the tune of *Highland Laddie*, the famous Buckeye song written by the poet Otway Curry."
—See Ohio Arch. and Hist. Quart., Jan., 1905.

Oh, who fell before him in battle, tell me who?
Oh, who fell before him in battle, tell me who?
He drove the savage legions, and British armies, too,
At the Rapids, and the Thames, and old Tippecanoe!

By whom, tell me whom, will the battle next be won?
By whom, tell me whom, will the battle next be won?
The spoilsmen and leg treasurers will soon begin to run!
And the "Log Cabin Candidate" will march to Washington!

FREDERICK WILLIAM THOMAS

FREDERICK WILLIAM THOMAS, a native of South Carolina, was born at Charleston, in the year 1811. He came of literary stock, his father, E. S. Thomas,— who died in 1847,— being the author of Reminiscences of the Last Sixty-five Years, and his grand-uncle, Isaiah Thomas, the author of a History of Printing. His brother, Lewis Foulke Thomas, was a poet of some mark, and his sister, Martha M. Thomas, wrote a novel entitled "Life's Lessons," published by Harper & Brothers, in 1855. In 1829 Frederick removed with his father from Baltimore to Cincinnati, in which city he resided for the next twelve years, devoting himself to literary pursuits and, irregularly, to the practice of law. "In 1840," writes his biographer, W. T. Coggeshall, "Mr. Thomas 'took the stump' in Ohio for William Henry Harrison, as a candidate for the Presidency, and won friends as a popular orator;" and subsequently he "lectured extensively with much success on 'Eloquence,' on 'Early Struggles of Eminent Men,' and other popular topics." Being appointed, in 1841, by Thomas Ewing, then Secretary of the United States Treasury, to select a library for that department of Government, Mr. Thomas removed to Washington, D. C., where he remained until 1850, when he returned to Cincinnati. Here for a brief period he occupied a pulpit in the Methodist Episcopal Church. After several years of residence in the Queen City he accepted a professorship in Rhetoric and English Literature, to which he was called by the Alabama University; but, having determined to resume the practice of law, he resigned his collegiate chair, and, in 1858, moved to Cambridge, Maryland, where he settled as an attorney. Two years later, however, he was induced again to engage in journalism, and in the spring of 1860 he became literary editor of the Richmond

(Virginia) Enquirer. His death occurred in Washington, D. C., September 30, 1866. After the lapse of some years his remains were brought to Cincinnati by his brother, Calvin W. Thomas, and placed beside those of his parents, in Spring Grove Cemetery.

Frederick W. Thomas is the author of two volumes of verse: The Beechen Tree, a Tale in Rhyme, published in 1844 by Harper & Brothers, and The Emigrant, or Reflections While Descending the Ohio, first published in Cincinnati in 1833, by Alexander Flash, and re-issued in that city by Josiah Drake, in 1872. In a critical estimate of Mr. Thomas's work, Rufus W. Griswold, in his volume, The Poets and Poetry of America (Phila., 1855), wrote: "He has a nice discrimination of the peculiarities of character which give light and shade to the surface of society, and a hearty relish for that peculiar humor which abounds in that portion of our country which undoubtedly embraces most that is original and striking in manners and unrestrained in conduct. He must rank with the first illustrators of manners in the Valley of the Mississippi." The author's most ambitious poem, "The Emigrant," contains many vigorous stanzas of realistic description, which are of historical interest as picturing certain general aspects of primitive life in the Western wilderness.

THE EMIGRANT

(Extracts)

DANIEL BOONE

Here once Boone trod — the hardy Pioneer —
The only white man in the wilderness:
Oh! how he loved, alone, to hunt the deer,
Alone at eve, his simple meal to dress;
No mark upon the tree, nor print, nor track,
To lead him forward, or to guide him back:
He roved the forest, king by main and might,
And looked up to the sky and shaped his course aright.

That mountain, there, that lifts its bald, high head
Above the forest, was, perchance, his throne;
There has he stood and marked the woods outspread,
Like a great kingdom, that was all his own;
In hunting-shirt and moccasins arrayed,
With bear-skin cap, and pouch, and needful blade,
How carelessly he lean'd upon his gun!
That scepter of the wild, that had so often won.

THE INDIAN

With front erect, up-looking, dignified —
Behold high Hecla in eternal snows!
Yet while the raging tempest is defied,
Deep in its bosom how the pent flame glows!
And when it bursts forth in its fiery wrath,
How melts the ice-hill from its fearful path,
As on it rolls, unquench'd, and all untamed! —
Thus was it with that Chief when his wild passions flamed.

Nature's own statesman — by experience taught,
He judged most wisely, and could act as well;
With quickest glance could read another's thought,
His own, the while, the keenest could not tell;
Warrior — with skill to lengthen, or combine,
Lead on, or back, the desultory line;
Hunter — he passed the trackless forest through,
Now on the mountain trod, now launch'd the light canoe.

To the Great Spirit, would his spirit bow,
With hopes that Nature's impulses impart;
Unlike the Christian, who just says his vow
With heart enough to say it all by heart.
Did we his virtues from his faults discern,
'Twould teach a lesson that we well might learn:
An inculcation worthiest of our creed,
To tell the simple truth, and do the promised deed.

How deeply eloquent was the debate,
Beside the council-fire of those red men!
With language burning as his sense of hate;
With gesture just; with eye of keenest ken;
With illustration simple but profound,
Drawn from the sky above him, or the ground
Beneath his feet; and with unfalt'ring zeal,
He spoke from a warm heart and made e'en cold hearts feel.

And this is Eloquence. 'Tis the intense,
Impassioned fervor of a mind deep fraught
With native energy, when soul and sense
Burst forth, embodied in the burning thought;
When look, emotion, tone, are all combined —
When the whole man is eloquent with mind —
A power that comes not to the call or quest,
But from the gifted soul, and the deep-feeling breast.

Poor Logan had it, when he mourned that none
Were left to mourn for him: —'twas his who swayed
The Roman Senate by a look or tone;
'Twas the Athenian's, when his foes, dismayed,
Shrunk from the earthquake of his trumpet call;
'Twas Chatham's, strong as either, or as all;
'Twas Henry's holiest, when his spirit woke
Our patriot fathers' zeal to burst the British yoke.

'TIS SAID THAT ABSENCE CONQUERS LOVE

'Tis said that absence conquers love!
  But, oh! believe it not;
I've tried, alas! its power to prove,
  But thou art not forgot.
Lady, though fate has bid us part,
  Yet still thou art as dear —
As fixed in this devoted heart
  As when I clasp'd thee here.

FREDERICK WILLIAM THOMAS

I plunge into the busy crowd,
    And smile to hear thy name;
And yet, as if I thought aloud,
    They know me still the same;
And when the wine-cup passes round,
    I toast some other Fair;—
But when I ask my heart the sound,
    Thy name is echoed there.

And when some other name I learn,
    And try to whisper love,
Still will my heart to thee return,
    Like the returning dove.
In vain! I never can forget,
    And would not be forgot;
For I must bear the same regret,
    Whate'er may be my lot.

E'en as the wounded bird will seek
    Its favorite bower to die,
So, Lady! I would hear thee speak,
    And yield my parting sigh.
'Tis said that absence conquers love!
    But, oh! believe it not;
I've tried, alas! its power to prove,
    But thou art not forgot.

LEWIS FOULKE THOMAS

LEWIS FOULKE THOMAS, son of E. S. Thomas and brother of Frederick W. and of Martha M. Thomas, was born in Baltimore, Md., about the year 1815. Removing to Cincinnati with his father's family in 1829, he assisted his brother in conducting the Commercial Advertiser and the Evening Post, and later he became a contributor to the Western Monthly and to the Cincinnati Mirror. In 1838 he wrote a drama entitled "Osceola," which was performed in Cincinnati, in Louisville, and in New Orleans. He is the author of two interesting books of verse: Inda, and Other Poems (1842), and Rhymes of the Routes, a small volume issued in Washington, D. C., about the year 1847. Mr. Thomas became an attorney at law and practiced his profession in Washingon, D. C., in which city he died, in 1868.

LOVE'S ARGUMENT

(Extract)

O love! it is the tender rose,
That for a little season blows,
  And withers, fades, and dies;
Then seize it in its budding grace,
And in thy bosom give it place,
  Ere its sweet perfume flies.

Love is the bubble that doth swim
Upon the wine-cup's flowing brim,
  A moment sparkling there;
Then haste thee, dear, its sweets to sip,
And let them melt upon thy lip,
  Or they will waste in air.

LEWIS FOULKE THOMAS

O love! it is the dew-drop bright
That steals upon the flower at night,
  And lingers there till morn;
The flower doth droop, when with the day
The sun dissolves the drop away:
  So love is killed by scorn.

CHARLES A. JONES

CHARLES A. JONES, son of George W. Jones, was born in Philadelphia, Pa., about the year 1815. In his childhood he accompanied his parents to Cincinnati, Ohio, where he resided during the greater part of his life. At an early age he was a frequent contributor to several local periodicals, including the Cincinnati Mirror, the Cincinnati Message, the Western Literary Journal, the Hesperian, and the Daily Gazette. He studied law, and, having been admitted to the bar in 1840, he entered upon the practice of his profession in the Queen City. He was married, in 1843, to Miss Charlotte Ludlow, daughter of James C. Ludlow, of Cincinnati. Some years later he removed with his wife to New Orleans, where he resumed his legal practice; but on account of failing health he returned to Cincinnati in 1851, in which year he died, in Millcreek Township, Hamilton County, "at the old Ludlow Station[1] of pioneer renown."

In a sketch of the poet's life, contributed to Coggeshall's historic volume, W. D. Gallagher says: "Charles A. Jones is to be honored above the generality of Western writers, because he explored extensively, and made himself well acquainted with Western character, and in the West, found the theme of his essay, the incident of his story, and the inspiration of his song. His principal poem is a stirring narrative of the exploits of the bold outlaws, who, in the infancy of the settlement of the West, had their common rendezvous in the celebrated Cave-in-Rock on the Ohio. The subjects of many of his lesser productions are the rivers, the mounds, the Indian heroes, and the pioneers of the Mississippi Valley."

---

[1] "A part of the original Indian fort, 'Ludlow Station,' erected in 1790, was built into the locally famous Ludlow Mansion, which is still standing in Cumminsville, near Mill Creek."—See History of Cincinnati and Hamilton County. Nelson & Co., Cincinnati, 1894.

CHARLES A. JONES

TECUMSEH

Where rolls the dark and turbid Thames [1]
  His consecrated wave along,
Sleeps one, than whose, few are the names
  More worthy of the lyre and song;
Yet o'er whose spot of lone repose
  No pilgrim eyes are seen to weep;
And no memorial marble throws
  Its shadow where his ashes sleep.

Stop, stranger! there Tecumseh lies;
  Behold the lowly resting-place
Of all that of the hero dies;
  The Cæsar — Tully, of his race,
Whose arm of strength, and fiery tongue,
  Have won him an immortal name,
And from the mouths of millions wrung
  Reluctant tribute to his fame.

Stop — for 'tis glory claims thy tear!
  True worth belongs to all mankind;
And he whose ashes slumber here,
  Though man in form was god in mind.
What matter he was not like thee,
  In race and color; 'tis the soul
That marks man's true divinity;
  Then let not shame thy tears control.

Art thou a patriot? — so was he!
  His breast was Freedom's holiest shrine;
And as thou bendest there thy knee,
  His spirit will unite with thine.

---

[1] **Thames.** A river in Ontario, Canada. Near its banks, October 5, 1813, the Americans, under William Henry Harrison, hero of Tippecanoe (1811), defeated the allied forces of the British, under Proctor, and the Indians, under Tecumseh, who was killed in the battle.

POETS OF OHIO

All that a man can give, he gave;
   His life: the country of his sires
From the oppressor's grasp to save:
   In vain — quench'd are his nation's fires.

Art thou a soldier? dost thou not
   O'er deeds chivalric love to muse?
Here stay thy steps — what better spot
   Couldst thou for contemplation choose?
The earth beneath is holy ground;
   It holds a thousand valiant braves;
Tread lightly o'er each little mound,
   For they are no ignoble graves.

Thermopylæ and Marathon,
   Though classic earth, can boast no more
Of deeds heroic than yon sun
   Once saw upon this lonely shore,
When in a gallant nation's last
   And deadliest struggle, for its own,
Tecumseh's fiery spirit passed
   In blood, and sought its Father's throne.

Oh, softly fall the summer dew,
   The tears of heaven, upon his sod,
For he in life and death was true,
   Both to his country and his God;
For oh, if God to man has given,
   From his bright home beyond the skies,
One feeling that's akin to heaven,
   'Tis his who for his country dies.

Rest, warrior, rest! — Though not a dirge
   Is thine, beside the wailing blast,
Time cannot in oblivion merge
   The light thy star of glory cast;

CHARLES A. JONES

While heave yon high hills to the sky,
　While rolls yon dark and turbid river,
Thy name and fame can never die —
　Whom Freedom loves, will live forever.
1838.

THE OLD MOUND [1]
(Extract)

Lonely and sad it stands:
　The trace of ruthless hands
Is on its sides and summit, and, around,
The dwellings of the white man pile the ground;
　And, curling in the air,
The smoke of thrice a thousand hearths is there:
　Without, all speaks of life,— within,
　Deaf to the city's echoing din,
Sleep well the tenants of that silent Mound,
Their names forgot, their memories unrenown'd.

　Upon its top I tread,
　And see around me spread
Temples and mansions, and the hoary hills,
Bleak with the labor that the coffer fills,
　But mars their bloom the while,
And steals from nature's face its joyous smile:
　And here and there, below,
　The stream's meandering flow
Breaks on the view; and westward in the sky
The gorgeous clouds in crimson masses lie.

---

[1] This prehistoric earth-work, which gave name to Mound Street, Cincinnati, stood near the site of Hughes High School. It was originally more than thirty-five feet in height. "About eight feet were cut off by General Wayne, in 1794, to prepare it for the reception of a centinel." In November, 1841, the tumulus was entirely levelled, "in order to extend Mound Street across Fifth, and grade an alley."—See Drake's Picture of Cincinnati (1815); also Ford's History of Cincinnati (1881).

The hammer's clang rings out,
Where late the Indian's shout
Startled the wild-fowl from its sedgy nest,
And broke the wild deer's and the panther's rest.
The lordly oaks went down
Before the ax — the cane-brake is a town:
The bark canoe no more
'Glides noiseless from the shore;
And, sole memorial of a nation's doom,
Amid the works of art rises this lonely tomb.

DANIEL DECATUR EMMETT

DANIEL DECATUR EMMETT was born at Mount Vernon, Ohio, October 29, 1815, and he died at the place of his birth, June 28, 1904. "His early schooling was of the most elementary character," writes his biographer, Hon. C. B. Galbreath. . . . "In the printing office his real education began. The training that he there received is revealed in the carefully and generally accurate punctuation of his manuscript papers. At the age of thirteen years he began work in the office of the Huron Reflector, at Norwalk, Ohio. Shortly afterward he returned to Mount Vernon and was employed by C. P. Bronson on the Western Aurora until he reached the age of seventeen years. Here he knew the Sherman boys, of whom he related interesting reminiscences. . . . He entered the army at the early age of seventeen years as fifer, and served until discharged, July 8, 1835. He was first stationed at Newport, Kentucky, and afterward at Jefferson Barracks, below St. Louis, Missouri. In the service he improved his opportunity to study music, a fact to which he has borne detailed and explicit testimony."

Emmett was but fifteen or sixteen years old when he composed the negro rhyme and melody, "Old Dan Tucker," which immediately caught the popular ear and was sung and played wherever banjo minstrelsy afforded entertainment. Being a natural musician and comic actor, he was readily induced to travel with circus shows, and, after a varied experience, he was drawn to New York City, where, in 1848, he organized a troupe which he named the "Virginia Minstrels," and began his independent career as manager and star singer. In 1857 he engaged with an organization known as "Bryant's Minstrels," at 470 Broadway, New York, to act as "musician" and composer of negro melodies and plantation "walk-arounds," and he continued his connection with this company until 1865. It was while with Bryant's Minstrels in New York, that he composed the celebrated song, "Dixie," which was first produced in public on September 19, 1859. Other compositions by Emmett, which had a run in their day, were: "Jordan is a Hard Road to Travel," "Billy Patterson," "Road to Richmond," "Dar's a Darkey in de Tent," "Go Way, Boys," "Here We Are, or Cross Ober Jordan," "Striking Ile," "Old K-Y-Ky," and "Black Brigade."

For further particulars relating to the subject of this sketch, the reader is referred to Galbreath's very entertaining volume: Daniel Decatur Emmett, Author of "Dixie," (illustrated,) Columbus, O., 1904.

DIXIE [1]

I wish I was in de land ob cotton.
Old times dar am not forgotten;
    Look away! Look away! Look away! Dixie Land!
In Dixie Land whar I was born in,
Early on one frosty mornin',
    Look away! Look away! Look away! Dixie Land!

CHORUS:

Den I wish I was in Dixie! Hooray! Hooray!
In Dixie's Land we'll take our stand, to lib an' die in Dixie.
Away! away! away down South in Dixie.
Away! away! away down South in Dixie.

In Dixie Land de darkies grow,
If white folks only plant dar toe;
    Look away! Look away! Look away! Dixie Land!
Dey wet de groun' wid 'bakkar smoke,
Den up de darkies head will poke.
    Look away! Look away! Look away! Dixie Land!

---

[1] The orginal version of "Dixie," here reproduced, was first published in a booklet entitled "Emmett's Inimitable Plantation Songs," issued by Firth, Pond & Co., New York, 1860.

Missus married Will de weaber,
Will, he was a gay deceaber;
   Look away! Look away! Look away! Dixie Land!
When he put his arms around 'er,
He look as fierce as a forty pounder.
   Look away! Look away! Look away! Dixie Land!

Ole missus die,— she took a decline,
Her face was de color ob bacon-rhine;
   Look away! Look away! Look away! Dixie Land!
How could she act de foolish part,
An' marry a man to broke her heart.
   Look away! Look away! Look away! Dixie Land!

Den here's a health to de next ole missus
An' all de gals dat want to kiss us;
   Look away! Look away! Look away! Dixie Land!
Den hoe it down an' scratch yoa grabble.
To Dixie Land I'm boun' to trabble.
   Look away! Look away! Look away! Dixie Land!

ALICE CARY

ALICE CARY, the fourth child of Robert and Elizabeth (Jessup) Cary, was born April 26, 1820, in a rude frame house built by her father, in 1813, on a farm situated within the present limits of Mount Healthy, Ohio, a suburban village on Hamilton Pike, some three miles north of Cincinnati. In 1832 the family moved to a new and more commodious residence located near the site of their former dwelling, and the homestead was christened "Clovernook," a name which it still retains.[1] Though denied the advantages of academic schooling, Alice early manifested a facile talent for literary composition, and in her eighteenth year she contributed her first poetic venture, a piece entitled "The Child of Sorrow," to the Sentinel and Star in the West, a Universalist paper issued in the Queen City. She later wrote for several other local periodicals, including the Casket, the Herald of Truth, and the Western Quarterly Review; and also for the National Era, Washington, D. C., edited by Dr. Gamaliel Bailey, who, after printing a number of her poems and sketches, paid her ten dollars, the first pecuniary reward of her literary ambition. Among the discriminating critics who early recognized the unusual merit of her verse and encouraged her to continued effort, were Otway Curry and Edgar Allen Poe. In 1848, Rufus W. Griswold greatly increased her reputation by extolling her genius and liberally exploiting her work in his notable book, The Female Poets of America; and through his influence a small collection of poems by Alice and Phoebe Cary was brought out, in 1850, by Moss & Brother, Philadelphia. With the publication of this joint volume dates the beginning

---

[1] The Cary property was purchased by William A. Procter, of Cincinnati, who, on March 11, 1903, presented it to the Trader sisters (Miss Georgia D. and Miss Florence B. Trader), to be used as an institution for the blind. The historic homestead is now known as the "Clovernook Home for the Blind."

of the Cary sisters' national renown, and of their wide acquaintance with distinguished thinkers and writers, conspicuous among whom were Horace Greeley, who, in 1849, called on the poets at their "lonesome and obscure" country home, and John G. Whittier, whom they met in the following year, when they made their first pilgrimage to the East. Recording his personal reminiscences of this visit, in a poem entitled "The Singer," Whittier long afterwards wrote:

> "Timid and young, the elder had
> Even then a smile too sweetly sad;
> The crown of pain that all must wear
> Too early pressed her midnight hair.
>
> "Yet, ere the summer eve grew long,
> Her modest lips were sweet with song,
> A memory haunted all her words
> Of clover-fields and singing-birds.
>
> "Her dark, dilating eyes expressed
> The broad horizons of the West;
> Her speech dropped prairie flowers; the gold
> Of harvest wheat about her rolled."

In November, 1850, Alice established her permanent residence in New York City, where in the spring of 1851 she was joined by Phoebe and Elmina, and where thenceforward the three sisters made their home together. Here, in the house which the earnings of her pen had purchased, at 53 East Twentieth Street, the author died, February 12, 1870. She was buried in Greenwood Cemetery, Brooklyn.

More than seventy years have elapsed since Alice Cary gathered her first laurels as a poet. At the very beginning of her literary career she was received with applause, and from year to year her reputation steadily advanced. It is doubtful whether any other American woman, through the accomplishment of verse, has ever attained so much popular celebrity as did this country girl of Clovernook. Even today she has numerous readers and admirers, not only in Ohio and the West, but in all parts of the Union. This is not because her verse invariably stands the test of exacting criticism, for it does not, though it frequently possesses the rare qualities essential to poetic composition as a fine art. Readers love her personality and feel instinctively that she understands their feelings, and that she writes of what she really knows, from direct observation and experience. She was one of the poets "sown by nature." Her songs "gush from the heart." Delicate in her sympathies, she was sensitive to all beauty and to all truth. Every product of her genius, whether in prose or in verse, reveals a noble and generous mind free from every taint of affectation.

BALDER'S WIFE

Her casement like a watchful eye
    From the face of the wall looks down,
Lashed round with ivy vines so dry,
    And with ivy leaves so brown.
Her golden head in her lily hand
    Like a star in the spray o' the sea,
And wearily rocking to and fro,
She sings so sweet and she sings so low
    To the little babe on her knee.
But let her sing what tune she may,
Never so light and never so gay,
It slips and slides and dies away
    To the moan of the willow water.

Like some bright honey-hearted rose
    That the wild wind rudely mocks,
She blooms from the dawn to the day's sweet close
Hemmed in with a world of rocks.
The livelong night she does not stir,
    But keeps at her casement lorn,

And the skirts of the darkness shine with her
  As they shine with the light o' the morn;
And all who pass may hear her lay,
But let it be what tune it may,
It slips and slides and dies away
  To the moan of the willow water.

And there, within that one-eyed tower,
  Lashed round with the ivy brown,
She droops like some unpitied flower
  That the rain-fall washes down:
The damp o' the dew in her golden hair,
  Her cheek like the spray o' the sea,
And wearily rocking to and fro,
She sings so sweet and she sings so low
  To the little babe on her knee.
But let her sing what tune she may,
Never so glad and never so gay,
It slips and slides and dies away
  To the moan of the willow water.

PICTURES OF MEMORY [1]

Among the beautiful pictures
  That hang on Memory's wall,
Is one of a dim old forest,
  That seemeth best of all:
Not for its gnarled oaks olden,
  Dark with the mistletoe;

---

[1] This piece was greatly admired by Edgar Allen Poe, who pronounced it one of the most melodious lyrics in the English language, and who, in his review of Griswold's The Female Poets of America (1848) wrote: "We are proud to be able to say that one of Miss Alice Cary's poems is *decidedly the noblest poem in the collection*—although the most distinguished poetesses in the land have here included their most praiseworthy compositions. Our allusion is to 'Pictures of Memory.' Let our readers see it and judge for themselves. We speak deliberately:—in all the higher elements of poetry—in true imagination—in the power of exciting the only real poetical effect—elevation of *the soul*, in contradistinction from mere excitement of the intellect or heart—the poem in question is the noblest in the book."

Not for the violets golden
    That sprinkle the vale below;
Not for the milk-white lilies
    That lean from the fragrant hedge,
Coquetting all day with the sunbeams,
    And stealing their shining edge;
Not for the vines on the upland
    Where the bright red berries be,
Nor the pinks, nor the pale, sweet cowslip,
    It seemeth the best to me.

I once had a little brother,
    With eyes that were dark and deep —
In the lap of that old dim forest
    He lieth in peace asleep:
Light as the down of the thistle,
    Free as the winds that blow,
We roved there the beautiful summers,
    The summers of long ago;
But his feet on the hills grew weary,
    And, one of the autumn eves,
I made for my little brother
    A bed of the yellow leaves.

Sweetly his pale arms folded
    My neck in a meek embrace,
As the light of immortal beauty
    Silently covered his face:
And when the arrows of sunset
    Lodged in the tree-tops bright,
He fell, in his saint-like beauty,
    Asleep by the gates of light.
Therefore, of all the pictures
    That hang on Memory's wall,
The one of the old dim forest
    Seemeth the best of all.

NOW, AND THEN

"Sing me a song, my nightingale,
  Hid in among the twilight flowers;
And make it low," he said, "I pray,
And make it sweet." But she said, "Nay;
  Come when the morn begins to trail
Her golden glories o'er the gray —
  Morn is the time for love's all-hail!"
  He said, "The morning is not ours!

"Then give me back, my heart's delight,
  Hid in among the twilight flowers,
The kiss I gave you yesterday —
  See how the moon this way has leant,
  As if to yield a soft consent.
Surely," he said, "you will requite
My love in this?" But she said, "Nay."
"Yea, now," he said. But she said, "Hush!
And come to me at morning-blush."
  He said, "The morning is not ours!

"But say, at least, you love me, love.
  Hid in among the twilight flowers;
No winds are listening, far or near —
The sleepy doves will never hear."
  "Ah, leave me in my sacred glen;
  And when the saffron morn shall close
  Her misty arms about the rose,
Come, and my speech my thought shall prove —
Not now," she said! "not now, but then."
  He said, "The morning is not ours!"

TRICKSEY'S RING

O what a day it was to us,—
  My wits were upside down,
When cousin Joseph Nicholas
  Came visiting from town!

His curls they were so smooth and bright,
  His frills they were so fine,
I thought perhaps the stars that night
  Would be ashamed to shine.

But when the dews had touched the grass,
  They came out, large and small,
As if our cousin Nicholas
  Had not been there at all!

Our old house never seemed to me
  So poor and mean a thing
As then, and just because that he
  Was come a-visiting!

I never thought the sun prolonged
  His light a single whit
Too much, till then, nor thought he wronged
  My face, by kissing it.

But now I sought to pull my dress
  Of faded homespun down,
Because my cousin Nicholas
  Would see my feet were brown.

The butterflies — bright airy things —
  From off the lilac buds
I scared, for having on their wings
  The shadows of the woods.

I thought my straight and jet black hair
  Was almost a disgrace,
Since Joseph Nicholas had fair
  Smooth curls about his face.

ALICE CARY

I wished our rosy window sprays
  Were laces, dropping down,
That he might think we knew the ways
  Of rich folks in the town.

I wished the twittering swallow had
  A finer tune to sing,
Since such a stylish city lad
  Was come a-visiting.

I wished the hedges, as they swayed,
  Were each a solid wall,
And that our grassy lane were made
  A market street withal.

I wished the drooping heads of rye,
  Set full of silver dews,
Were silken tassels all to tie
  The ribbons of his shoes!

And when, by homely household slight,
  They called me Tricksey True,
I thought my cheeks would blaze, in spite
  Of all that I could do.

Tricksey!— that name would surely be
  A shock to ears polite;
In short, I thought that nothing we
  Could say or do was right.

For injured pride I could have wept,
  Until my heart and I
Fell musing how my mother kept
  So equable and high.

She did not cast her eyelids down,
  Ashamed of being poor;
To her a gay young man from town
  Was no discomfiture.

She reverenced honor's sacred laws
  As much, ay, more than he,
And was not put about because
  He had more gold than she;

But held her house beneath a hand
  As steady and serene,
As though it were a palace, and
  As though she were a queen.

And when she set our silver cup
  Upon the cloth of snow,
For Nicholas, I lifted up
  My timid eyes, I know;

And saw a ring, as needs I must,
  Upon his finger shine;
O how I longed to have it just
  A minute upon mine!

I thought of fairy folk that led
  Their lives in sylvan shades,
And brought fine things, as I had read,
  To little rustic maids.

And so I mused within my heart,
  How I would search about
The fields and woodlands, for my part,
  Till I should spy them out.

And so, when down the western sky
  The sun had dropped at last,
Right softly and right cunningly
  From out the house I passed.

It was as if awake I dreamed,
  All Nature was so sweet
The small round dandelions seemed
  Like stars beneath my feet.

ALICE CARY

Fresh greenness as I went along
  The grass did seem to take,
And birds beyond the time of song
  Kept singing for my sake.

The dew o'erran the lily's cup,
  The ground-moss shone so well,
That if the sky were down or up,
  Was hard for me to tell.

I never felt my heart to sit
  So lightly on its throne;
Ah, who knew what would come of it,
  With fairy folk alone!

An hour,— another hour went by,
  All harmless arts I tried,
And tried in vain, and wearily
  My hopes within me died.

No tent of moonshine, and no ring
  Of dancers could I find,—
The fairy rich folk and their king
  For once would be unkind!

My spirit, nameless fear oppressed;
  My courage went adrift,
As all out of the low dark west
  The clouds began to lift.

I lost my way within the wood,—
  The path I could not guess,
When, Heaven be praised, before me stood
  My cousin Nicholas!

Right tenderly within his arm
  My shrinking hand he drew;
He spoke so low, "These damps will harm
  My little Tricksey True."

I know not how it was: my shame
    In new delight was drowned;
His accent gave my rustic name
    Almost a royal sound.

He bent his cheek against my face,—
    He whispered in my ear,
"Why came you to this dismal place?
    Tell me, my little dear!"

Betwixt the boughs that o'er us hung
    The light began to fall;
His praises loosed my silent tongue,—
    At last I told him all.

I felt his lips my forehead touch;
    I shook and could not stand;
The ring I coveted so much
    Was shining on my hand!

We talked about the little elves
    And fairies of the grove,
And then we talked about ourselves,
    And then we talked of love.

'T was at the ending of the lane,—
    The garden yet to pass,
I offered back his ring again
    To my good Nicholas.

"Dear Tricksey, don't you understand,
    You foolish little thing,"
He said, "that I must have the hand,
    As well as have the ring?"

"Tonight — just now! I pray you wait!
    The hand is little worth!"
"Nay darling — now! we're at the gate!"
    And so he had them both!

THE GRAY SWAN

"Oh tell me, sailor, tell me true,
  Is my little lad, my Elihu,
    A-sailing with your ship?"
The sailor's eyes were dim with dew,—
"Your little lad, your Elihu?"
    He said with trembling lip,—
    "What little lad? what ship?"

"What little lad! as if there could be
  Another such a one as he!
    What little lad, do you say?
Why, Elihu, that took to the sea
The moment I put him off my knee!
    It was just the other day
    The *Gray Swan* sailed away."

"The other day?" the sailor's eyes
Stood open with a great surprise,—
    "The other day? the *Swan?*"
His heart began in his throat to rise.
"Ay, ay, sir, here in the cupboard lies
    The jacket he had on."
    "And so your lad is gone?"

"Gone with the *Swan.*" "And did she stand
With her anchor clutching hold of the sand,
    For a month, and never stir?"
"Why, to be sure! I've seen from the land,
Like a lover kissing his lady's hand,
    The wild sea kissing her,—
    A sight to remember, sir."

"But, my good mother, do you know
  All this was twenty years ago?
    I stood on the *Gray Swan's* deck,

And to that lad I saw you throw,
Taking it off, as it might be, so!
    The kerchief from your neck."
"Ay, and he'll bring it back!"

"And did the little lawless lad
That has made you sick and made you sad,
    Sail with the *Gray Swan's* crew?"
"Lawless! the man is going mad!
The best boy ever mother had,—
    Be sure he sailed with the crew!
    What would you have him do?"

"And he has never written line,
    Nor sent you word, nor made you sign
    To say he was alive?"
"Hold! if 't was wrong, the wrong is mine;
Besides, he may be in the brine,
    And could he write from the grave?
    Tut, man! what would you have?"

"Gone twenty years,— a long, long cruise,—
'T was wicked thus your love to abuse;
    But if the lad still live,
And come back home, think you you can
Forgive him?"—"Miserable man,
    You're mad as the sea,— you rave,—
    What have I to forgive?"

The sailor twitched his shirt so blue,
And from within his bosom drew
    The kerchief. She was wild.
    "My God! my Father! is it true?
My little lad, my Elihu!
    My blessed boy, my child!
    My dead, my living child!"

IDLE

I heard the gay spring coming,
I saw the clover blooming,
   Red and white along the meadows,
   Red and white along the streams;
I heard the bluebird singing,
I saw the green grass springing,
   All as I lay a-dreaming,—
   A-dreaming idle dreams.

I heard the ploughman's whistle,
I saw the rough burr thistle
   In the sharp teeth of the harrow,
   Saw the summer's yellow gleams
In the walnuts, in the fennel,
In the mulleins, lined with flannel,
   All as I lay a-dreaming,—
   A-dreaming idle dreams.

I felt the warm, bright weather,
Saw the harvest, saw them gather
   Corn and millet, wheat and apples,
   Saw the gray barns with their seams
Pressing wide,— the bare-armed shearers,
The ruddy water-bearers,
   All as I lay a-dreaming,—
   A-dreaming idle dreams.

The bluebird and her nestling
Flew away; the leaves fell rustling,
   The cold rain killed the roses,
   The sun withdrew his beams:
No creature cared about me,
The world could do without me,
   All as I lay a-dreaming,—
   A-dreaming idle dreams.

NOBILITY [1]

True worth is in *being,* not *seeming,*—
    In doing each day that goes by
Some little good — not in the dreaming
    Of great things to do by and by.
For whatever men say in blindness,
    And spite of the fancies of youth,
There's nothing so kingly as kindness,
    And nothing so royal as truth.

We get back our mete as we measure —
    We cannot do wrong and feel right,
Nor can we give pain and gain pleasure,
    For justice avenges each slight.
The air for the wing of the sparrow,
    The bush for the robin and wren,
But alway the path that is narrow
    And straight, for the children of men.

'Tis not in the pages of story
    The heart of its ills to beguile,
Though he who makes courtship to glory
    Gives all that he hath for her smile.
For when from her heights he has won her,
    Alas! it is only to prove
That nothing's so sacred as honor,
    And nothing so loyal as love!

We cannot make bargains for blisses,
    Nor catch them like fishes in nets;
And sometimes the thing our life misses,
    Helps more than the thing which it gets.

---

[1] This familiar piece is a good example of the numerous poems of a moral and didactic character, by Alice Cary, which for half a century have exercised a wholesome and elevating influence in many American schools and homes. Of kindred theme and motive are the poems entitled: "A Sermon to Young Folks," "Work," "Old Maxims," "Take Care," "Proverbs in Rhyme," "Faith and Works."

For good lieth not in pursuing,
  Nor gaining of great nor of small,
But just in the doing, and doing
  As we would be done by, is all.

Through envy, through malice, through hating,
  Against the world, early and late,
No jot of our courage abating —
  Our part is to work and to wait.
And slight is the sting of his trouble
  Whose winnings are less than his worth;
For he who is honest is noble,
  Whatever his fortunes or birth.

AN ORDER FOR A PICTURE
(Extract)

Oh, good painter, tell me true,
  Has your hand the cunning to draw
  Shapes of things that you never saw?
Ay? Well, here is an order for you.

Woods and corn-fields, a little brown,—
  The picture must not be over-bright,—
  Yet all in the golden and gracious light
Of a cloud, when the summer sun is down.
  Alway and alway, night and morn,
  Woods upon woods, with fields of corn
    Lying between them, not quite sere,
And not in the full, thick, leafy bloom,
When the wind can hardly find breathing-room
  Under their tassels,— cattle near,
Biting shorter the short green grass,
And a hedge of sumach and sassafras,
With bluebirds twittering all around,
(Ah, good painter, you can't paint sound!)
  These, and the house where I was born,

Low and little, and black and old,
With children, many as it can hold,
All at the windows, open wide,—
Heads and shoulders clear outside,
And fair young faces all ablush:
   Perhaps you may have seen, some day,
   Roses crowding the selfsame way,
Out of a wilding, wayside bush.

Thy works, O Lord, interpret Thee,
   And through them all Thy love is shown;
Flowing about us like a sea,
   Yet steadfast as the eternal throne.

Out of the light that runneth through
   Thy hand, the lily's dress is spun;
Thine is the brightness of the dew,
   And Thine the glory of the sun.

MY DREAM OF DREAMS
(Extract)

Alone within my house I sit;
   The lights are not for me,
The music, nor the mirth; and yet
   I lack not company.

So gayly go the gay to meet,
   Nor wait my griefs to mend —
My entertainment is more sweet
   Than thine, tonight, my friend.

Whilst thou, one blossom in thy hand,
   Bewail'st my weary hours,
Upon my native hills I stand
   Waist-deep among the flowers.

PHOEBE CARY

PHOEBE CARY, the sixth child in a family of two sons and seven daughters, was born September 4, 1824, in the "old brown homestead" at Clovernook, near Mount Healthy, Hamilton County, Ohio, where, with her elder sister, she received her elementary education in a log schoolhouse, and where, surrounded by the homely environments of country life, she grew to womanhood. In the spring of 1851, following the ambitious example of Alice, she removed to New York City, and there the two poets, united by the double bond of common literary aspiration and of lifelong mutual devotion, established their permanent home together. Phoebe outlived her sister by less than a year and a half, dying July 31, 1871. She was buried by the side of Alice, in Greenwood Cemetery, Brooklyn.

Critics and appraisers of literary genius have seldom done justice to the exceptional talent of Phoebe Cary, whose reputation as a poet has been somewhat obscured by the greater luster of her sister's fame. Though the amount of her work is relatively small, Phoebe was possessed of natural gifts scarcely inferior to those of Alice, nor was her artistic instinct less refined than that of her sister. Sincerity, directness, and genuine poetic feeling are qualities never absent from her verse. "No singer," writes her biographer, Mary Clemmer Ames, "was ever more thoroughly identified with her own songs than Phoebe Cary. With but few exceptions, they distilled the deepest and sweetest music of her soul. They uttered, besides, the cheerful philosophy which life had taught her, and the sunny faith which lifted her out of the dark region of doubt and fear, to rest forever in the loving kindness of her Heavenly Father."

OUR HOMESTEAD [1]

Our old brown homestead reared its walls
    From the wayside dust aloof,
Where the apple-boughs could almost cast
    Their fruit upon its roof;
And the cherry-tree so near it grew
    That when awake I've lain
In the lonesome nights, I've heard the limbs
    As they creaked against the pane;
And those orchard-trees, oh those orchard trees!
    I've seen my little brothers rocked
In their tops by the summer breeze.

The sweet-brier, under the window-sill,
    Which the early birds made glad,
And the damask rose, by the garden fence,
    Were all the flowers we had.
I've looked at many a flower since then,
    Exotics rich and rare,
That to other eyes were lovelier,
    But not to me so fair;
For those roses bright, oh those roses bright!
    I have twined them in my sister's locks,
That are hid in the dust from sight.

We had a well, a deep old well,
    Where the spring was never dry,
And the cool drops down from the mossy stones
    Were falling constantly;
And there never was water half so sweet
    As the draught which filled my cup,
Drawn up to the curb by the rude old sweep
    That my father's hand set up.

---

[1] The birthplace of the Cary sisters. No vestage of this house remains. A pleasant glimpse of the old homestead is given by Alice Cary in the poem entitled "An Order for a Picture."

And that deep old well, oh that deep old well!
    I remember now the plashing sound
Of the bucket as it fell.

Our homestead had an ample hearth,
    Where at night we loved to meet;
There my mother's voice was always kind,
    And her smile was always sweet;
And there I've sat on my father's knee,
    And watched his thoughtful brow,
With my childish hand in his raven hair,—
    That hair is silver now!
But that broad hearth's light, oh that broad hearth's light!
    And my father's look, and my mother's smile,
They are in my heart tonight!

THE ONLY ORNAMENT

Even as a child, too well she knew
    Her lack of loveliness and grace;
So, like an unprized weed she grew,
    Grudging the meanest flower its face.

Often with tears her sad eyes filled,
    Watching the plainest birds that went
About her home to pair, and build
    Their humble nests in sweet content.

No melody was in her words;
    You thought her, as she passed along,
As brown and homely as the birds
    She envied, but without their song.

She saw, and sighed to see how glad
    Earth makes her fair and favored child;
While all the beauty that she had
    Was in her smile, nor oft she smiled.

So seasons passed her and were gone,
　　She musing by herself apart;
Till the vague longing that is known
　　To woman came into her heart.

That feeling born when fancy teems
　　With all that makes this life a good,
Came to her with its wondrous dreams,
　　That bless and trouble maidenhood.

She would have deemed it joy to sit
　　In any home, or great or small,
Could she have hoped to brighten it
　　For one who thought of her at all.

At night, or in some secret place,
　　She used to think, with tender pain,
How infants love the mother's face,
　　And know not if 't is fair or plain.

She longed to feast her hungry eyes
　　On anything her own could please;
To sing soft, loving lullabies
　　To children lying on her knees.

And yet beyond the world she went,
　　Unmissed, as if she had not been,
Taking her only ornament,
　　A meek and quiet soul within.

None ever knew her heart was pained,
　　Or that she grieved to live unsought;
They deemed her cold and self-contained,
　　Contented in her realm of thought.

Her patient life, when it was o'er,
　　Was one that all the world approved;
Some marveled at, some pitied her,
　　But neither man nor woman loved.

Even little children felt the same;
  Were shy of her, from awe or fear;—
I wonder if she knew they came
  And scattered roses on her bier!

TRUE LOVE

I think true love is never blind,
  But rather brings an added light;
An inner vision quick to find
  The beauties hid from common sight.

No soul can ever clearly see
  Another's highest, noblest part,
Save through the sweet philosophy
  And loving wisdom of the heart.

Your unanointed eyes shall fall
  On him who fills my world with light;
You do not see my friend at all,
  You see what hides him from your sight.

I see the feet that fain would climb,
  You, but the steps that turn astray;
I see the soul unharmed, sublime,
  You, but the garment, and the clay.

You see a mortal, weak, misled,
  Dwarfed ever by the earthly clod;
I see how manhood, perfected,
  May reach the stature of a god.

Blinded I stood, as now you stand,
  Till on mine eyes, with touches sweet,
Love, the deliverer, laid his hand,
  And lo! I worship at his feet!

SONG

I see him part the careless throng,
   I catch his eager eye;
He hurries towards me where I wait; —
   Beat high, my heart, beat high!

I feel the glow upon my cheek,
   And all my pulses thrill;
He sees me, passes careless by; —
   Be still, my heart, be still!

He takes another hand than mine,
   It trembles for his sake;
I see his joy, I feel my doom; —
   Break, oh my heart-strings, break!

VAIN REPENTANCE

Do we not say, forgive us, Lord,
   Oft when too well we understand
Our sorrow is not such as Thou
   Requirest at the sinner's hand?

Have we not sought Thy face in tears,
   When our desire hath rather been
Deliverance from the punishment,
   Than full deliverance from the sin?

Alas! we mourn because we fain
   Would keep the things we should resign:
And pray, because we cannot pray —
   Not my rebellious will, but Thine!

A WEARY HEART

Ye winds, that talk among the pines,
   In pity whisper soft and low;
And from my trailing garden vines
   Bear the faint odors as ye go;

Take fragrance from the orchard trees,
  From the meek violet in the dell;
Gather the honey that the bees
  Had left you in the lily's bell;

Pass tenderly as lovers pass,
  Stoop to the clover-blooms your wings,
Find out the daisies in the grass,
  The sweets of all insensate things;

With muffled feet, o'er beds of flowers,
  Go through the valley to the height,
Where frowning walls and lofty towers
  Shut in a weary heart tonight;

Go comfort her, who fain would give
  Her wealth below, her hopes above,
For the wild freedom that ye have
  To kiss the humblest flower ye love!

THOMAS BUCHANAN READ

THOMAS BUCHANAN READ was born in Chester County, Pa., March 12, 1822. At the age of seventeen he came to Cincinnati, Ohio, where he began his art career as a pupil of the sculptor Clevinger, and as a portrait-painter under the patronage of Nicholas Longworth. He afterwards lived, by turns, in New York, Boston, Philadelphia, London, Paris, Florence, and Rome, but Cincinnati was always his favorite social harbor and resort, and the source of his best inspiration. In 1852, Mr. Read became a member of the Literary Club of Cincinnati, and from 1861 to 1867 he was a resident of the Queen City, making his home with his brother-in-law, Mr. Cyrus Garrett, at the old Garrett house, (now "The Sheridan,") 23 East Eighth Street. It was here that he wrote many of his poems, including the spirited and patriotic lines in reminiscence of which the historic homestead has been given its present name. Perhaps the most interesting episode of Read's life in Cincinnati relates to the composition of the poem, "Sheridan's Ride," which was written at the suggestion of Mr. Garrett, on the afternoon of October 31, 1864, and read on the evening of the same day by James E. Murdoch, before an enthusiastic audience of "two or three thousand of the warmest hearts in Cincinnati," at Pike's Opera House. According to Mr. Murdoch, the piece was struck off in about three hours, and was not afterwards altered, excepting to introduce the stanza recording the fifteen-mile stage of the ride. On November 3, Mr. Read was in New York, where he attended the birthday reception given to William Cullen Bryant, on which occasion the new war-poem was again read. At the close of the reading Mr. Bryant grasped the author by the hand with great warmth, exclaiming, "That poem will live as long as Lochinvar!" Referring to the origin of the piece, Gen. Sheridan is reported to have said: "The incident was mine, the poem Murdoch's; Read wrote it for him:—see!"

In 1862, when Cincinnati was threatened by Kirby Smith's troops, Mr. Read was on the military staff of Gen. Lew Wallace, commander of the Union forces in and near the city, and he subsèquently contributed to the Atlantic Monthly a lucid account of the "Siege" of Cincinnati. Of historical and literary interest is the author's occasional poem entitled "Pons Maximus," which was written to commemorate the completion of the great Suspension Bridge uniting Cincinnati and Covington, Ky., and which appeared in the Daily Commercial on New Year's Day, 1868.

Thomas Buchanan Read died in New York City, May 11, 1872.

For further particulars relating to the poet's career in Cincinnati, see article by W. H. Venable, in the Ohio Educational Monthly, May, 1898.

SHERIDAN'S RIDE [1]

Up from the South at break of day,
Bringing to Winchester fresh dismay,
The affrighted air with a shudder bore,
Like a herald in haste, to the chieftain's door,
The terrible grumble, and rumble, and roar,
Telling the battle was on once more,
And Sheridan twenty miles away.

And wider still those billows of war
Thundered along the horizon's bar;
And louder yet into Winchester rolled
The roar of that red sea uncontrolled,
Making the blood of the listener cold,
As he thought of the stake in that fiery fray,
And Sheridan twenty miles away.

---

[1] Copyright, 1894, by Harriet Dennison Read.

But there is a road from Winchester town,
A good broad highway leading down;
And there, through the flush of the morning light,
A steed as black as the steeds of night,
Was seen to pass, as with eagle flight,
As if he knew the terrible need;
He stretched away with his utmost speed;
Hills rose and fell, but his heart was gay,
With Sheridan fifteen miles away.

Still sprung from those swift hoofs, thundering South,
The dust, like smoke from the cannon's mouth;
Or the trail of a comet, sweeping faster and faster,
Foreboding to traitors the doom of disaster.
The heart of the steed, and the heart of the master
Were beating like prisoners assaulting their walls,
Impatient to be where the battle-field calls;
Every nerve of the charger was strained to full play,
With Sheridan only ten miles away.

Under his spurning feet the road
Like an arrowy Alpine river flowed,
And the landscape sped away behind
Like an ocean flying before the wind,
And the steed, like a bark fed with furnace ire,
Swept on, with his wild eye full of fire.
But lo! he is nearing his heart's desire;
He is snuffing the smoke of the roaring fray,
With Sheridan only five miles away.

The first that the general saw were the groups
Of stragglers, and then the retreating troops.
What was done? what to do? a glance told him both;
Then striking his spurs, with a terrible oath,
He dashed down the line, 'mid a storm of huzzas,
And the wave of retreat checked its course there, because

THOMAS BUCHANAN READ

The sight of the master compelled it to pause.
With foam and with dust, the black charger was gray;
By the flash of his eye, and the red nostril's play,
He seemed to the whole great army to say,
"I have brought you Sheridan all the way
From Winchester, down to save the day!"

Hurrah! hurrah for Sheridan!
Hurrah! hurrah for horse and man!
And when their statues are placed on high,
Under the dome of the Union sky,
The American soldiers' Temple of Fame;
There with the glorious general's name,
Be it said, in letters both bold and bright,
"Here is the steed that saved the day,
By carrying Sheridan into the fight,
From Winchester, twenty miles away!"

DRIFTING [1]

My soul to-day
Is far away,
Sailing the Vesuvian Bay;
My wingèd boat,
A bird afloat,
Swings round the purple peaks remote:—

Round purple peaks
It sails, and seeks
Blue inlets and their crystal creeks,
Where high rocks throw,
Through deeps below,
A duplicated golden glow.

Copyright, 1894, by Harriet Dennison Read.

Far, vague, and dim,
The mountains swim;
While on Vesuvius' misty brim,
With outstretched hands,
The gray smoke stands
O'erlooking the volcanic lands.

Here Ischia smiles
O'er liquid miles;
And yonder, bluest of the isles,
Calm Capri waits,
Her sapphire gates
Beguiling to her bright estates.

I heed not, if
My rippling skiff
Float swift or slow from cliff to cliff;
With dreamful eyes
My spirit lies
Under the walls of Paradise.

Under the walls
Where swells and falls
The Bay's deep breast at intervals,
At peace I lie,
Blown softly by,
A cloud upon this liquid sky.

The day, so mild,
Is Heaven's own child,
With Earth and Ocean reconciled;
The airs I feel
Around me steal
Are murmuring to the murmuring keel.

Over the rail
My hand I trail
Within the shadow of the sail,
A joy intense,
The cooling sense
Glides down my drowsy indolence.

With dreamful eyes
My spirit lies
Where Summer sings and never dies,—
O'erveiled with vines
She glows and shines
Among her future oil and wines.

Her children, hid
The cliffs amid,
Are gambolling with the gambolling kid;
Or down the walls,
With tipsy calls,
Laugh on the rocks lie waterfalls.

The fisher's child,
With tresses wild,
Unto the smooth, bright sand beguiled,
With glowing lips
Sings as she skips,
Or gazes at the far-off ships.

Yon deep bark goes
Where traffic blows,
From lands of sun to lands of snows;
This happier one,—
Its course is run
From lands of snow to lands of sun.

O happy ship,
To rise and dip,
With the blue crystal at your lip!

O happy crew,
My heart with you
Sails, and sails, and sings anew!

No more, no more
The worldly shore
Upbraids me with its loud uproar:
With dreamful eyes
My spirit lies
Under the walls of Paradise!

THE CLOSING SCENE [1]

Within his sober realm of leafless trees
　　The russet year inhaled the dreamy air;
Like some tanned reaper in his hour of ease,
　　When all the fields are lying brown and bare.

The gray barns looking from their lazy hills
　　O'er the dim waters widening in the vales,
Sent down the air a greeting to the mills,
　　On the dull thunder of alternate flails.

All sights were mellowed and all sounds subdued,
　　The hills seemed farther and the streams sang low;
As in a dream the distant woodman hewed
　　His winter log with many a muffled blow.

The embattled forests, erewhile armed in gold,
　　Their banners bright with every martial hue,
Now stood, like some sad beaten host of old,
　　Withdrawn afar in Time's remotest blue.

On slumbrous wings the vulture held his flight;
　　The dove scarce heard his sighing mate's complaint;
And, like a star slow drowning in the light,
　　The village church-vane seemed to pale and faint.

[1] Copyright, 1894, by Harriet Dennison Read.

The sentinel-cock upon the hill-side crew,—
  Crew thrice, and all was stiller than before,
Silent till some replying warder blew
  His alien horn, and then was heard no more.

Where erst the jay, within the elm's tall crest,
  Made garrulous trouble round her unfledged young,
And where the oriole hung her swaying nest,
  By every light wind like a censer swung;

Where sang the noisy masons of the eaves,
  The busy swallows, circling ever near,
Foreboding, as the rustic mind believes,
  An early harvest and a plenteous year;

Where every bird which charmed the vernal feast
  Shook the sweet slumber from its wings at morn,
To warn the reaper of the rosy east,—
  All now was songless, empty, and forlorn.

Alone from out the stubble piped the quail,
  And croaked the crow through all the dreamy gloom;
Alone the pheasant, drumming in the vale,
  Made echo to the distant cottage loom.

There was no bud, no bloom upon the bowers;
  The spiders wove their thin shrouds night by night;
The thistle-down, the only ghost of flowers,
  Sailed slowly by, passed noiseless out of sight.

Amid all this, in this most cheerless air,
  And where the woodbine shed upon the porch
Its crimson leaves, as if the Year stood there
  Firing the floor with his inverted torch;

Amid all this, the centre of the scene,
  The white-haired matron, with monotonous tread,
Plied the swift wheel, and with her joyless mien,
  Sat, like a Fate, and watched the flying thread.

She had known Sorrow,— he had walked with her,
  Oft supped and broke the bitter ashen crust;
And in the dead leaves still she heard the stir
  Of his black mantle trailing in the dust.

While yet her cheek was bright with summer bloom,
  Her country summoned and she gave her all;
And twice War bowed to her his sable plume,—
  Regave the swords to rust upon her wall.

Regave the swords,— but not the hand that drew
  And struck for Liberty its dying blow,
Nor him who, to his sire and country true,
  Fell mid the ranks of the invading foe.

Long, but not loud, the droning wheel went on,
  Like the low murmur of a hive at noon;
Long, but not loud, the memory of the gone
  Breathed through her lips a sad and tremulous tune.

At last the thread was snapped — her head was bowed;
  Life dropped the distaff through his hands serene,—
And loving neighbors smoothed her careful shroud,
  While Death and Winter closed the autumn scene.

WILLIAM JAMES SPERRY

WILLIAM JAMES SPERRY, son of James Sperry, was born January 25, 1823, at Henrietta, N. Y. His residence in Ohio dates from the year 1840, when he entered Oberlin College, which institution he attended for three consecutive years, and from which he graduated in 1843, receiving the degree of Bachelor of Arts. According to the recollection of his cousin, Mrs. E. M. Webster, of Spencerport, N. Y., he was for a time engaged with his brother, Henry H. Sperry, in the publication of a newspaper in Cincinnati; and from a reference to his work by his friend, the poet W. D. Gallagher, in 1884, it appears that Mr. Sperry was associated editorially with Dr. Gamaliel Bailey, who, in 1837, became proprietor of the Philanthropist, (the organ of the Ohio Antislavery Society,) a journal which in 1843 was merged into the Cincinnati Morning Herald, also an abolitionist paper. In 1847 Bailey removed to Washington City, and there conducted the National Era, (in which Uncle Tom's Cabin was originally published,) to the columns of which Sperry was a contributor. After the cholera epidemic of 1850, which demoralized business in the Queen City, Mr. Sperry went to San Francisco, Cal., where he died, in the month of March, 1856. His memory has been kept alive by the melodious lyric, "A Lament for the Ancient People," a poem which, after going the rounds of the newspaper press, was given deserved conspicuity by James W. Taylor, in his History of Ohio, 1854, and which has since been frequently reprinted, no less on account of its musical charm than because of its peculiar historical interest.

A LAMENT FOR THE ANCIENT PEOPLE

 Sad are fair Muskingum's waters,
  Sadly, blue Mahoning raves;
 Tuscarawas' plains are lonely,
  Lonely are Hockhocking's waves.
 From where headlong Cuyahoga
  Thunders down its rocky way,
 And the billows of blue Erie
  Whiten in Sandusky's bay,
 Unto where Potomac rushes
  Arrowy from the mountain side,
 And Kanawha's gloomy waters
  Mingle with Ohio's tide,
 From the valley of Scioto,
  And the Huron sisters three,
 To the foaming Susquehanna
  And the leaping Genesee;
 Over hill and plain and valley —
  Over river, lake and bay —
 On the water — in the forest —
  Ruled and reigned the Seneca.

 But sad are fair Muskingum's waters,
  Sadly, blue Mahoning raves;
 Tuscarawas' plains are lonely,
  Lonely are Hockhocking's waves.
 By Kanawha dwells the stranger,
  Cuyahoga feels the chain,
 Stranger ships vex Erie's billows,
  Strangers plow Scioto's plain.
 And the Iroquois have wasted
  From the hill and plain away;
 On the waters,— in the valley,—
  Reigns no more the Seneca.
 Only by the Cattaraugus,
  Or by Lake Chautauqua's side,

Or among the scanty woodlands
  By the Alleghany's tide,—
There, in spots, like sad oases,
  Lone amid the sandy plains,
There the Seneca, still wasting,
  Amid desolation reigns.

WILLIAM PENN BRANNAN

WILLIAM PENN BRANNAN, poet and artist, was born in Cincinnati, Ohio, March 22, 1825. Of his efforts with the pen, W. T. Coggeshall wrote, in 1860: "Mr. Brannan is a regular poetical contributor to several leading literary journals, and is the author of humorous sketches in prose, which have been read wherever American newspapers are circulated." One of Brannan's laughter-provoking pieces, a burlesque sermon, or extravaganza, entitled "The Harp of a Thousand Strings," was immensely popular on the school stage, and with professional elocutionists. The only book published by this author is a volume, issued in Cincinnati in 1865, bearing the title, "Vagaries of Vandyke Brown; an Autobiography in Verse." The poet died in St. Mary's Hospital, Cincinnati, in 1866.

SAINT MARY'S HOSPITAL
(Extracts)

The east is red with beacon-fires,
    And night's deep shadows are withdrawn
From silent streets and hill and lawn;
And sunlight gilds the heavenward spires,
    Where sweet bells ring another dawn.

Now, struggling from the arms of sleep,
    I wake once more to joy and pain —
    I wake to mortal life again,
And look abroad o'er heaven's blue deep
    Where sunlight sheds its golden rain.

WILLIAM PENN BRANNAN

The sunshine flashes down the walls,
   And matin bells peal forth again
   Return of prayer — return of pain —
Like troubled sounds of waterfalls,
   Baptizing all the heart and brain.

And wandering thought returns once more;
   The day is wearing into noon,
   Yet health, that ever-precious boon,
Has fled beyond my chamber-door
   Away into the fields of June.

And where is he that died today?
   Whose form was borne away from hence,
   Bereft of mortal life and sense,—
As cold and stark as potter's clay,—
   His dead remains a rank offense?

We all must follow in his wake,
   'Wherever gone or whither bound;
   We all will meet on common ground,
And take our chance through Jesus' sake,
   To reach where heavenly joys abound.

Yet life is dear to all that groan;
   They long and yet they fear to go
   To endless bliss or endless woe —
A leap into the dark unknown
   That clouds the skeptic's stolid brow.

Thus, struggling on through doubts and fears,
   Now daring all — now doubting naught,
   'My soul is swayed by varied thought,
And drifts along the tide of years
   With all the teachers and the taught.

I will not bow with patient knees
  To mouldering laws or bigot creeds;
  My nature knows its wants and needs,
And scorns all cant hypocrisies
  Of hollow words and empty deeds.

I am unto myself a law;
  No mortmain reaching from the grave,
  Shall drag me down where demons rave,
Or bow my soul with servile awe
  To that which has no power to save.

   * * *

A larger breadth of heart and mind,
  A genial grasp, a loving law,
  Would melt each stubborn soul, and draw
In bonds of peace all human-kind
  'Not stultified by slavish awe.

A larger love for those who fall,
  A faith that reaches from the sod
  Of Adam-nature up to God,
And finds the germ of good in all —
  'From angels to an outcast clod.

   * * *

Where Truth and Error, hand in hand,
  Have sped along the shores of time,
  And scattered seeds of peace and crime,
I, too, have overwalked the land,
  And planted thorns and buds sublime.

The footprints of a world gone by,
  The records of a golden age,
  The deeds of savage, saint, and sage,
The pyramids that pierce the sky,
  Are landmarks of my pilgrimage.

WILLIAM PENN BRANNAN

I envy every bird that flies
    And clips the air on soaring wings;
    I envy every lark that sings
Away in cool eternal skies,
    Where heavenly music reigns and rings.

And I would cool my burning brow
    Beneath a roaring waterfall
    O'ershadowed by a forest tall,
Where not a ray of sunlit glow
    E'er warmed the rocky, dripping wall:

No sound of woe could reach me there,
    No human eye would mark the spot,
    No search would find the hidden grot,
Afar from wasting pain and care,
    Where I might rest and be forgot.

HELEN LOUISA BOSTWICK BIRD

AMONG the biographical and critical notices in Coggeshall's The Poets and Poetry of the West, there is a brief sketch of Helen Louisa Bostwick, contributed by W. D. Howells, who says: "No woman poet of our country, as the writer of this sketch thinks, has surpassed Mrs. Bostwick in those graces of thought and style which distinguish her poems. Her choice of words is extremely felicitous; her rhyme is rich and full; her verse is always sweet and harmonious. . . . If her faculty does not amount to genius, it is at least transcendent talent."

Mrs. Helen Louisa Bostwick Bird, a daughter of Dr. Putnam Barrow, was born January 5, 1826, at North Charlestown, New Hampshire, where the first twelve years of her girlhood were passed. Here she received an elementary common-school education, which was supplemented by special private tuition under Rev. A. A. Miner, of Boston. In 1838 she removed with her father and mother to a farm near Ravenna, Portage County, Ohio, where, in 1844, at the age of eighteen, she was married to Mr. Edwin Bostwick. Her husband died September 9, 1860, leaving two daughters,— Florence, who lived to be only fifteen years old, and Marion, who died at the age of thirty. Mrs. Bostwick remained in widowhood until 1875, when she became the wife of Dr. John F. Bird, and removed with him to Philadelphia, where he died January 20, 1904, and where the subject of this sketch continued to reside during the remainder of her life. She died December 20, 1907.

Nearly all of Mrs. Bird's literary work was done in Ohio, chiefly within the period of her first widowhood. She began writing for the press at the age of eighteen, and was for many years a valued contributor to various newspapers and magazines, including the National Era, the New York Independent, the

Home Monthly, the Ohio Farmer, the Home Journal, the Saturday Evening Post, and the Atlantic Monthly.

Mrs. Bird's best poems, most of which were produced subsequently to the publication of Coggeshall's pioneer collection, are to be found in a little volume entitled Four O'Clocks, which was issued in Philadelphia in 1888. That the brilliant promise which Mr. Howells discovered in the author's earlier verse was not illusory, but betokened the unfolding of original powers so exceptional as to entitle their possessor to a place of distinction among the women poets of her time, is demonstrated by the contents of the volume just named, several typical selections from which are here given.

DRAFTED

Who's drafted? Not Harry! my son! Why man, 'tis a boy
    at his books;
No taller, I think, than your Annie; as delicate, too, in his looks.
Why, it seems but a day since he helped me, girl-like, in my
    kitchen, at tasks;
He drafted! Great God — can it be that our President knows
    what he asks?

He never could wrestle — this boy — though in spirit as bold
    as the best;
Narrow-chested a little, you notice, like him who has long
    been at rest.
Too slender for over-much study; why, his master has made
    him to-day
Go out with his ball on the common,— and you've drafted a
    child at his play!

Not a patriot? Fie! did I whimper when Robert stood up
    with his gun,
And the hero-blood chafed in his forehead, the evening we
    heard of Bull Run?

Pointing his finger at Harry, but turning his eyes to the wall,
"*There's* a staff growing up for your age, mother," said Robert,
"if I should fall."

Eighteen? Oh, I know; and yet narrowly,— just a wee babe
on the day
When his father got up from a sick bed, and cast his last
ballot for Clay;
Proud of his boy and his ticket! Said he: "A new morsel
of fame
We'll lay on our candidate's altar," and christened the child
with his name.

Oh, what have I done, a weak woman, in what have I meddled
with harm,
Troubling only my God for the sunshine and rain on my rough
little farm,
That my ploughshares are beaten to swords, and whetted
before my eyes?
That my tears must cleanse a foul nation, my lamb be a sacrifice?

Oh, 'tis true there's a country to save, man, and 'tis true there
is no appeal;
But did God see my boy's name lying the uppermost one in
the wheel?
Five stalwart sons has my neighbor, and never the lot upon one!
Are these things Fortune's caprices, or is it God's will that is
done?

Are the others too precious for resting where Robert is taking
his rest?
With the pictured face of your Annie lying over the rent in
his breast;
Too tender for parting with sweethearts, too fair to be crippled
and scarred?
My boy! thank God for these tears; I was growing so bitter
and hard!

Let us sit by the firelight, Harry; let us talk in the firelight's shine
Of something that's nobler than living, of a Love that is higher than mine,
That shall go with my soldier to battle, shall stand with my picket on guard;—
My boy! thank God for these tears; I was growing so bitter and hard!

MY MOUNTAIN

My mountain's base has goodly breadth of green;
Laps of lush grass and lilied sacristies,
Groves rapturous with music. Sharp from these
Steep crags uprise and dizzy cliffs o'erlean,
And pallid cataracts totter out between.
Far up — its lofty summits loom, stark white;
They know the storm-clouds, thunders, and great light.
Midway —'tis belted by a broad plateau,
My zone of calms. Short turf, few flowers, but fair,
Are here; cold waters and swift wholesome air.
Here in thin, grateful shade, I sit and dream,
While tawny August tans the fields below.
"How cold!" I say, "my mountain summits gleam."
Almost I seem to touch their caps of snow.
Then, smiling, mark far downward, 'neath my feet,
The steel blue verges shimmering in the heat,
And distant reapers resting by their wheat.

MY ISLAND

My feet have never trod thy flowery ways,
  O my fair Island, situate in the sea,
  Whose green curled tongues still lap thee back from me,
Strive how I may. Yet oft in wintry days
I stretch my hands toward thee as toward a blaze

That warms and cheers. I know what beauty fills
　Those groves of thine, what flash of crimson bills
Adrip with music; what sweet wind delays
　Among the bashful lilies cloistered there.
In summer heats I watch, through dust and glare,
The grey mists wrap thee, and across thy crest
The rainy grass blown slantwise toward the west,
　While mutinous fountains shake their jeweled hair.
Sometimes I seek thee ill, (oh, deaf and blind!)
　And cannot find thee, lovliest, anywhere;
　Yet — whether by some vague, stirred pulse of air,
Or fugitive sweet odor undefined —
　Even then I know thee, O thou rare and fair,
That thou dost lie between me and the wind!

MY RIVER

Sing out, laugh out, O River, glad and new,
Sing out, ring out, the wooded gorges through;
Sing, sing, and bring from meadows morning-sweet,
The green of mosses on your twinkling feet.
White gleam your dainty shallops in the sun,
And deftly row the rowers, all as one.
— Sing louder, River, for the noon is high,
And swiftly speed the freighted barges by,
And deftly row the rowers as they sing,
"That which we bear away we never bring."
— O River, widening toward an unseen tide,
Your slowing current seeks the yielding side,
And heavily row the rowers as they feel
The long waves lapsing underneath the keel.
Sing low — sing low — O River, winding slow,
The sea is near — the darkness falls — sing low!

MY LAKE

My little lake doth in a valley lie,
   Bowered deep in green of ancient solitudes;
No dust nor din of highway cometh nigh,
   No reek of towns can pass these winnowing woods.
One stilly nook it has whose borders keep
   Trace of a shape to human outline true;
As if some Queen of Naiads, fallen asleep,
   Veiled her soft beauty 'neath the dimpling blue.
And see — upon the cove's remotest edge,
A single lily trembling in the sedge;
As if the gracious sleeper lightly slept,
   And from beneath her garment's tremulous hem
One fair white instep in a dream had crept,
   Lighting up all the dim place like a gem.

SO MANY TIMES

To-day, beloved, if one should say to me,
"Some great, new joy awaits thy friend and thee,"
Perchance I should turn wearily, and say,
"Nay; let to-morrow be as yesterday."
So many times have we two feared to touch
   The summer's largesse, purpling o'er the lands,
Lest our pale blood be colored overmuch;
   So many times sat still with heavy hands,
Watching the mellow vintage go to waste,
And we too tired, dear heart, too tired to taste.

'Twill not be thus, O friend, 'twill not be thus
In distant summers, ripening slow for us;
When we shall walk beside the fruited vines
Full-handed, and press out the cordial wines.
Nor drop the cup from hands too weak to hold,
   Nor fear to taste, nor tasting, fear to stop;

"O cup so new," our lips shall cry, "yet old;
  O cup so sweet, and yet no cloying drop!
O cup so full, and yet no overflow —
How could we know, dear heart, how could we know!"

HOW THE GATES CAME AJAR

'Twas whispered one morning in Heaven,
  How the little child-angel, May,
By the side of the great white portal,
  Sat sorrowing night and day.
How she said to the stately warden
  (Keeper of key and bar),—
"O angel, sweet angel, I pray you,
  Set the beautiful gates ajar.
Only a little, I pray you,
  Set the beautiful gates ajar!

"I can hear my mother weeping;
  She is lonely — she cannot see
One glimmer of light in the darkness,
  Where the gates closed after me.
One gleam of the golden splendor,
  O warden! would shine so far;"
But the warden answered: "I dare not
  Set the beautiful gates ajar."
Spoke low as he answered: "I dare not
  Set the beautiful gates ajar."

Then up arose Mary the Blessèd,
  Sweet Mary, Mother of Christ;
Her hand on the hand of the angel
  She laid, and her touch sufficed.
Turned was the key in the portal,
  Fell ringing the golden bar;

And lo! in the little child's fingers
  Stood the beautiful gates ajar.
In the little child-angel's fingers
  Stood the beautiful gates ajar!

"And this key, forever and ever,
  To my blessèd Son shall be given;"
Said Mary, Mother of Jesus —
  Tenderest heart in Heaven.
Now, never a sad-eyed mother
  But may catch the glory afar,
Since safe in the Lord Christ's bosom
  Are the keys of the gates ajar;
Safe hid in the dear Christ's bosom,
  And the gates forever ajar!

THE LOST IMAGE

A wandering singer at my door
  Asked leave to try her minstrelsy;
  Small pain the discord was to me,
And still the children begged for more.

Some coins I gave for peace at last;
  But, as she thrust them in her dress,
  Striving to make its scantiness
Hold all her gathered treasures fast,

Some sudden terror o'er her crept;
  Apart her ragged robe she tore,
  Felt all its foldings o'er and o'er,
And still so bitterly she wept;

So oft her swarthy brow she crossed,
  So scanned the turf about her feet
  With "Misereres" mournful-sweet,
That from her bosom she had lost

Some precious thing I gathered well;
  But speech so strangely did she mix,
  That if it were a crucifix,
Or book, or beads, I could not tell.

She went away disconsolate,
  Searching her tattered tunic o'er,
  Wailing and moaning, more and more,
And looking backward from the gate.

Next morning —'midst the lilac slips,
  The children found, and brought in haste,
  An image, rude and time-defaced,
Yet with strange sweetness on the lips.

So then, those wretched rags, we knew
  Had held our faith's sublimest sign;
  As glimpses of the One Divine
Oft peep some moral ruin through.

So, when for meaner gains, we lose
  That faithful presence in our breast,
  Vain words of moaning and unrest
Are all the cheated soul can use.

THE LITTLE COFFIN

'Twas a tiny rosewood thing,
Ebon bound, and glittering
With its stars of silver white,
Silver tablet, blank and bright,
Downy pillowed, satin lined,
That I, loitering, chanced to find
'Mid the dust, and scent, and gloom
Of the undertaker's room,
Waiting empty — ah! for whom?

Ah! what love-watched cradle-bed
Keeps to-night the nestling head;
Or, on what soft, pillowing breast
Is the cherub form at rest,
That ere long, with darkened eye,
Sleeping to no lullaby,
Whitely robed, and still, and cold,
Pale flowers slipping from its hold,
Shall this dainty couch enfold?

Ah! what bitter tears shall stain
All this satin sheen like rain,
And what towering hopes be hid
'Neath this tiny coffin lid,
Scarcely large enough to bear
Little words, that must be there,
Little words, cut deep and true,
Bleeding mothers' hearts anew —
Sweet, pet name, and "Agèd Two."

Oh! can sorrow's hovering plume
Round our pathway càst a gloom
Chill and darksome as the shade
By an infant's coffin made!
From our arms an angel flies,
And our startled, dazzled eyes
Weeping round its vacant place,
Cannot rise its path to trace,
Cannot see the angel's face!

IN THE FISHER'S HUT

Storm blowing wild without, waves at fearful height,
Three little frightened ones keeping watch and light;
Ill fare the fishermen out of port to-night!

 Winsome maid is Blonde-hair, scarcely turned eleven,
 Sturdy boy is Brown-hair, lacks a month of seven;
 Baby girl is Gold-hair, one year out of Heaven.

Fast drives the little boat; there are rocks ahead —
How beats the father's heart in that hour of dread!
"Christ, they are motherless!" were the words he said.

"Christ — they are motherless!" Did an angel bear
Heavenward that anguished cry? — yet a little prayer,
"Please God, keep father safe," was before it there.

Anxious maiden Blonde-hair heaps the driftwood higher,
Fearful heart has Brown-hair, holding closely by her;
Sleepy baby Gold-hair, winking at the fire.

O ruddy cottage light, pierce the blinding storm,
Wreathe round the headlands dim, like a rosy form;
Hands make a gallant fight when the heart is warm.

Crash! parts the little boat amidst breakers white!
Strike bravely, fisherman! for the home in sight.
Love nerves the father's arm — love will win to-night.

Happy eyes has Blonde-hair, pouring father's tea,
Noisy tongue has Brown-hair, nestling on his knee;
"Goo," says baby Gold-hair, waking up to see!

TOO FINE FOR MORTAL EAR

"Heard melodies are sweet, but those unheard
    Are sweeter," sang a gentle poet, well;
And somewhere in Arabia lives a bird
    Whose little throat seems evermore to swell
With music, while the tender, golden tongue
Throbs in the parted beak as if she sung;
Yet ne'er by sound the brooding air is stirred
    Save when on almond trees she folds her wings;
    Yet men do follow her, and cry "She sings!
Yea always sings had we but ears to hear;"
And when across the vacant morning clear
    Her rare and rapturous melody she flings,
"Ah God!" they cry, low listening 'neath her tree,
"How ravishing sweet the unheard notes must be!"

WILLIAM HAINES LYTLE [1]

WILLIAM HAINES LYTLE, son of General Robert Todd and Elizabeth (Haines) Lytle, and grandson of General William Lytle, was born, November 2, 1826, in Cincinnati, Ohio, at the old Lytle homestead,[2] on Lawrence Street. Inheriting from paternal ancestors a martial spirit and a gift of eloquence, and from his mother a poetic strain, he early manifested a tendency to express himself in oratorical prose and in romantic verse, the favorite themes on which he exercised his boyish invention being patriotic. Young Lytle received his academic training at the Cincinnati College, (of which his grandfather was one of the founders and in which his father was educated,) where he devoted himself with zeal to the study of languages,— English, Latin, Greek, German, and French,— and where, before he had reached his seventeenth year, he had completed the prescribed course, graduating with honors, the youngest in his class. In 1843 he began the study of law in the office of his uncle, E. S. Haines, under whose guidance he was prepared for admission to the bar.

The Mexican War, which broke out in 1846, had a romantic, adventurous, and spectacular character irresistibly attractive to young men of cavalier instincts, and the call for volunteers did not fail to arouse the martial blood and patriotic enthusiasm of Lytle, summoning him to don the sword of his fathers. From October 5, 1847, until July 25, 1848, he was engaged in active military duty, serving for a time as First Lieutenant and afterward as Captain, of Company L, Second Ohio Volunteer Cavalry, a regiment which was disbanded on the fifth of October, 1848.

---

[1] See Poems of William Haines Lytle, edited, with Memoir, by W. H. Venable, (The Robert Clarke Co., 1894,) from which the material of this sketch is mainly derived.

[2] This historic mansion, built in 1810 by the poet's grandfather, was the first brick house of its grade erected in Cincinnati. It was still standing, in the then newly dedicated Lytle Park, until the year 1908, when it was torn down by authority of the City Council.

Returning to Cincinnati at the close of the war, Lytle entered into a law partnership with the firm of Haines, Todd & Lytle, and was soon recognized in the Queen City as one of the ablest members of the legal profession. In 1852 he was elected to a seat in the Ohio Legislature, in which body he served with distinction. His growing popularity, among both Democrats and Whigs, led to his nomination, in 1857, as the Democratic candidate for Lieutenant-Governor of Ohio, but the ticket was defeated by a few hundred votes. In the same year he received from Governor Chase the commission of Major-General of the First Division of the Ohio Militia.

The period of Lytle's greatest literary activity dates from the time of his return from the Mexican War to the outbreak of the Rebellion, and it was signalized by the production of most of his poems, including the masterful lyric, "Antony and Cleopatra," which brought its author national fame, and which, perhaps, has served, more than all his other achievements, either of sword or of pen, to keep Lytle's name in lasting remembrance. This poem was dashed off in a glow of poetic inspiration, at the Lytle homestead, one afternoon in July, 1858, and was first published on the 29th of that month, in the Cincinnati Commercial.

The story of Gen. Lytle's splendid career from the day when Fort Sumter yielded, to the day of his death on the field of Chickamauga — a period of less than two years and eight months — covers the events of three principal campaigns, each signalized by a terrible battle. He was wounded at Carnifex Ferry, in the conflict of September 10, 1861, and again in the battle of Perryville, October 7, 1862. On November 27, of the latter year, he was promoted from the rank of Colonel to that of Brigadier-General, in which capacity he served until his death, which occurred on September 20, 1863, when he received a fatal shot while directing the movements of his brigade, being the only Union officer of high rank who fell that day.

His body was buried, with loving care, by a Confederate officer who had been a comrade of Lytle in Mexico. After a lapse of twenty days his remains were recovered, under a flag of truce, and were conveyed to Cincinnati, where, with solemn and imposing obsequies, they were consigned to a final resting-place in Spring Grove Cemetery, October 22, 1863. The Lytle monument, a shaft of Carrara marble, erected near his grave, shows, in symbolic sculpture, the sword, the scroll, the pen, and, surmounting all, the eagle sustaining a garland of laurel. In Chickamauga Park there stands another memorial to the "warrior poet,"— a pyramid of cannon balls piled upon a base of granite, distinguishing the spot where the hero fell in battle.

ANTONY AND CLEOPATRA

I am dying, Egypt, dying!
   Ebbs the crimson life-tide fast,
And the dark Plutonian shadows
   Gather on the evening blast;
Let thine arm, oh Queen, enfold me,
   Hush thy sobs and bow thine ear,
Listen to the great heart secrets
   Thou, and thou alone, must hear.

Though my scarred and veteran legions
   Bear their eagles high no more,
And my wrecked and scattered galleys
   Strew dark Actium's fatal shore;
Though no glittering guards surround me,
   Prompt to do their master's will,
I must perish like a Roman,
   Die the great Triumvir still.

Let not Cæsar's servile minions
   Mock the lion thus laid low;
'T was no foeman's arm that felled him,
   'T was his own that struck the blow —
His who, pillowed on thy bosom,
   Turned aside from glory's ray —
His who, drunk with thy caresses,
   Madly threw a world away.

Should the base plebeian rabble
  Dare assail my name at Rome,
Where the noble spouse, Octavia,
  Weeps within her widowed home,
Seek her; say the gods bear witness,—
  Altars, augurs, circling wings,—
That her blood, with mine commingled,
  Yet shall mount the thrones of kings.

And for thee, star-eyed Egyptian —
  Glorious sorceress of the Nile!
Light the path to Stygian horrors
  With the splendors of thy smile;
Give the Cæsar crowns and arches,
  Let his brow the laurel twine,
I can scorn the senate's triumphs,
  Triumphing in love like thine.

I am dying, Egypt, dying;
  Hark! the insulting foeman's cry;
They are coming; quick, my falchion!
  Let me front them ere I die.
Ah, no more amid the battle
  Shall my heart exulting swell;
Isis and Osiris guard thee,—
  Cleopatra, Rome, farewell!

POPOCATAPETL

  Pale peak, afar
Gilds thy white pinnacle, a single star,
While sharply on the deep blue sky thy snows
  In death-like calm repose.

  The nightingale
Through "Mira Flores" bowers repeats her tale,
And every rose its perfumed censer swings
  With vesper offerings.

WILLIAM HAINES LYTLE

But not for thee,
Diademed king, this love-born minstrelsy,
Nor yet the tropic gales that gently blow
    Through these blest vales below.

Around thy form
Hover the mid-air fiends, the lightning warm,
Thunder, and by the driving hurricane,
    In wrecks thy pines are lain.

Deep in thy heart
Burn on vast fires, struggling to rend apart
Their prison walls, and then in wrath be hurled
    Blazing upon the world.

In vain conspire
Against thy majesty tempest and fire;
The elemental wars of madness born,
    Serene, thou laugh'st to scorn.

Calm art thou now
As when the Aztec, on thine awful brow,
Gazed on some eve like this from Chalco's shore,
    Where lives his name no more.

And thou hast seen
Glitter in dark defiles the ominous sheen
Of lances, and hast heard the battle-cry
    Of Castile's chivalry.

And yet again
Hast seen strange banners steering o'er the main,
When from his eyrie soared to conquest forth
    The Eagle of the North.

Yet at thy feet,
While rolling on, the tides of empire beat,
Thou art, oh mountain, on thy world-piled throne,
    Of all, unchanged alone.

Type of a power
Supreme, thy solemn silence at this hour
Speaks to the nations of the Almighty Word
Which at thy birth was stirred.
Prophet sublime!
Wide on the morning's wings will float the chime
Of martial horns; yet 'mid the din thy spell
Shall sway me still — farewell!

MACDONALD'S DRUMMER [1]

A drummer-boy from fair Bayonne
By love of glory lured,
With bold Macdonald's stern array
The pains of war endured.
And now amid those dizzy heights
That girt the Splugen dread,
The silent columns struggled on,
And he marched at their head.

Then in those regions cold and dim,
With endless winter cursed,
The Alpine storm arose and scowled
And forth in fury burst —
Burst forth on the devoted ranks,
Ambition's dauntless brood,
That thus with sword and lance profaned
Old Winter's solitude.

"Down! down! upon your faces fall;
Cling to the guns! for, lo,
The chamois on this slippery track
Would dread yon gulf below!"
So speeds the word from front to rear,
And veterans to the storm
Bowed low, who ne'er in battle bowed
To aught in foeman's form.

---
[1] See Headley's account of the passage of the Splugen, by Marshal Macdonald.

But hark! what horror swells the gale —
  Beware, oh sons of France!
Beware the avalanche whose home
  Is 'mid these mountain haunts.
Yon distant thunder —'tis its voice!
  The bravest held his breath,
And silently a prayer put up
  To die a soldier's death.

And near and nearer with a roar
  That loud and louder swelled,
The avalanche down glaciers broad
  Its lightning pathway held;
And through the shivering ranks it crashed,
  And then with one vast stride
Swept down the gulf, till far below
  Its muttering thunders died.

In vain Italia's sunny plains
  And reeling vines invite;
Full many a soldier found his shroud
  'Mid Alpine snows that night;
And he, his comrades' pride and boast,
  The lad from fair Bayonne,
The roll was called, no voice replied,—
  The drummer-boy was gone.

Gone! gone! but hark, from the abyss,
  What sounds so faintly come,
Amid the pauses of the storm?
  It is — it is — the drum!
He lives, he beats for aid, he sounds
  The old familiar call,
That to the battery's smoking throat
  Had brought his comrades all.

Over the dizzy verge that eve
  With straining eyes they peered,
And heard the rattling of the drum,
  In echoes strange and weird;
The notes would cease, and then again
  Would sound — again to fail,
Until no more their fainting moan
  Came wafted on the gale.

And when red Wagram's fight was fought,
  And the big war was o'er,
A dark-haired matron in Bayonne
  Stood watching by her door;
Stood watching, praying many an hour,
  Till hair and heart grew gray,
For the bright-eyed boy who, 'mid the Alps,
  Was sleeping far away.

And still, belated peasants tell
  How, near that Alpine height,
They hear the drum-roll loud and clear
  On many a storm-vexed night.
This story of the olden time
  With sad eyes they repeat,
And whisper by whose ghostly hands
  The spirit-drum is beat.

BRIGAND'S SONG

Through the Sierra's wild ravines
  An old grandee of Spain
Is passing with his dark-eyed girls
  And all his gorgeous train;
The spoil is rich, the guard is weak,
  The way is rough and long,
So bathe your lips in foaming wine,
  And chant your parting song.

WILLIAM HAINES LYTLE

    Drink, brothers, drink,
      Drink, men, and away;
    Adieu, señoras, in your smiles
      We'll bask before the day.

The moon is in the azure skies,
    The stars are by her side,
They glitter in her path of light
    Like maids around a bride;
Like night-birds let us sally forth
    Where booty may be won;
So whet the poignard's polished edge,
    And gird your carbines on.
      Arm, brothers, arm,
        Arm, men, and away;
      Adieu, señoras, in your smiles
        We'll bask before the day.

All hail to-night; for since the world
    Was made in times of old,
The day has been for coward knaves,
    The night time for the bold;
Hark! to the mule-bells' distant chime,
    Our Lady, grant a boon,
That ere an hour the ring of steel
    May drown their jingling tune.
      Mount, brothers, mount,
        Mount, men, and away;
      Adieu, señoras, in your smiles
        We'll bask before the day.

To horse! Hurra —with thundering press
    Over the plain we glide,
Around the startled hamlet's edge
    And up the mountain side;
With waving plumes and clanking spurs,
    We sweep along like wind;

Our beacon on the rugged cliff
  Is flaming far behind.
    Ride, brothers, ride,
      .   Ride, men, and away;
    Adieu, señoras, in your smiles
      We'll bask before the day.

ANACREONTIC

Nay, frown not fairest, chide no more,
  Nor blame the blushing wine;
Its fiery kiss is innocent,
  When thrills the pulse with thine.
So leave the goblet in my hand,
  But vail thy glances bright,
Lest wine and beauty mingling
  Should wreck my soul to-night.

Then, Ida, to the ancient rim
  In sculptured beauty rare,
Bow down thy red-arched lip and quaff
  The wine that conquers care;
Or breathe upon the shining cup
  Till that its perfume be
Sweet as the scent of orange groves,
  Upon some tropic sea.

And while thy fingers idly stray
  In dalliance o'er the lyre,
Sing to me, love, some rare old song
  That gushed from heart of fire —
Song such as Grecian phalanx hymned
  When freedom's field was won,
And Persia's glory with the light
  Faded at Marathon.

WILLIAM HAINES LYTLE

Sing till the shouts of armèd men
   Ring bravely out once more:
Sing till again the ghost-white tents
   Shine on the moon-lit shore;
Bid from their melancholy graves
   The buried hopes to start,
I knew ere many a storm had swept
   The dew-drops from my heart.

Sing the deep memories of the past,
   My soul shall follow thee,
Its boundless depths re-echoing
   Thy glorious minstrelsy;
And as the wild vibrations hang
   Enfettered on the air,
I'll drink, thy white arms round me, love,
   The wine that conquers care.

IN CAMP

I gazed forth from my wintry tent
Upon the star-gemmed firmament;
I heard the far-off sentry's tramp
Around our mountain-girdled camp,
And saw the ghostly tents uprise
Like specters 'neath the jeweled skies.
And thus upon the snow-clad scene,
So pure and spotless and serene,
Where locked in sleep ten thousand lay
Awaiting morn's returning ray,—
I gazed, till to the sun the drums
Rolled at the dawn, "He comes, he comes."

BARDSTOWN, KY., 1862.

"WHEN THE LONG SHADOWS"

When the long shadows on my path are lying,
  Will those I love be gathered at my side;
Clustered around my couch of pain, and trying
  To light the dark way, trod without a guide?

Shall it be mine, beyond the tossing billow,
  'Neath foreign skies, to feel the approach of death,
Will stranger hands smooth down my dying pillow,
  And watch with kindly heart my failing breath?

Or shall, perchance, the little stars be shining
  On some lone spot, where, far from home and friends,
The way-worn pilgrim on the turf reclining,
  His life and much of grief together ends?

Ah! wheresoe'er the closing scene may find me,
  'Mid friends or foemen or in deserts lone,
May there be some of those I leave behind me
  To shed a tear for me when I am gone.

Full well I know life's current, onward rushing,
  Sweeps hearts away from spots where they would cling,
And by life's shores fair flowers are ever blushing,
  That o'er the waves a Lethean fragrance fling.

Yet when the thousand gales of morn are blowing,
  Or when the bright moon gilds the solemn sea,
And the sweet stars their smiles on earth are throwing,
  In the wide world, will none remember me?

COATES KINNEY

COATES KINNEY was born November 24, 1826, at Kinney's Corners, Yates County, N. Y., in the picturesque region of Keeuka Lake. His father, Giles Kinney, sprang from two old Connecticut families, dating back to the time of the landing of the Mayflower — the families of Kinney and Coates. The poet's mother, Myra (Cornell) Kinney, a native of New York, belonged to a branch of the Cornells who are numerous in that State. In the spring of 1840, when the subject of this sketch was thirteen years old, his parents moved from New York to Ohio, settling at Springboro, Warren County, where he attended the district school and, later, a local academy,— though his studies were interrupted by long periods of manual employment, first in a saw-mill, next as a cooper's apprentice, and then in a woolen-factory. His eagerness for knowledge kept all his leisure hours engaged with intense though desultory studies in algebra, geometry, Latin, Greek, and general literature. Kinney taught school at Ridgeville, at Mount Holly, and in other country districts, and also found time to begin the study of law at Lebanon, Ohio, under the auspices of the famous "Tom" Corwin. Subsequently he pursued his legal studies with the Hon. William Lawrence, of Bellefontaine, Ohio, and much later, with Donn Piatt, of Cincinnati.

His other occupations, however, did not prevent the ambitious youth from applying his mind to literary composition, and he was early a contributor to newspapers and magazines. While living at Bellefontaine, in the summer of 1849, he wrote the famous lyric, "Rain on the Roof," which first appeared in print on September 22 of the same year, being published by E. Penrose Jones, in the Great West, a Cincinnati weekly, edited by Emerson Bennett. This poem, which at once became a popular favorite, and which perhaps has been reproduced in type more frequently than any other lyric ever written in the Ohio Valley, is deserving of special notice on account of its melodious charm and its tender appeal to the home-bred affections, and because it was the earliest of the author's writings to attract general attention.

On July 17, 1851, Coates Kinney married Miss Hannah Kelly, of Waynesville, Ohio. During the eight years of struggle and comparative poverty in which his young wife lived to inspire him with her sympathetic coöperation, he devoted his energies to various literary and educational effort, and to those intellectual pursuits which equipped him thoroughly for the public duties he afterwards discharged with distinguished ability in several important stations. In this period he wrote much for the press, contributing poems, short stories, and critical essays to the National Era, the Philadelphia Post, the Yankee Blade, Willis's Home Journal, and the Ladies' Repository. For a time he was associated with Charles S. Abbott and William T. Coggeshall, in Cincinnati, in the editorship of the Genius of the West. In 1854 he purchased a half interest in Abbott's printing office, where, with his own hand, he set up the type of his first book, Keeuka and Other Poems, which was issued from the press, as a private edition, in 1855. Desiring to extend his knowledge of Greek and of French, the young author, in the same year, went to Yellow Springs, where he took courses in Antioch College, of which institution Horace Mann was at that time the President. Admitted to the bar in 1856, Kinney opened an office in the Debolt Building, Cincinnati, where he was engaged in law practice for a year or more, keeping his family at Waynesville. Shortly after the death of his wife, which occurred in 1859, the poet was called to take the editorship of the Xenia News, a position just vacated by Whitelaw Reid.

At the outbreak of the Civil War, Kinney applied for a commission, and, upon the recommendation of Secretary Chase, President Lincoln, June 1, 1861, appointed him Major and Paymaster, U. S. A., in which capacity he served until the close of the war, retiring, November 14, 1865, with the brevet rank of Lieutenant-Colonel.

In the spring of 1862 Col. Kinney was married to Miss Mary C. Allen, of Xenia, Ohio, in which city he afterwards resided for many years, and where his three daughters, Myra, Lestra, and Clara, were born.

A trenchant and influential journalist, Kinney was successively connected with the West Liberty Banner, the Xenia News, the Genius of the West, the Xenia Torch-Light, the Cincinnati Daily Times, the Ohio State Journal, and the Springfield Globe Republic. In 1868 he was a delegate from Ohio to the Republican National Convention at Chicago, which nominated Grant for President, and he was Ohio Secretary of that convention. Elected in 1881 to represent the Fifth Ohio District in the State Senate, he served for one term in that body, where he took a leading part in legislation, being especially distinguished for his eloquence, and for strength and clearness in debate.[1]

Coates Kinney devoted the last seven years of his life chiefly to literary pursuits, spending much of his leisure in the Queen City, where he occupied apartments first at the Oxford Hotel and afterwards at the Munro.

The poet died in the Presbyterian Hospital, Cincinnati, January 24, 1904. He was buried in Miami Cemetery, Waynesville, Ohio, by the side of his first wife, and near the little graves of the three children whom she had borne to him and who had all died in their infancy.

The poetical work of Coates Kinney, thus far published, is comprised in three volumes: Keeuka, and Other Poems (1855); Lyrics of the Ideal and Real (1887); and Mists of Fire, a Trilogy; and Some Eclogs (1899). It is impossible for the reader of critical discernment to peruse these volumes without recognizing on every page evidence of an original genius, bold

---

[1] Col. Kinney was recognized in the Senate and throughout the State as a bold and aggressive antagonist of all forms of public corruption and injustice, and as the zealous champion of several reformatory measures. Memorable on account of its far-reaching influence in molding popular sentiment and in determining the course of later legislation, was his powerful speech on "The Official Railroad Pass," delivered March 29, 1882, in support of a bill "to prohibit unjust discrimination in favor of persons in public employment traveling on railroads." The fundamental principles of this bill have since been embodied in the provisions of an act passed by the Ohio Legislature, April 21, 1908.

in thought, daring in imagination, and unique in the consummate mastery of song which has for its supreme purpose not merely art for art's sake, but "art for the sake of utterance, to the uttermost." In his special domain of thought and poetic invention, Kinney stands unrivaled. The more intently the deep-meaning cadences of his philosophic muse are studied, the more clearly will they reveal those qualities of substance and style which demonstrate the justice of the opinion expressed by William Dean Howells, that "Coates Kinney is a truly great poet, subtle and profound,"— one of "the few who think in the electrical flushes known only to the passion of most men," and whose work brings to the reader "the thrill imparted by mastery in an art which has of late seemed declining into clever artistry."

In a review of the author's second volume, Lyrics of the Ideal and the Real, Julian Hawthorne wrote, in 1887: "These lyrics are a genuine surprise, and, to my thinking, are among the most powerful and original poems of this generation. . . . Mr. Kinney's name is not widely known; and it is scarcely possible that he has made his living by literature. And yet he has the gifts of imagination, passion, and spiritual insight that are entrusted only to poets, and of which the poetasters and versifiers of the day possess no trace. His book is profoundly interesting. It expands the brain and touches the heart. It is genuine thought and feeling uttered with strength, beauty, and tenderness. It does not at all resemble any contemporary volume of verse. Its forms are always simple, and sometimes rugged or harsh. The writer is reticent, and yet few poets have so effectively communicated their inmost souls to the reader — if the reader have apprehension to receive the communication. He has felt or sympathized with all the deeper human thoughts and emotions; the story of the longings, the regrets, the love, the fear and hope of human beings is reflected in these few pages. The deep speculations of philosophy, the intuitions of religion, the homely pathos and tenderness of daily life, the charm of fancy and the splendor of imaginative revery, find their echo here. It is a book to be felt and acknowledged rather than read. Its prevailing tone is grave and sad; but there is in it an inner voice of hope and consolation. . . . Whatever may be thought of the philosophy of the remarkable poem 'Pessim and Optim,' the largeness of its scope can not be questioned; and Mr. Kinney has no need to fear comparison with Tennyson's 'Two Voices' on the score of originality, earnestness, and depth."

Coates Kinney's most important published work is contained in the volume, Mists of Fire, a Trilogy; and Some Eclogs, issued in 1899 by Rand, McNally & Company, Chicago. The author's masterpiece, "Mists of Fire," an elaborate production in three parts entitled, respectively, "Kapnisma," "Pessim and Optim," and "A Keen Swift Spirit," has for its theme the immortal soul of man, its origin, vicissitudes, exaltations, despairs, and conjectured destiny. In this great work, the ripe fruition of the poet's genius, the whole gamut and diapason of intellectual life is sounded. Thought surcharges every sentence. The thought is usually calm, logical, guided by scientific safeguards; but now and again imagination kindles the philosophic facts, and the glowing pile mounts to the sky, a daring chariot of fire. The prevailing mood of the poem is solemn, devout, religious, rising at times to the high seriousness of oracular utterance. Unique in design and in poetic method, "Mists of Fire" is, in fact, the autobiography of a prophetic nature, the thought and feeling of a profound and speculative soul, who, like Wordsworth, Tennyson, and Browning, seeks to embody in adventurous song a new gospel of freedom and of faith, which shall reconcile the postulates of science with the intuitions of religion.

Shortly before his death Coates Kinney entrusted to the keeping of an intimate friend unpublished literary property including: a novel entitled "A Drama of Doubles;" a philosophical essay entitled "Unthinkable Data of Human Thought;" a short treatise on "Grammar;" an essay on "The English Language and Its Correct Use;" a long poem entitled "Apparitions;" and several lyrics of extraordinary beauty and power, written within the years 1903-04.

MISTS OF FIRE
A TRILOGY
(Extracts)

There is no glory worth a moment's thought
  Save that which links the memory of a man
To some fair order out of chaos wrought
  By him creating on creation's plan.

His work it is that lifts the human life:
  While others lead by law's and battle's might
He rises into calm above the strife
  And sets new guiding-stars along the night.

Though to the vision of his time and race
  Be only darkness where his far thoughts fly,
Yet, looking through himself, he well may trace
  The constellation men shall know him by.

ONEIRODE

To think! to think and never rest from thinking!
  To feel this great globe flying through the sky
And reckon by the rising and the sinking
  Of stars how long to live, how soon to die!

This, this is life. Is life, then, worth the living?
  This plotting for his freedom by the slave!
This agony of loving and forgiving!
  This effort of the coward to be brave!

Our freedom! We are sin-scourged into being,
  And ills of birth enslave us all our days;
No chance of flying and no way of fleeing,
  Until the last chance and the end of ways.

We are walled in by darkness — wall behind us,
   From whose sprung dungeon-gates Fate dragged us in,
And wall before us, where Fate waits to bind us
   And thrust us out through swinging gates of sin.

But what is Fate? It is a mere breath spoken,
   To echo clamoring between the walls
Of darkness — blind phrase uttered to betoken
   This blind Unreason which our life enthralls.

Out through abysmal depths of heaven around us
   We think our way past orbs of day and night,
Till skies of empty outer darkness bound us
   And place and time are fixed pin-points of light;

But nowhere from the silent planets wheeling;
   And nowhere from the thundering hells of suns,
And nowhere from the darkness comes revealing
   Itself a Fate that through all being runs.

No ghostly presence, no mysterious voices,
   The midnight of these infinite spaces thrill;
And even Chaos flies hence and rejoices
   To find and feel yon Universe's Will.

Thought follows chaos — nay, without the places
   And times of matter globed and motion whirled,
Thought chaos is, a spread dead wing in space is,
   Drifting for wafture somewhere toward a world.

Where shall it reach and touch the Will Universal?
   How with its confines bound the Infinite Mind?
One atom of the Allsoul's whole dispersal
   Assuming how the whole shall be defined!

Such thinkings are not Thought; they are but dreamings
   Of what perchance may be itself but dream:
Our truths are to the Truth as moonlight's gleamings
   In dungeon are to open noonday's beam.

All worlds of matter, all the world of spirit,
    How these are one, eternal, increate —
Soul can not clutch it, sense come never near it;
    It is unthinkable, and it is Fate!

This awful riddle, wherewith we have struggled
    Since the dim dawn of human consciousness,
With whatsoever dread words we have juggled —
    Ptah, Zeus, Jove, God — we fail, we fail to guess.

Whether there be of all intelligences
    A total Sum, a comprehending Whole —
Great sea, wherefrom rise all these mists, the senses,
    And back whereto flow all the streams of soul?

Whether this lives a selfexistent Essence,
    With its own passions, wills, imaginings,
Or is but everlasting evanescence,
    But perfume of the bloom of living things?

How cosmic spirit can take hold of matter
    And give dead elements the living breath?
How gather into selfhoods, and how scatter,
    To work the miracles of life and death?

Poets in grand imagination's trances
    Conceive the gods and give them wondrous birth,
And martyrs bleed for faith's divine romances,
    And priests go forth to proselyte the earth;

But what terrestrial religion reaches
    Out into heavenly majesty so far
That it may guess what god strange nature teaches
    To the strange dwellers on the nearest star?

Is Buddha known to denizens of Saturn?
    Is Jesus preached upon the Jovian moons?
And what are gods of any earthly pattern
    To far spheres drifting in the Force-monsoons?

Yon sun's flame, in whose light our worlds go darkling
    To eyes that from another system gaze —
Yon flaming sun is but a glimmer sparkling
    To like worlds blotted in the Dogstar's blaze.

And, howsoever gravitation labors,
    It lets a million suns from vision slip;
While the ten million systems are not neighbors
    Even by light's fine far swift fellowship.

How these immensities dwarf and obscure us!
    What, what are we amid such scenes as these?
Our Earth unguessed in planets of Arcturus,
    Undreamed in orbs around the Pleiades!

By such infinitudes of distance bounded
    (These chasms of darkness that no light can leap!)
We seem a dream with glooms of sleep surrounded —
    Our life a dream surrounded with a sleep!

ANTONEIRODE

Ay, we are dreamed; and if ever the Dreamer
    Wake from the sleep to remember the dream,
We of His waking shall thrill in the tremor,
    Dawn with His memory, mingle and stream.

What though He slumber through eon on eon?
    When He has dreamed all the infinite full,
Dreamed all the worlds and the lives there to be on,
    Out to dreamed gravity's uttermost pull;

Dreamed forth of matter and force interblended
    (Storm-drifts of matter and torrents of force)
Cyclones of flame, globed, exploded, and rended —
    Wide wild beginnings of Time's endless course;

Dreamed out of chaos the suns in the spaces,
  Dreamed down the suns to their white molten cores,
Dreamed off the worlds in their systemal places,
  Over them dreaming the continent-floors

Out of their pulps of fire — dreaming the oceans
  Out of the rain from their heavens of steam,
And of their mad elemental commotions
  Molding the motions of life in His dream;

Dreaming the marvelous atoms together
  Into the miracles feeling and thought,
Hitching, with matter's mysterious tether,
  Selfhoods of sense to insensible naught;

Dreaming the span of the measureless chasm
  Yawning between the alive and the dead —
Wonder of dreams in the organless plasm
  Crawling to soul from the sea's oozy bed —

Feeling to soul in the sea's vital foment,
  Feeling to form and to faculties dim,
Till, at the touch of a consummate moment,
  Loosed into freedom to rise and to swim —

Swimming of dreams in the nightmare of waters!
  Hydras, chimeras, and gorgons of sleep,
That by transitions of mutual slaughters
  Play the dream-tragedy Life in the deep;

When His long dream through the spawning and swarming
  Sea-generations has passed into things
Creeping aland, and has risen transforming
  Into the slow apparition of wings;

When from the budding of nerves in the banded
  Spirals of earth-crawling pleasure and pain
Upward has issued His dream and expanded
  Into the glorified blooming of brain —

Flower of all the world's forces and ages,
  Top-bloom of matter exhaling the soul,
Opening volume whose unopened pages
  Yet of God's being shall utter the whole,—

Here from His dream shall He start into waking —
  Dream of the universe waking in Me —
Me as a shore where the great billows breaking
  Leap out of silence in sounds of the sea!

Here, in the self of Me, here wakes the Dreamer,
  Wakes and shall wake as the brain shall unfold;
Here is the Christ of God, here the Redeemer,
  Spirit incarnate that Faith has foretold.

Growth of the brain shall be God manifested
  Here in the flesh, when the dead shall arise,
By an inherited memory vested
  With the immortal life dreamed of the skies.

What so has ever with being been gifted,
  Since the first givings of being began,
Living again shall be gathered and lifted
  Into the Sovereign Consciousness, Man.

* * * * *

TO AN OLD APPLETREE

This grim old appletree which many a May
  Has greened between my window and the morn
Seems to me thinking now in every spray
  A thought that is to be a blossom born.

Those maimed limbs plead thy story;
  The wounds upon thy body speak for thee:
Thou art a veteran soldier scarred with glory,
  My brave old Appletree!

Oft hast thou borne up under
  Onset of storming wind and shot of hail;
And once a sword-lunge of assailant thunder
  Slashed down thy barken mail.

Old age, disease, and battle
  Have scathed and crooked and crippled all thy form,
And thy Briarean bare arms clash and rattle
  Tossed in the wintry storm.

I seem to feel thee shiver,
  As on thy nakedness hang rags of snow:
May charitable Spring, the gracious giver,
  O'er thee her mantle throw.

She will; and sunshine spilling
  From blue skies thou again shalt drink as wine,
To feel afresh the rush of young blood thrilling
  Through that old heart of thine.

For in the season duly
  Each year there rises youth's perennial power
Within thee, and thou then rejoicest newly
  In robes of leaf and flower.

Ay, though thy years are many
  And sorrows heavy, yet from winter's gloom
Thou issuest with the young trees, glad as any,
  As quick of green and bloom.

The bluebird, warbling mellow
  Refrains, like memory comes and calls thy name;
And like first love, the oriole's pomp of yellow
  Flits through thy shade a flame.

Thou quiverst in the sunny
  June mornings to the welcoming of song,
And bees about their business of the honey
  Whisper thee all day long.

Thus thou art blest and blessest —
  Thy grace of blossoms fruiting into gold;
And thus in touch with nature, thou possessest
  The art of growing old.

MISCELLANEOUS EXTRACTS

It is my faith that man shall yet receive
  Even through the pains of sin and pangs of birth
And throes of death, the virtue to achieve
  The deed of immortality on earth.

Though this poor body shall not witness it,
  The tree of life, which has eternal growth
By evolution that is infinite,
  Must sometime come to amaranthine blowth.

And this my soul, though held long in the gloom
  Of the slow growth's expansion, shall not sink,
But, flushing upward, through that final bloom
  Shall taste the skies and wines of sunlight drink.

But, ah, the gloom! this darkness which shall yawn
  Between my day of life now soon to close
And that unspeakably far future dawn
  Which I must wait for in the dread repose!

The horror of it who is there that scapes
  In age? — sun setting, death's Pacific deep
Stretching out skyward from the western capes,
  And on the beach his little boat of sleep!

'There is no God'— the flippant fool's old saying,
  The blinkard's logic, or the coward's curse!
What, then, this procreant Life-Force intraplaying
  Throughout the matter of the universe?

I Am! The Hebrew seer's clairvoyant seeing
  Flashed to the depths in that one fulgent phrase:
I Am — the Consciousness! I Am — the Being!
  Whatever comes or goes, I Am — that stays!

I Am — in all things! and whenever, thinking,
  Mind so forth-stars its being as to find
Its own form I-am, then begins it drinking
  The influx of the Omnisplendent Mind.

———

O selfish soul of me! the thought thou knowst
  As duty to the neighbor shall be warmed
With the quick comfort of the Holy Ghost,
  And heaven shall catch thee in the good performed.

But what is good? — grand question that has tasked
  All time's best wisdom, and yet rests involved
With 'What is truth?' the question Pilate asked
  Of Jesus, nor without it shall be solved.

Jesus was silent; let the Roman law
  Declare his answer from the Roman cross —
And ruled Rome, though his dying vision saw
  Round him the Cæsar's brazen eagles toss.

His good was life that all men's hearts applaud,
  His truth was innocence' victorious death:
In three days both arose and walked abroad,
  To fill Rome and the world with Nazareth.

———

But what is goodness? Is it selfishness?
  How vainly questioned! Duty understood
Waits outdoors in the snow and under stress
  Of winds of winter, and I dream it good.

Again here, in my fire's caressing hold,
  To watch my fancies as in smoke they float
About my chamber's mellow glow of gold
  Or stop and swirl, sucked up the chimney's throat.

Too precious in the brain my life has grown;
  And the left moments of it look so scarce and small
That I no more can bear to see them sown
  Like seed afield, lest they unfertile fall.

But who would save his life shall lose it! Yea,
  I know — the treasure that is buried gives
No increase — and I know there comes a day
  When each shall answer for the life he lives.

Yet so I love my world — this world of thought,
  This business of my dreams, this drowse in books
Over the lore of life the dead have taught —
  That all my selfhood shrinks from outward looks.

My selfhood, ay and selfishness, it is —
  The German Goethe's yearning to absorb
More life, without that Sungod's-thirst of his
  To drain the light from every starry orb.

The egotism of culture was his cult —
  Worship of self with others' sacrifice
And can it be that such supreme result
  Commends the priest through whom the victim dies?

From Jesus down to Goethe — down or up! —
  Between the thought Semitic and the Greek,
The soul asks, shall compassion drink the cup,
  Or passion pour it for the lowly weak?

It was my grandsire reaching from his grave
  That pulled me back to darkness when I willed
An utterance of light and was not brave
  Enough to word the thought with which I thrilled.

A million voices from ancestral tombs,
  A million forces round me in the air,
Control my nature, and a million looms
  Have woven this life-vesture which I wear.

I am obedient to all the powers
  Of universal being; for I go
Back to its roots, as forward to its flowers
  I shall, through all its bole and branches, grow.

The Oriental fancy, in its dream,
  Nirvana, whereinto the souls ascend,
Lets Lethe through their selfhoods flow and stream
  To cleanse them of beginning as of end.

That tenet of the Hindoo wisdom feels
  Toward the unutterable truth: the peace
Of God, round which the Western reason reels,
  Is the All-Self, wherein all selves shall cease.

As years increase, the wont of solitude
  Wins on the thinker — portals ear and eye
Shutting against the world, to interclude
  The common show and noise we know it by.

Pity for age when it grows garrulous
  With memories of the dead, and in eclipse
Of intellect gropes miserably thus
  To seek old friends in new companionships.

Rather smoke so alone amid the leaves
   Here where the moonshine flickers on the grass,
And feel the heavenly old remembered eves
   Like yonder westering star-streams overpass.

CONSUMMATION
(Extract)

Death had sunk the world from under my feet;
   Love had given thee wings to fly;
And we met as the dawn and the darkness meet —
   Thou the dawn, and the darkness I.

My soul was a gloom that had blotted heaven;
   And thine was a fine ascending fire
That streamed it through with a luminous leaven
   Of hope of morning and day's desire.

Love wrought the miracle of raising the dead;
   Though on the tomb the seal had been put,
Thine eyes to my buried passion said,
   'Come forth!' and it came, bound hand and foot.

Sad memory drowned itself in those eyes —
   Fell into their liquid deeps and sunk;
And the darkness of all the earth and skies
   To those two crystals of darkness shrunk.

When we met our fate — rememberst the place?
   My day was barren, my dream was done;
But the bright warm flush of thy radiant face
   On my frozen heart flamed like a sun.

That look! it created the world anew:
   Thy presence came to me like the sweep
Of a full white sail to the sudden view
   Of a shipwrecked man on the deep.

I knew I was saved; I knew that thy voice
  Should sing the cries in the night to peace;
But I felt it almost a guilt to rejoice
  That love from the dead had love's release.

Thou hadst never suffered, and couldst not know
  How past and present in me were whirled —
How the breeze out of sunrise semed to blow
  From the sundown of the underworld.

* * * * *

"DID I NOT REALIZE"

Did I not realize, as you do now
  By your straight speed east on it these four days,
  How vast the world is, I should dread the haze
Which glooms this morning; but your vessel's prow
  May point to clear sun, and its forenoon-blaze
May pour your sea-floored sky-tent full of gold:
  So there for you were youth and Orient,
While west the sad sky mists, and I am old.
  I dream it so; but dreams do not content;
For in my thought, clouds darken, great winds rise,
  And billows toss you, and I long to stand
Beside you there, and hold you in my eyes,
  And cling to you with father's heart and hand,
  Dear mariners a thousand miles from land!
XENIA, 5 October, 1890.

SHIPS COMING IN

I lay upon a rock that jutted to the sea.
Twilight came down from out the pine-woods back of me,
And, stealing on the waters, met the sudden moon,
Rushed into her kiss, and sank to a dead white swoon.
I lay there on the rock and thought of all had been,
I lay and watched my ships come, my ships come in.

Sail, O ships! my home-voyaging ships!
  Sail from the sunlit side of the world;
    Climb the watery bulge of the globe;
Pass the line where the orient dips
  In the sea, and, with canvas unfurled,
    Take yon moon's glory on as a robe:
From wherever your sailing has been,
Sail, ships, hither, sail hither, sail in.

Ship! that flew out of port with thy wings
  Dipt in morning, is yon phantom thou —
    Moonlit phantom that drifts to the strand
And no freight and no passenger brings?
  Yet see! one there alive on the prow,
    In his gaze the sick hunger for land:
Hope! my Captain! that sailed out to win
All our world — conquered Captain, sail in.

Ship! that pushed to the tropical zone,
  Touched spice-islands in summery seas,
    Then, in mad equatorial gales,
Went adrift with one mariner lone —
  Bring him back from the sunned Caribbees,
    Bring him in with thy storm-tattered sails:
Love! my Sailor! once life's happy twin,
Now sweet ghost of life, specter! sail in.

Ship! that steered for the boreal stars,
  And, bewitched by the weird northern-lights,
    Cramped through ice-packs and wintered in snows
Heaped to the deck and piled to the spars,
  Thou hast brought from the long arctic nights
    Only one, and him famished and froze:'
Fame! my Helmsman! Anatomy thin
Propt to the wheel, stark Helmsman, sail in.

Ship! that went out to traffic with Ind,
   Hugged the Gold Coast, and doubled Good Hope,
   When full sail on the Asian sea,
Thou wast caught by a contrary wind
   And blown down the world's southerly slope
   And thence upward and hither to me:
Ship, whose lading did never begin,
With this moonshine for cargo! sail in.

Ship! that searched round the world for new lands,
   Sounded new seas and charted new skies,
   Studied new stars, new sights of the sun,
Then plowed keel in the ooze and the sands —
   There in shallows thy mastery lies,
   When all the deeps thy sailing has done:
Psyche wove but the Parcae did spin
Warp and woof of thy sail sailing in.

Ship! that struck the horizon's sea-line
   And there vanished away in the blue,
   Seemed that thy sail went into the sky,
And not down the east ocean's decline:
   Is naught, then, but the underworld true,
   And yon overworld naught but a lie?
Faith! my Anchor! all rusted with sin,
There on deck of this ship sailing in!

CHILD LOST

She came the sweet fulfillment of a dream;
   She bloomed upon me like a flower;
   Her life was my life's gift and dower,
Her love was my love's meed supreme.

She seemed a precious memory of mine
   Waked from the holiness of death
   And quickened back to pulse and breath
By working of love's miracle divine.

I took her babehood as a gift of God;
   And when her tiny toddling feet
   Began my coming-home to meet,
My heart lay under every step she trod.

Her life was light to me where night had been;
   It was herself she heralded
   When from her little crib she said
Each morning, "Papa, light is coming in."

She was a newness and a solace deep —
   A newness like the dawning light,
   A solace like the lulling night,
A joy like waking, and a bliss like sleep.

Her being was around me as a sky
   Of summer is around the earth:
   I never thought of any worth
Of life without her love to price it by.

But suddenly I missed the child one day;
   I looked, and lo a stranger stood
   There stately in full womanhood
Where I had left the little maid at play.

'EGYPT'[1]

Nile in far source of it,
Nile in flood-force of it;
   Eyes of the lynx,
   Eyes of the sphinx
     (Future and history);
   Isis, the mystery,
'Egypt,' my Gypsy.

---

[1] This poem now for the first time appears in print.

Pyramids loom in her,
Blast of simoom in her;
  Sand-storms and calms,
  Shade of green palms;
    Now blaze of noon to me,
    Then stars and moon to me,
      Gypsy, my Gypsy.

What may seem base of her,
That is the race of her;
  Cataracts' flood
  Swirls in her blood —
    Thrills and revives in her
    Old Egypt's lives in her,
      Gypsy, my Gypsy.

Wild as a leopardess,
Mild as a shepherdess
  Leading a lamb —
  Lamb that I am! —
    Mild, wild and beautiful,
    Obstinate, dutiful,
      Gypsy, my Gypsy.

Mothers me, brothers me,
Comrades me, others me,
  Counters me, mates,
  Loves me, and hates;
    She is the test of me,
    She is the best of me,
    She is the zest of me,
    She is the pest of me,
      And — all the rest of me!
  'Egypt,' my Gypsy.

1903.

RAIN ON THE ROOF

When the hovering humid darkness
   Over all the starry spheres
Flows and falls like sorrow softly
   Breaking into blessèd tears,
Then how sweet to press the pillow
   Of a cottage-chamber bed
And lie listening to the rain-drops
   On the low roof overhead.

To the pitpat on the shingles
   Answer echoes in the heart;
And dim dreamy recollections
   Into form and being start,
And the busy fairy, Fancy,
   Weaves her air-threads, warp and woof,
As I listen to the patter
   Of the light rain on the roof.

Now in memory comes my mother
   As she used in summers gone,
Taking leave of little faces
   That her loving look shone on;
And I feel that fond look on me
   As I feel the old refrain
Here repeated on the shingles
   By the patter of the rain.

Then my little seraph-sister,
   With the wings and waving hair
And her star-eyed cherub-brother —
   A serene angelic pair —
Glide around my wakeful pillow
   With sweet praise or mild reproof,
As I shut my eyes and listen
   To the soft rain on the roof.

And another comes, to thrill me
   With her eyes' bewitching blue,
And I mind not, musing on her,
   That my heart she never knew;
I remember but to love her
   With a passion kin to pain,
And my quickened pulses quiver
   To the patter of the rain.

Art hath naught of tone or cadence,
   Naught of music's magic spell,
That can thrill the secret fountain
   Whence the tears of rapture well,
Like that weird nocturne of Nature,
   That subdued, subduing strain
Which is played upon the shingles
   By the patter of the rain.

1849.   1899.

FLORUS BEARDSLEY PLIMPTON

FLORUS BEARDSLEY PLIMPTON, journalist and poet, the third son of Rev. Billings O. and Eliza (Merwin) Plimpton, was born in Elmira, Portage County, Ohio, September 4, 1830. He received a common school and academic education, remaining on his father's farm in Hartford, Trumbull County, Ohio, till seventeen years of age, when he entered Allegheny College, Meadville, Pa. In 1851 he began his career as a newspaper-man, in the office of the Western Reserve Transcript, at Warren, Ohio, and in the summer of 1852 he became editor of a Whig campaign paper at Niles, Mich. Later he was associated with John S. Herrick, at Ravenna, Ohio, in conducting the Portage Whig. Mr. Plimpton was married June 2, 1853, to Miss Cordelia A. Bushnell, of Hartford, Ohio, and in the following spring he moved to Elmira, N. Y., where he was engaged in the management of the Elmira Daily Republic until the spring of 1857, when he went to Pittsburg, Pa., in which city he took a position on the staff of the Pittsburg Daily Dispatch. In 1860, at the solicitation of M. D. Potter, proprietor of the Cincinnati Daily Commercial, he removed to Cincinnati to assist in the editorship of that newspaper, with which, and its successor, the Commercial-Gazette, he was connected during the remainder of his life, in constant association with the eminent journalist, Murat Halstead. Mr. Plimpton died in Cincinnati, April 23, 1886. His body was cremated in Washington, Pa.

"The time of the work of Mr. Plimpton on the Cincinnati Commercial and the Commercial Gazette," to quote the words of Mr. Halstead, "was just about twenty-five years. He was well trained before he came, in North-eastern Ohio, in Elmira, New York, and in Pittsburg. His labors in Cincinnati extended over the most interesting period of the history of our country, and were addressed to the enlightenment of our constituency on a vast variety of subjects. Volumes of his writings might be selected from the files which form for each old established paper a library of its own; and there are veins of gold, that the historians who turn over the ample leaves upon which he wrote, will have need to appropriate for the fine metal of the coin of truth that is to circulate through the generations that will not, and indeed could not, search for themselves into the mass of newspaper literature."

Besides being a master of elegant and incisive prose, Mr. Plimpton was gifted to no small degree with that "vision and faculty divine" which distinguishes the poet born. "To devote himself to poetry," wrote J. W. Miller, his friend and fellow-journalist, "would doubtless have been the ideal life for him. There was about him at times a poetic abstraction that his associates understood, and often, after the paper went to press, at three or four o'clock in the morning, he would write two or three stanzas on a subject that had at some time of the busy day flashed into his mind, and had been put aside to wait for a moment of leisure. These poetic subjects were most varied. He did not seek to control them, nor reduce them to any system. Generally they were left unfinished; yet they forced a hearing since he could not resist them entirely. Sometimes he would repeat to an intimate friend a couplet that had darted into his mind ready made, and he would complete the stanza, giving it, more than likely, an amusing turn. Vigorous as he was in the prose of journalism, and great as were his resources as a writer of masculine leaders and paragraphs with the keenest edge, he yet impressed those who knew him well as one who would never cease to feel the fascination of poetry and belles-lettres. . . . His poetry is graceful and gentle, the reflex of happy moods, or of tender seriousness. It is characterized by an intense love of natural scenery, especially far-reaching pastoral or forest loveliness. He was master, too, of the pathos that is 'twixt a smile and a tear. . . . His poems will give him a place of honor among Ohio singers."

FLORUS BEARDSLEY PLIMPTON

Though Mr. Plimpton contributed verse to various newspapers and periodicals, including the Knickerbocker Magazine, Godey's Lady's Book, the Genius of the West, the New York Tribune, the Ohio State Journal, and the Cincinnati Commercial, no collection of his poems was published during his lifetime. An elegantly illustrated memorial volume of his verse, however, comprising seventy of the author's best lyrics, compiled and edited by his widow, with an introduction by Murat Halstead, and containing eulogistic tributes from Mr. J. W. Miller, Mr. J. M. Cochran, and Hon. Jacob D. Cox, was issued in Cincinnati in 1886. One of the dedicatory pages of this elaborate volume is devoted to the following lines contributed by Edith M. Thomas:

> "He who hath told his mortal days
> And passed beyond the voice of praise,
> From song's full service was debarred.
> He toilsome days and nights did guard,
> To which the records in these leaves
> Were welcome periods and reprieves.
> Yet none the less, in hour of need,
> With generous faith he bade them speed,
> Who, half in fear and hopeful half,
> Pierian waters sought to quaff."

We may appropriately close this sketch by again quoting from Mr. Halstead's memorial tribute: "I knew well long ago that while I should ask the forgiveness of forgetfulness for my crude Indian and rural stories, . . . there was something in the poetry of Plimpton that was rare and precious. Boy and man, through the changes of forty years, he found in poetry the finer, higher, truer expression of himself. Loving hands have preserved with wonderful care that has rewarded itself, the poems that were the flowers of a life of labor always hard and often barren, and that was full of the inherent and impulsive qualities that are the springs of poetry — a life whose chief happiness was in the fervent faith that the earth was beautiful and mankind good. . . . He touched the harp because it comforted him.

There were things to say that could not otherwise be said; there were tones, rays of light, to trace through melodies unheard by, and illuminations invisible to, others — pathways into the infinite space that seemed to promise the divine achievement of the humanly unattainable. . . . For the audience of the fit, whether many or few, these utterances will be refreshing like a mountain rill or a bough laden with roses, or the flavor of the clover fields and tasseling corn, or the bloom of the locust and apple trees of Ohio."

SUMMER DAYS

In summer, when the days were long,
    We walked together in the wood;
Our heart was light, our step was strong;
    Sweet flutterings then were in our blood,
In summer when the days were long.

We strayed from morn till evening came;
    We gathered flowers and wove us crowns;
We walked 'mid poppies red as flame,
    Or sat upon the yellow downs;
And always wished our lives the same.

In summer, when the days were long,
    We leaped the hedge-row, crossed the brook;
And still her voice flowed forth in song,
    Or else she read some graceful book,
In summer when the days were long.

And then we sat beneath the trees,
    With shadows lessening in the noon;
And in the sunlight and the breeze
    We rested many a gorgeous June,
While larks were singing o'er the leas.

FLORUS BEARDSLEY PLIMPTON

We loved, and yet we knew it not —
   For loving seemed like breathing then;
We found a heaven in every spot;
   Saw angels, too, in all good men,
And dreamed of God in grove and grot.

In summer, when the days are long,
   Alone I wander,— muse alone —
I see her not; but that old song
   Under the fragrant wind is blown,
In summer when the days are long.

Alone I wander in the wood;
   But one fair spirit hears my sighs;
And half I see, so glad and good,
   The honest daylight of her eyes,
That charmed me under earlier skies.

In summer, when the days are long,
   I love her as we loved of old;
My heart is light, my step is strong;
   For love brings back those hours of gold
In summer when the days are long.

THE REFORMER
(Extract)

Oh, large of heart! oh, nobly great!
   He scorns the thrall of sect and clan,
Shakes off the fetters forged in hate,
   And claims a brotherhood with man.

Dwarfed Ignorance fills the world with wail,
   Opinion sneers at his advance;
And Error, rusted in his mail,
   Strides forth to meet him, lance to lance.

For him the tyrant's guard is set,
    For him the bigot's fagots fired,
For him the headsman's ax is whet,
    And chains are forged and minions hired.

Invincible in God and Truth,
    To smite the errors of his age
He gives the fiery force of youth,
    The tempered wisdom of the sage.

He sees, as prophets saw afar,
    In faith and vision rapt sublime,
The coming of the Morning Star,
    The glory of the latter time.

His faith, outreaching circumstance,
    Beholds, beyond the narrow range
Of present time, the slow advance
    Of cycles bringing wondrous change.

He hears the mighty march of mind,
    The stately steppings of the free,
Where glorious in the sun and wind,
    Their blazoned banners yet shall be.

Well can he wait: the seed that lies
    Hid in the cold, repulsive clay,
Shall burst in after centuries,
    And spread its glories to the day.

Well can he wait: though sown in tears
    And martyred blood, with scourge and stripe,
God watches through the whirling years,
    And quickens when the hour is ripe.

Man's hands may fail, the slackened rein
    Drop from his nerveless grasp, but still
The wheels shall thunder on the plain,
    Rolled by the lightning of his will.

PITTSBURG

Veiled in thick clouds, shut in by shelving hills,
  The city of a thousand forges lies,
  Nor feels the pleasant glow of sunny skies.
Hard toil have they who, in her thundering mills,
Stir the white-heated metal or draw out
  The lengthening bar, or at the ponderous wheel
  Turn the huge shaft and shape the edging steel.
How like a hell from pit and chimney spout
The tumbling smoke and lapping flames that light
  The sky like torches, and reflecting quiver
  Along the tremulous surface of the river.
Unlovely though she be, in Freedom's might
Her strong hands build — buttress and tower and crest—
  The iron gateway to the golden West.

IN REMEMBRANCE
J. P., Feb. 11, 1878

If only she were here, who knew
  The secret paths of fields and woods,
And where the earliest wild flowers through
  Cool mosses push their dainty hoods;
Whose voice was like a mother's call
  To them, and bade them wake and rise,
And mark the morning's splendors fall
  In mists of pearl from tender skies: —

If only she were here, to see
  The landscape freshening hour by hour,
And watch in favorite plant and tree
  The bud unfold in leaf and flower;
To welcome back from sunny lands
  The bluebirds that have tarried long,
Or feed with her own loving hands
  The bright, red-breasted prince of song: —

If, brightening down th' accustomed walk,
  She came to welcome friend and guest,
To share our light, unstudied talk,
  And sparkle at the rising jest;
Or, leading on to nobler themes,
  In art and science play the sage,
And rapt, as in prophetic dreams,
  Foretell the wonders of the age: —

Could she return, as now the spring
  Returns in robes of green and gold,
When love and song are on the wing,
  And hearts forget that they are old —
How bright were all the days! how fair
  This miracle of life would be!
Whose pulsings thrill the glowing air
  And quicken over land and sea.

And shall we doubt thy presence here,
  Spirit of light, because our eyes,
Veiled in this earthly atmosphere,
  See not the heaven that near us lies?
More living thou than we, who stand
  Within the shadow of the years,
Whose glimpses of a better land
  Are caught through eyelids wet with tears.

* * * * *

RETURN

Return — return! nor longer stay thy feet,
  Where rugged hills shut in the peaceful dale,
  And chattering runnels riot through the vale,
And lose themselves in meadows violet sweet.
Or does the oriole charm thee; or the lark
  Lure thee to green fields, where the gurgling brook
  Leaps up to kiss thy feet, the while we look

FLORUS BEARDSLEY PLIMPTON

For thee with tearful eyes from morn till dark?
O winds, that blow from out th' inconstant west,
  O birds, that eastward wing your heavenly way,
  Tell her of our impatience — her delay,
And woo the wanderer to her humble nest;
Come, as the dove that folds her wings in rest,
When holy evening sets her watch-star in the west.

SPRINGTIME
(Extract)

The robin rests its northward wing,
  And twittering in the quickened tree,
  Pipes all its sweetest notes for me —
The merriest prophet of the spring.

I knew that it would come once more
  When nights grew short and days were long,
  To wake the morning with its song,
And feed its fledglings round my door.

From all the fields the snows have fled,
  And thro' the grasses gray and sere,
  Peeps the green promise of the year —
The hope that slumbered with the dead.

In every nook the crocus springs —
  The dandelions star the hills,
  And round the golden daffodils
I hear the bee's industrious wings.

WAITING TO DIE

Lonely the hearthstone,
Silent the halls,
Faded the pictures
Hung on the walls.

Rusty the door-hinge,
Pathways grass-grown —
O, it is weary
Dwelling alone!

Sadly he goeth —
Thus do they say —
Locks, once an auburn,
Silvered and gray;
Feebly he's leaning
Now on his cane,
Wrinkled with sorrows,
Bending with pain.

Heavily stepping,
Stiffened with years,
Sightless his dark eyes,
Deafened his ears,
Slowly he moveth —
Let him pass by!
Pity an old man
Waiting to die.

BENJAMIN RUSSEL HANBY

BENJAMIN RUSSEL HANBY, conspicuous among the song-writers of Ohio, was born July 22, 1833, in Rushville, Fairfield County, Ohio, and he died in Westerville, Franklin County, March 16, 1867. In 1858 he graduated from Otterbein College, Westerville, Ohio, and soon thereafter became a school-teacher. Later he entered the ministry in the United Brethren Church, but after a brief service he left the pulpit, to engage in business as musical composer, finding congenial employment first with the John Church Company, Cincinnati, and then with Root & Cady, Chicago. He wrote many popular pieces, sentimental, political, and religious,— but is best known by the lyric, "Darling Nelly Gray," which was composed in 1856. Among other of Hanby's songs, "Little Tillie's Grave," "Now den! Now den!" and "Ole Shady" may be mentioned as having once been much in public favor.

DARLING NELLY GRAY

There's a low, green valley, on the old Kentucky shore,
    Where I've whiled many happy hours away,
A-sitting and a-singing by the little cottage door,
    Where lived my darling Nelly Gray.

CHORUS

Oh! my poor Nelly Gray, they have taken you away,
    And I'll never see my darling any more;
I am sitting by the river and I'm weeping all the day,
    For you've gone from the old Kentucky shore.

When the moon had climbed the mountain and the stars were shining, too,
    Then I'd take my darling Nelly Gray,
And we'd float down the river in my little red canoe,
    While my banjo sweetly I would play.

One night I went to see her, but "She's gone!" the neighbors say,
  The white man bound her with his chain;
They have taken her to Georgia for to wear her life away,
  As she toils in the cotton and the cane.

My canoe is under water, and my banjo is unstrung;
  I'm tired of living any more;
My eyes shall look downward, and my song shall be unsung,
  While I stay on the old Kentucky shore.

My eyes are getting blinded, and I cannot see my way.
  Hark! there's somebody knocking at the door —
Oh! I hear the angels calling, and I see my Nelly Gray,
  Farewell to the old Kentucky shore.

CHORUS
Oh, my darling Nelly Gray, up in heaven there they say
  That they'll never take you from me any more;
I'm a-coming, coming, coming, as the angels clear the way,
  Farewell to the old Kentucky shore.

JOHN JAMES PIATT

JOHN JAMES PIATT, son of John Bear and Emily (Scott) Piatt, and a great-grandson of Captain William Piatt, (an officer in the Revolutionary army and an original member of the Society of the Cincinnati,) was born at James's Mills, Dearborn County, (now Ohio County,) Ind., March 1, 1835. He first attended school at Rising Sun, Ind., but in his tenth year his parents removed to Columbus, Ohio, where his education was continued chiefly under private instruction. Then another removal, three or four miles northward from the capital of the State, gave him some experience in the old-fashioned, Western, log school-house. At the age of fourteen he was placed in the family of his uncle, Charles Scott, at Columbus, where for brief periods he attended the High School and the Capital University, going thence to Kenyon College, Gambier, Ohio, where he first began writing verses, having been stimulated thereto by reading Leigh Hunt's "Imagination and Fancy." In 1856 he accompanied his parents to Shelby County, Ill., where he remained for about a year, several months of which he spent with his uncle Scott, who had previously moved from Columbus to Chicago. In Illinois Mr. Piatt, whose early life had been pretty equally divided between town and country, wrote "The Morning Street," "The Forgotten Street," "Fires in Illinois," and several other poems referring to the prairie region. The two lyrics last named were contributed to the Louisville Journal, the editor of which, George D. Prentice, pronounced "The Forgotten Street" the work of "one of the most subtle spirits of our time." A year or two later, Mr. Prentice,— with whom, in the meanwhile, Piatt had become editorially associated,— forwarded a copy of "The Morning Street" to James Russell Lowell, who, in a letter to the author, expressed great admiration for the poem, and who, in

March, 1859, published the same in the Atlantic Monthly, of which he was then the editor.

Revisiting Columbus in 1859, Mr. Piatt there met Mr. William Dean Howells, with whom he had formed a slight acquaintance some eight or nine years previously, in the State Journal office, and the result of the literary relations which were soon established between the young writers, was a joint volume of verse entitled "Poems of Two Friends," issued in Columbus, in 1859,— a publication now rare and valuable as a "first book" of each author.

In March, 1861, Mr. Piatt was appointed, by Secretary Chase, to a clerkship in the Treasury Department, at Washington, D. C. Soon afterward, June 18, 1861, he was married, at Newcastle, Ky., to Miss Sarah Morgan Bryan. The young couple resided in Washington for about six years, at the close of which period, in 1867, they established their home at North Bend, Ohio, on the picturesque heights overlooking the Ohio River, a few miles below Cincinnati.

In March, 1864, Mr. Piatt published The Nests at Washington, a collection of poems by himself and Mrs. Piatt, which elicited the cordial praise of Longfellow, and greatly widened the reputation of "the wedded poets." This book was followed, in 1866, by the volume, Poems in Sunshine and Firelight, which was issued in Cincinnati; and, later, by Western Windows and Other Poems, dedicated to the author's old friend, George D. Prentice, and also issued in the Queen City. In the years 1868-9 Piatt was connected editorially with the Cincinnati Chronicle; and, from 1869 to 1878, he was a frequent contributor to the Cincinnati Commercial.

From 1871 to 1875 Mr. Piatt was Librarian of the United States House of Representatives; and in 1882 he was appointed United States Consul at Cork, Ireland, where the government retained him in office until 1893. During their residence abroad Mr. and Mrs. Piatt enjoyed the acquaintance and friendship of many distinguished literary people, including Jean Ingelow, Aubrey de Vere, Edward Dowden, Lady Wilde, Philip Bourke

Marston, Edmund Gosse, Austin Dobson, Alice Meynell, Katherine Tynan, and Professor John Stuart Blackie. From April to September, 1893, Mr. Piatt served as Consul at Dublin, Ireland. He remained abroad until the following year, when he returned to America and to his home at North Bend, Ohio, where he has resided ever since, devoting himself to literary pursuits, being latterly engaged as book-reviewer for the Cincinnati Enquirer and as associate editor of Midland.

John James Piatt holds a deservedly conspicuous place among contemporary American poets. In the words of a Western critic: "He is one of those 'planters of celestial plants,' who have never lost faith in high ideals or in the divinity of the Muses. He has exerted an elevating influence on the literary profession in the Ohio Valley, both by his discriminating work as an editorial writer, and by his many publications in prose and verse. The country owes him a debt of gratitude for compiling that notably elegant and comprehensive volume, The Union of American Poetry and Art, (1880,) and for issuing the more recent volumes of The Hesperian Tree, An Annual of the Ohio Valley, (1900, 1903,) which contain some of the best literature of the locality and period they represent. Mr. Piatt's reputation as a poet is established; he needs no new encomium. Proud and jealous of the region in which he was born and educated, he has chosen to write on local themes, and has given subtle and delicate poetic expression to thoughts and emotions evoked by the idyllic, the home-bred, and the pensive."

Mr. Piatt's poetical work, which has won for its author a multitude of admiring and appreciative readers, is held in high estimation by critics, not only in the United States, but also in Great Britain and Ireland. That his verse has received a cordial welcome in transatlantic circles is amply testified in the following extracts from representative foreign periodicals: "The 'Great West,' of which Mr. Piatt is a native, is preëminently a land of poetic inspiration. Its boundless prairies, its vast depths of impenetrable forests, its gigantic rivers, its gorgeous sunsets and sunrises, its quiet scenes of natural beauty, and its pathetic traditions of the pioneer colonists, are all meet subjects for the poet's contemplation, . . . and the impressions they have left on him he has reproduced with no less grace than freshness. But chiefly does he seem to love the simple home-life of the West, which he describes with a depth and refinement of feeling that are equally rare and admirable."—*The Nation* (Dublin). "For us Europeans these poems have the additional charm of describing scenes with which we are comparatively unfamiliar. But while some of the scenes are alien, the human sentiment of the book is never remote. Mr. Piatt glories in the poetry of common life. He will not allow familiarity to rob family bonds, or patriotism, or childhood's associations of any of their sacredness or grandeur. . . . He plays with a firm hand on these universal heartstrings, and holds us unwearied by his music."—*The Literary World* (London). "The writer is, taken altogether, as unlike Crabbe, as unlike Gray, as unlike Wordsworth, as one poet can be unlike another, for he is quite original, with a distinct individuality; but there are in his writings touches that call to mind Crabbe, Gray, and Wordsworth. This means no more, of course, than that he is rustic, idyllic, pathetic, domestic; that he plays, for the most part, on the oaten reed, and that, though self-taught and unimitative, he plays sometimes like the masters of that simple instrument."—*The Illustrated London News.* "He draws his inspiration from the romance which always clings to the childhood of men and nations, to the mystery of the beginning. . . . His verses, which are free from any taint of folly or false taste, breathe the freshness of the Western scenery with which he is familiar; and while they suggest that touch of melancholy, which is characteristic of all poems descriptive of American scenery, they are to be commended for a wholesome moderation in style and sentiment."—*The Westminster Review.*

JOHN JAMES PIATT

KING'S TAVERN

Far-off spires, a mist of silver, shimmer from the far-off town;
Haunting here the dreary turnpike, stands the tavern, crumbling
    down.

Half a mile before you pass it, half a mile when you are gone,
Like a ghost it comes to meet you, ghost-like still it follows on.

Never more the sign-board, swinging, flaunts its gilded wonder
    'there:
"Philip King"— a dazzled harvest shocked in Western sunset air!

Never, as with nearer tinkle through the dust of long ago
Creep the Pennsylvania wagons up the twilight — white and slow.

With a low, monotonous thunder, yonder flies the hurrying train —
Hark, the echoes in the quarry! — in the woodland lost again!

Never more the friendly windows, red with warmth and Chris-
    tian light,
Breathe the traveler's benediction to his brethren in the night.

Old in name, The Haunted Tavern holds the barren rise alone;—
Standing high in air deserted, ghost-like long itself has grown.

Not a pane in any window — many a ragged corner-bit:
Boys, the strolling exorcisors, gave the ghost their notice—"Quit."

Jamestown-weeds have close invaded, year by year, the bar-room
    door,
Where, within, in damp and silence gleams the lizard on the floor.

Through the roof the drear Novembers trickle down the midnight
    slow;
In the summer's warping sunshine green with moss the shingles
    grow.

Yet in Maying wind the locust, sifting sunny blossom, snows,
And the rose-vine still remembers some dear face that loved the rose,—

Climbing up a southern casement, looking in neglected air;
And, in golden honey-weather, careful bees are humming there.

In the frozen moon at midnight some have heard, when all was still —
Nothing, I know! A ghostly silence keeps the tavern on the hill!

HONORS OF WAR

Wails of slow music move along the street,
Before the slow march of a myriad feet
    Whose mournful echoes come;
Banners are muffled, hiding all their sight
Of sacred stars — the century's dearest light —
    And, muffled, throbs the drum.

Proud is the hearse our Mother gives her son,[1]
On the red altar laid her earliest one!
    Wrapp'd in her holiest pall
He goes: her household guardians follow him;
Eyes with their new heroic tears are dim;
    The stern to-morrows call!

Well might the youth who saw his coffined face,
Lying in state within the proudest place,
    Long for a lot so high:
He was the first to leap the treacherous wall;
First in the arms of Death and Fame to fall —
    To live because to die!

---

[1] Ephriam Elmer Ellsworth, an American officer of Zouaves, shot at Alexandria, Va., May 24, 1861.

Pass on, with wails of music, moving slow,
Thy dark dead-march, O Mother dress'd in woe!
    Lo, many another way
Shall blacken after, many a sacred head
Brightly thy stars shall fold, alive though dead,
    From many a funeral day!

Weep, but grow stronger in thy suffering:
From their dead brothers' graves thy sons shall bring
    New life of love for thee:
The long death-marches herald, slow or fast,
The resurrection-hour of men at last
    New-born in Liberty!

WASHINGTON, May, 1861.

SONNET — IN 1862

Stern be the Pilot in the dreadful hour
  When a great nation, like a ship at sea
  With the wroth breakers whitening at her lee,
Feels her last shudder if her Helmsman cower;
A godlike manhood be his mighty dower!
  Such and so gifted, Lincoln, may'st thou be
  With thy high wisdom's low simplicity
And awful tenderness of voted power:
From our hot records then thy name shall stand
  On Time's calm ledger out of passionate days —
With the pure debt of gratitude begun
  And only paid in never-ending praise —
One of the many of a mighty Land
Made by God's providence the Anointed One.

THE GOLDEN HAND [1]

Lo, from the city's heat and dust
A Golden Hand forever thrust,
Uplifting from a spire on high
A shining finger in the sky!

I see it when the morning brings
Fresh tides of life to living things,
And the great world awakes: behold,
That lifted Hand in morning gold!

I see it when the noontide beats
Pulses of fire in busy streets;
The dust flies in the flaming air:
Above, that quiet Hand is there.

I see it when the twilight clings
To the dark earth with hovering wings:
Flashing with the last fluttering ray,
That Golden Hand remembers day.

The midnight comes — the holy hour;
The city, like a giant flower,
Sleeps full of dew: that Hand, in light
Of moon and stars, how weirdly bright!

Below, in many a noisy street,
Are toiling hands and striving feet;
The weakest rise, the strongest fall:
That equal Hand is over all.

---

[1] The lofty steeple of the First Prebyterian Church, on the north side of Fourth Street, between Main and Walnut, Cincinnati, terminates in a "golden hand"—the inspiration of this poem.

Below, in courts to guard the land,
Gold buys the tongue and binds the hand;
Dropping in God's great scales the gold,
That awful Hand, above, behold!

Below, the Sabbaths walk serene,
With the great dust of days between;
Preachers within their pulpits stand;
See, over all, that heavenly Hand!

But the hot dust, in crowded air
Below, arises never there: —
O speech of one who can not speak!
O Sabbath-witness of the Week!
CINCINNATI, OHIO, 1859.

THE MORNING STREET

Alone I walk the Morning Street,
Filled with the silence vague and sweet:
All seems as strange, as still, as dead,
As if unnumbered years had fled,
Letting the noisy Babel lie
Breathless and dumb against the sky.
The light wind walks with me, alone,
Where the hot day, flame-like, was blown;
Where the wheels roared, the dust was beat:—
The dew is in the Morning Street!

Where are the restless throngs that pour
Along this mighty corridor
While the noon shines?— the hurrying crowd
Whose footsteps make the city loud?—
The myriad faces, hearts that beat
No more in the deserted street?

Those footsteps, in their dreaming maze,
Cross thresholds of forgotten days;
Those faces brighten from the years
In rising suns long set in tears;
Those hearts — far in the Past they beat,
Unheard within the Morning Street!

Some city of the world's gray prime,
Lost in some desert far from Time,
Where noiseless ages, gliding through,
Have only sifted sand and dew,—
Yet a mysterious hand of man
Lying on all the haunted plan,
The passions of the human heart
Quickening the marble breast of Art,—
Were not more strange, to one who first
Upon its ghostly silence burst,
Than this vast quiet, where the tide
Of Life, upheaved on either side,
Hangs trembling, ready soon to beat
With human waves the Morning Street!

Ay, soon the glowing morning flood
Breaks through the charmèd solitude:
This silent stone, to music won,
Shall murmur to the rising sun;
The busy place, in dust and heat,
Shall roar with wheels and swarm with feet;—
The Arachne-threads of Purpose stream,
Unseen, within the morning gleam;
The life shall move, the death be plain;
The bridal throng, the funeral train,
Together, face to face, shall meet
And pass, within the Morning Street!
1858.

THE OPEN SLAVE-PEN

We start from sleep in morning's buoyant dawn,
  And find the horror which our sleep oppress'd
A vanish'd darkness, in the daylight gone —
  The nightmare's burthen leaves the stifled breast.

Yet still a presence moves about the brain,
  Some frightful shadow lost in hazy light,
And in the noonday highway comes again
  The loathsome phantom of the breathless night.

So, while before these hateful doors I stand,
  I feel the burdening darkness which is pass'd,
Or passing surely from the awaken'd land:
  The nightmare clutches me and holds me fast.

Back from the years that seem so long ago
  Return the dark processions which have been;
Lifting again lost manacles of woe
  They enter here — they vanish, going in.

Hark to the smother'd murmur of a race
  Within these walls — its helpless wail and moan —
Which, for the ancient shadow on its face,
  Call'd not the morning's new-born light its own!

Imprison'd here, what unforgotten cries
  Of hopeless torture and what sights of woe,
From cotton-field and rice-plantation rise!—
  These walls have heard, and seen, and witness show.

The human drove, the human driver, see!
  Hark, the dread bloodhound in the swamp at bay!
The whipping-post reëchoes agony;
  The slave-mart blackens all the shameful day.

The wife and husband, see, asunder thrust;
  The mother dragg'd from her far children's wail;
The maiden torn from love and given to lust —
  The Human Family in a bill of sale!

All sounds reëcho, all sights reappear:
  (O blindness, deafness! that ye can not be!)
All sounds of woe, that have been heard, I hear;
  All sights of shame, that have been seen, I see!

O sounds, be still! O visions, leave the day! —
  What thunder trembled on the sultry air?
What lightnings went upon their breathless way?
  Behold the stricken gates of old despair!

The writing on these barbarous walls was plain;
  The curse has fallen none would understand:
God's deluge ere another happier rain;
  His plow of fire before the reaper's land!

The awful nightmare slips into its night,
  With cannon-flash and noise of hurrying shell:
O prisons, open for returning light,
  The sun is in the world, and all is well!

A LOST KINGDOM OF GODS

The vast Olympian Heaven vanishes
Like the frail wreck of clouds that travel slow
After a thunder-storm, when eastward far
They sink, forever fainter, lower, down
In evening dusk among dark mountain peaks,
With vague unpurposed thunders, nerveless bolts
Of dull forgetful lightnings; and its King,
Who made an earthquake if he bent his brows,
Moves with his kind in half-forgotten dreams,
Such as we dream, and, waking, find are naught,
But feel their nothing present in all the air.

JOHN JAMES PIATT

FARTHER

Far-off a young State rises, full of might:
   I paint its brave escutcheon. Near at hand
   See the log-cabin in the rough clearing stand;
A woman by its door, with steadfast sight,
Trustful, looks Westward, where, uplifted bright,
   Some city's Apparition, weird and grand,
   In dazzling quiet fronts the lonely land,
With vast and marvelous structures wrought of light,
Motionless on the burning cloud afar: —
   The haunting vision of a time to be,
After the heroic age is ended here,
Built on the boundless, still horizon's bar
   By the low sun, his gorgeous prophecy
Lighting the doorway of the pioneer!

THE BOOK OF GOLD

If I could write a Book made sweet with thee,
And therefore sweet with all that may be sweet,
With lingering music never more complete
Should turn its golden pages: each should be
Like whispering voices, beckoning hands, and he
Who read should follow, while his heart would beat
For some new miracle, with most eager feet
Through loving labyrinths of mystery.
Temple and lighted home of Love should seem
The Book wherein my love remember'd thine:
There holiest visions evermore should gleam,
Vanishing wings, with wandering souls of sound
And breaths of incense from an inmost shrine
Sought nearer evermore and never found.

SUNDOWN
(Extract)

Low sounds of autumn creep along the plains,
  Through the wide stillness of the woodlands brown,
    Where the weird waters hold
    The melancholy gold;
The cattle, lingering slow through river lanes,
  Brush yellowing vines that swing through elm-trees down.

On many a silent circle slowly blown,
  The hawk, in sun-flushed calm suspended high,
    With careless trust of might
    Slides wing-wide through the light,—
Now golden through the restless dazzle shown,
  Now drooping down, now swinging up the sky.

With evening bells that gather, low or loud,
Some village, through the distance, poplar-bound,
    O'er meadows silent grown,
    And lanes with crisp leaves strown,
Lifts up one spire, aflame, against a cloud
  That slumbers eastward, slow and silver-crowned.

A VOICE IN OHIO [1]
(Extract)

By my quick firelight rapt and still,
High on this black Ohio hill,
  I think of him who crossed to-day
  The snow-roofed boundary of our way,
    (His book upon my table lies,
    Look from my wall his grave, sweet eyes,)

---

[1] Read at the "Atlantic Dinner" in Boston, December 17, 1877, the seventieth anniversary of John G. Whittier's birthday.

JOHN JAMES PIATT

The poet, who, in many a song,
Quickening unnumbered hearts so long,
Has breathed New England's spirit forth
From East to West, through South and North—
Not the witch-burning bigot's rage,
That soiled her first heroic page,
But that sweet, tender, warm and good,
Confirming, human brotherhood;
Religious with diviner scope;
Wide-armed with charity and hope;
Lighter of household fires that bless
The fast-withdrawing wilderness
(Keeping old home-stars burning clear
In Memory's holy atmosphere);
Sowing the waste with seeds of light;
Righteous with wrath at wrongful might:
Such is thy better spirit, known
Wherever Whittier's songs have flown;—
Thy greater, larger, nobler air,
New England, thus is everywhere!

* * * * *

Blessings be with him — praise, less worth;
Why ask long-added hours of earth?
Grateful, if given, these shall come,
Birds, sing to the reaper going home,
Singing himself — his work well-done.
Shine on him, slow, soft-setting sun!
NORTH BEND, OHIO.

TAKING THE NIGHT-TRAIN

A tremulous word, a lingering hand, the burning
  Of restless passion smouldering — so we part;
Ah, slowly from the dark the world is turning
  When midnight stars shine in a heavy heart.

The streets are lighted, and the myriad faces
  Move through the gaslight, and the homesick feet
Pass by me, homeless; sweet and close embraces
  Charm many a household — laughs and kisses sweet.

From great hotels the stranger throng is streaming,
  The hurrying wheels in many a street are loud;
Within the depot, in the gaslight gleaming,
  A glare of faces, stands the waiting crowd.

The whistle screams; the wheels are rumbling slowly,
  The path before us glides into the light:
Behind, the city sinks in silence wholly;
  The panting engine leaps into the night.

I seem to see each street a mystery growing,
  In mist of dreamland — vague, forgotten air:
Does no sweet soul, awaking, feel me going?
  Loves no dear heart, in dreams, to keep me there?

READING THE MILESTONE

I stopped to read the Milestone here,
  A laggard school-boy, long ago;
I came not far — my home was near —
  But ah, how far I longed to go!

Behold a number and a name,—
  A finger, Westward, cut in stone:
The vision of a city came,
  Across the dust and distance shown.

Around me lay the farms asleep
  In hazes of autumnal air,
And sounds that quiet loves to keep
  Were heard, and heard not, everywhere.

JOHN JAMES PIATT

I read the Milestone, day by day:
  I yearned to cross the barren bound,
To know the golden Far-away,
  To walk the new Enchanted Ground!

THE THREE WORK-DAYS

So much to do, so little done!
In sleepless eyes I saw the sun;
His beamless disk in darkness lay,
The dreadful ghost of Yesterday!

So little done, so much to do!
The morning shone on harvests new;
In eager light I wrought my way,
And breathed the spirit of Today!

So much to do, so little done!
The toil is past, the rest begun;
Though little done, and much to do,
Tomorrow Earth and Heaven are new!

USE AND BEAUTY

Who would have a treadmill measure every golden-sanded hour?
Who would find a purpose busy deep in every fragrant flower?

Yet we sometimes (ay, and often) gladly find the two agree;
Clasped together, Use and Beauty — in the rose the honey bee.

Factory-bells in yonder city, wind-blown music, far away
Waken soft enchanted sleepers in the charmèd breast to-day;

See the river's quiet water, lovely mirror, slowly steal,
Dance with sunshine to its task-work; — Beauty overflows the
        wheel!

TORCH-LIGHT IN FALL-TIME

I lift this sumach-bough with crimson flare,
  And, touch'd with subtle pangs of dreamy pain,
Through the dark wood a torch I seem to bear
  In Autumn's funeral train.

AT HOME.

Far off the sunset-smitten spires
Breathe through the wood their golden fires;
Hither the noisy city swells
A dreamy tide of vesper bells.

THE GUERDON

To the quick brow Fame grudges her best wreath,
While the quick heart to enjoy it throbs beneath.
On the dead forehead's sculptured marble shown,
Lo, her choice crown — its flowers are also stone.

SARAH MORGAN BRYAN PIATT

SARAH MORGAN BRYAN PIATT, daughter of Talbot N. and Mary A. (Spiers) Bryan, and wife of John James Piatt, was born August 11, 1836, at Lexington, Kentucky. Her paternal grandfather, Morgan Bryan, was one of the pioneer settlers of that State — a proprietor of "Bryan's Station," famous in the old Indian wars — and he was a brother-in-law of Daniel Boone, whom the Bryans accompanied from North Carolina into Kentucky. Mrs. Piatt's childhood was passed near Versailles, Ky., where her mother, a young and beautiful woman, died, in 1844, when the subject of this sketch was but eight years old. Shortly thereafter the father placed Sarah and a younger sister in the care of their aunt, Mrs. Annie Boone, who lived at Newcastle, Henry County. Here the poet received her school-education and here graduated from Henry Female College, an institution then under the directorship of a cousin of Charles Sumner. At an early age Miss Bryan produced poems of extraordinary merit, not a few of which were published and praised by George D. Prentice, the distinguished editor of the Louisville Journal, who confidently predicted of their author her eventual recognition as first in rank of women poets of America.

"It is since her marriage, in June, 1861," says Mrs. Piatt's biographer in R. H. Stoddard's Poets' Homes, "that her more individual characteristics of style have manifested themselves, especially the dramatic element, so delicate, subtle and strong, which asserts her intellectual kinship with Mrs. Elizabeth Barrett Browning."

Mrs. Piatt's poems are introspective and personal to the last degree. They depict the essential life of woman, in its various phases, voicing her ambitions, longings, joys, disappointments, doubts, anguish, prayer. The tone of the verse is often sorrowful, sometimes deeply tragic. "In the rush of these hopeless tears," writes William Dean Howells, "this heart-broken scorn of comfort, this unreconcilable patience of grief, is the drama of the race's affliction; in the utter desolation of one woman's sorrow, the universal anguish of mortality is expressed. It is not pessimism; it does not assume to be any sort of philosophy or system; it is simply the bitter truth, to a phrase, of human experience through which all men must pass, and the reader need not be told that such poems were lived before they were written."

Another admirer of Mrs. Piatt's masterful verse, in a critical survey of the literature of Ohio, (1903,) says of the author and her work: "Mrs. Piatt is a woman of original and exceptional genius — a poet whose name shines in American literature

'Like some great jewel full of fire.'

She is unrivaled, in her pròvince of song, by any living writer of her sex, whether native to this country or of foreign birth. . . . She is inimitable in her own vivid, bold, and suggestive invention and manner. Whatever she writes has meaning — and the significance is often deep — sometimes strange and elusive — never commonplace. . . . Mrs. Piatt's rare artistic skill has been admired by many who appreciate the technical difficulties of the poetic craft."

Equally emphatic is the praise accorded her genius by a contemporary English critic, who, in an article contributed to the London Saturday Review, commenting on the volume of select verse entitled "A Voyage to the Fortunate Isles, and Other Poems," says: "Of all the concourse of women singers Mrs. Piatt is the most racy and, in a word, the most American. . . . The new selections of her poems should be most welcome to all who seek in American poetry something more than a pale reflex of the British commodity. . . . Her poems, with all their whim and inconstancy of mood, are charmingly sincere, artless, piquant, and full of quaint surprise." And in like commendatory strain another English critic, reviewing the same book in the Pictorial World (London), pronounces her verse "not easy to equal, much less to surpass, on either side of the Atlantic," and characterizes her poetical achievement in the following words: "Mrs. Piatt studies no model, and takes no pattern for her work; she simply expresses herself; hence her verse is just the transparent mantle of her individuality. The natural refinement, the ready sympathy, the tender sentiment, the quiet grace of a thoroughly womanly woman reveal themselves quite unconsciously in every poem; and the musical quality of the verse increases the impression that the reader is listening to the heart-utterances of one of the Imogens or Mirandas to be met with now seldom outside the radiant land where Shakespeare's imagination reigns supreme. . . . Mrs. Piatt will, we doubt not, as her poems become known to English readers, become popular, or, we should rather say, dear to a wide circle mainly composed of members of her own sex, for she supplies the adequate expression for women whose hearts are tender and true like her own."

LEAVING LOVE

"If one should stay in Italy awhile,
 With bloom to hide the dust beneath her feet,
 With birds in love with roses to beguile
  Her life until its sadness grew too sweet;

"If she should, slowly, see some statue there,
 Divine with whiteness and with coldness, keep
 A very halo in the hovering air;
  If she should weep — because it could not weep;

"If she should waste each early gift of grace
 In watching it with rapturous despair,
 Should kiss her youth out on its stony face,
  And feel the grayness gathering toward her hair:

"Then fancy, though it had till now seemed blind,
   Blind to her little fairness, it could see
How scarred of soul, how wan and worn of mind,
   How faint of form and faded, she must be;

"If she should moan: 'Ah, land of flower and fruit,
   Ah, fiercely languid land, undo your charm!
Ah, song impassioned, make your music mute!
   Ah, bosom, shake away my clinging arm!'

"Then swiftly climb into the mountains near,
   And set her face forever toward the snow,
And feel the North in chasm and cliff, and hear
   No echo from the fairyland below;

"If she should feel her own new loneliness,
   With every deep-marked, freezing step she trod,
Nearing (and in its nearness growing less)
   The vast and utter loneliness of God;

"If back to scented valleys she should call,
   This woman that I fancy — only she —
Would it remind one statue there at all,
   O cruel Silence in the South, of — me?"

A DOUBT

It is subtle, and weary, and wide;
It measures the world at my side;
  It touches the stars and the sun;
  It creeps with the dew to my feet;
    It broods on the blossoms, and none,
Because of its brooding, are sweet;
It slides as a snake in the grass,
Whenever, wherever I pass.

It is blown to the South with the bird;
At the North, through the snow, it is heard;
　With the moon from the chasms of night
It rises, forlorn and afraid;
　If I turn to the left or the right
I can not forget or evade;
When it shakes at my sleep as a dream,
If I shudder, it stifles my scream.

It smiles from the cradle; it lies
On the dust of the grave, and it cries
　In the winds and the waters; it slips
In the flush of the leaf to the ground;
　It troubles the kiss at my lips;
It lends to my laughter a sound;
It makes of the picture but paint;
It unhaloes the brow of the saint.

The ermine and crown of the king,
The sword of the soldier, the ring
　Of the bride, and the robe of the priest,
The gods in their prisons of stone,
　The angels that sang in the East —
Yea, the cross of my Lord, it has known;
And wings there are none that can fly
From its shadow with me, till I die!

TRANSFIGURED

Almost afraid they led her in
　(A dwarf more piteous none could find);
Withered as some weird leaf, and thin,
　The woman was — and wan and blind.

Into his mirror with a smile —
　Not vain to be so fair, but glad —
The South-born painter looked the while,
　With eyes than Christ's alone less sad.

"Mother of God," in pale surprise
  He whispered, "What am I to paint!"
A voice, that sounded from the skies,
  Said to him: "Raphael, a saint."

She sat before him in the sun:
  He scarce could look at her, and she
Was still and silent. . . . "It is done,"
  He said,—"Oh, call the world to see!"

Ah, this was she in veriest truth —
  Transcendent face and haloed hair.
The beauty of divinest youth,
  Divinely beautiful, was there.

Herself into her picture passed —
  Herself and not her poor disguise,
Made up of time and dust. . . . At last
  One saw her with the Master's eyes.

THE THOUGHT OF ASTYANAX BESIDE IULUS
(After reading Virgil's Story of Andromache in Exile.)

Yes, all the doves begin to moan,—
But it is not the doves alone.
Some trouble, that you never heard
In any tree from breath of bird,
That reaches back to Eden lies
Between your wind-flower and my eyes.

I fear it was not well, indeed,
Upon so sad a day to read
So sad a story. But the day
Is full of blossoms, do you say,—
And how the sun does shine? I know.
These things do make it sadder, though.

You'd cry, if you were not a boy,
About this mournful tale of Troy?
Then do not laugh at me, if I —
Who am too old, you know, to cry —
Just hide my face a while from you,
Down here among these drops of dew.

. . . Must I for sorrow look so far?
This baby headed like a star,
Afraid of Hector's horse-hair plume
(His one sweet child, whose bitter doom
So piteous seems — oh, tears and tears!—)
Has he been dust three thousand years?

Yet when I see his mother fold
The pretty cloak she stitched with gold,
Around another boy, and say:
"He would be just your age to-day,
With just your hands, your eyes, your hair"—
Her grief is more than I can bear.

NO HELP

When will the flowers grow there? I cannot tell.
  Oh, many and many a rain will beat there first,
Stormy and dreary, such as never fell
  Save when the heart was breaking that had nursed
Something most dear a little while, and then
Murmured at giving God his own again.

The woods were full of violets, I know;
  And some wild sweet-briers grew so near the place:
Their time is not yet come. Dead leaves and snow
  Must cover first the darling little face
From these wet eyes, forever fixed upon
Your last still cradle, O most precious one!

Is he not with his Father? So I trust.
   Is he not His? Was he not also mine?
His mother's empty arms yearn toward the dust.
   Heaven lies too high, the soul is too divine.
I wake at night and miss him from my breast,
And — human words can never say the rest.

Safe? But out of the world, out of my sight!
   My way to him through utter darkness lies.
I am gone blind with weeping, and the light —
   If there be light — is shut inside the skies.
Think you, to give my bosom back his breath,
I would not kiss him from the peace called Death?

And do I want a little Angel? No,
   I want my Baby — with such piteous pain,
That were this bitter life thrice bitter, oh!
   I could not choose but take him back again.
God cannot help me, for God cannot break
His own dark Law — for my poor sorrow's sake.

CALLING THE DEAD

My little child, so sweet a voice might wake
So sweet a sleeper for so sweet a sake.
Calling your buried brother back to you,
You laugh and listen — till I listen too!

. . . Why does he listen? It may be to hear
Sounds too divine to reach my troubled ear.
Why does he laugh? It may be he can see
The face that only tears can hide from me.

Poor baby faith — so foolish or so wise:
The name I shape out of forlornest cries
He speaks as with a bird's or blossom's breath.
How fair the knowledge is that knows not Death!

. . . Ah, fools and blind — through all the piteous years
Searchers of stars and graves — how many seers,
Calling the dead, and seeking for a sign,
Have laughed and listened, like this child of mine?

A PIQUE AT PARTING

Why, sir, as to that — I did not know it was time for the moon
 to rise,
 (So, the longest day of them all can end, if we will have
  patience with it.)
One woman can hardly care, I think, to remember another one's
 eyes,
 And — the bats are beginning to flit.
 . . . We hate one another? It may be true.
What else do you teach us to do?
Yea, verily, to love you.

My lords — and gentlemen — are you sure that after we love
 quite all
 There is in your noble selves to be loved, no time on our hands
  will remain?
Why, an hour a day were enough for this. We may watch the
 wild leaves fall
 On the graves you forget. . . . It is plain
That you were not pleased when she said — Just so;
Still, what do we want, after all, you know,
But room for a rose to grow?

You leave us the baby to kiss, perhaps; the bird in the cage
 to sing;
 The flower on the window, the fire on the hearth (and the
  fires in the heart) to tend.
When the wandering hand that would reach somewhere has
 become the Slave of the Ring,
 You give us — an image to mend;

Then shut with a careless smile, the door —
(There's dew or frost on the path before;)
We are safe inside. What more?

If the baby should moan, or the bird sit hushed, or the flower
  fade out — what then?
Ah? the old, old feud of mistress and maid would be left
  though the sun went out?
You can number the stars and call them by names, and, as
  men, you can wring from men
The world — for they own it, no doubt.
We, not being eagles, are doves? Why, yes,
We must hide in the leaves, I guess,
And coo down our loneliness.

God meant us for saints? Yes — in Heaven. Well, I, for one,
  am content
  To trust Him through darkness and space to the end — if
  an end there shall be;
But, as to His meanings, I fancy I never knew quite what He
  meant.
And — why, what were you saying to me
Of the saints — or *that* saint? It is late;
The lilies look weird by the gate.
  . . . Ah, sir, as to that — we will wait.

CAPRICE AT HOME

No, I will not say good-by —
  Not good-by, nor anything.
He is gone. . . . I wonder why
  Lilacs are not sweet this spring.
  How that tiresome bird will sing!

I might follow him and say
  Just that he forgot to kiss
Baby, when he went away.

Everything I want I miss.
Oh, a precious world is this!

. . . What if night came and not he?
Something might mislead his feet.
Does the moon rise late? Ah me!
There are things that he might meet.
Now the rain begins to beat:

So it will be dark. The bell? —
Some one some one loves is dead.
Were it he — ! I cannot tell
Half the fretful words I said,
Half the fretful tears I shed.

Dead? And but to think of death! —
Men might bring him through the gate:
Lips that have not any breath,
Eyes that stare — And I must wait!
Is it time, or is it late?

I was wrong, and wrong, and wrong;
I will tell him, oh, be sure!
If the heavens are builded strong,
Love shall therein be secure;
Love like mine shall there endure.

. . . Listen, listen — that is he!
I'll not speak to him, I say.
If he choose to say to me,
"I was all to blame today;
Sweet, forgive me," why — I may!

THE HOUSE BELOW THE HILL

You ask me of the farthest star,
    Whither your thought can climb at will,
Forever questioning child of mine.
I fear it is not half so far
    As is the house below the hill,
Where one poor lamp begins to shine,—
The lamp that is of death the sign.

Has it indeed been there for years,
    In rain and snow, with ruined roof
For God to look through, day and night,
At man's despair and woman's tears,
    While with myself I stood aloof,
As one by some enchanted right
Held high from any ghastly sight?

. . . One of my children lightly said:
    "Oh nothing, (Why must we be still?)
Only the people have to cry
Because the woman's child is dead
    There in the house below the hill.
I wish that we could see it fly;—
It has gold wings, and that is why!"

Gold wings it has? I only know
    What wasted little hands it had,
That reached to me for pity, but
Before I thought to give it—oh,
    On earth's last rose-bud, faint and sad,
Less cold than mine had been, they shut.
Sharper than steel some things should cut!

. . . I thought the mother showed to me,
    With something of a noble scorn
(When morning mocked with bird and dew),

That brief and bitter courtesy
  Which awes us in the lowliest born.
Ah, soul, to thine own self be true; —
God's eyes, grown human, look thee through!

"We need no help — we needed it.
  You have not come in time, and so
The women here did everything.
You did not know? You did not know!"
  I surely saw the dark brows knit.
— To let the living die for bread,
Then bring fair shrouds to hide the dead!

What time I cried with Rachel's cry,
  I wondered that I could not wring,
While sitting at the grave forlorn,
Compassion from yon alien sky,
  That knows not death nor anything
That troubles man of woman born,
Save that he wounded Christ with thorn.

My sorrow had the right to find
  Immortal pity? I could sit,
Not hearing at my very feet
The utter wailing of my kind,
  And dream my dream high over it!
O human heart! what need to beat,
If nothing save your own is sweet?

Ah me, that fluttering flower and leaf,
  That weird, wan moon and pitiless sun,
And my own shadow in the grass
Should hide from me this common grief!
  Was I not dust? What had I done?
In that fixed face, as in a glass,
I saw myself to judgment pass!

SAD WISDOM — FOUR YEARS OLD

"Well, but some time I will be dead;
    Then you will love me, too!"
Ah! mouth so wise for mouth so red,
    I wonder how you knew.
(Closer, closer, little brown head —
    Not long can I keep you!)

Here, take this one poor bud to hold
    Take this long kiss and last;
Love cannot loosen one fixed fold
    Of the shroud that holds you fast —
Never, never; oh, cold, so cold!
    All that was sweet is past.

Oh, tears, and tears, and foolish tears,
    Dropped on a grave somewhere!
Does not the child laugh in my ears
    What time I feign despair?
Whisper, whisper — I know he hears;
    Yet this is hard to bear.

O world, with your wet face above
    One veil of dust, thick-drawn!
O weird voice of the hapless dove,
    Broken for something gone!
Tell me, tell me, when will we love
    The thing the sun shines on?

"TO BE DEAD"

If I should have void darkness in my eyes
    While there were violets in the sun to see;
If I should fail to hear my child's sweet cries,
    Or any bird's voice in our threshold tree;

If I should cease to answer love or wit:
Blind, deaf, or dumb, how bitter each must be!
Blind, deaf, or dumb — I will not think of it!
  . . . Yet the night comes when I shall be all three.

A LOOK INTO THE GRAVE

I look, through tears, into the dust to find
  What manner of rest man's only rest may be.
The darkness rises up and smites me blind.
  The darkness — is there nothing more to see?

Oh, after flood, and fire, and famine, and
  The hollow watches we are made to keep
In our forced marches over sea and land —
  I wish we had a sweeter place to sleep.

THE HIGHEST MOUNTAIN

I know of a higher Mountain. Well?
  "Do the flowers grow on it?" No, not one.
"What is its name?" But I can not tell.
  "Where —— ?" Nowhere under the sun!

"Is it under the moon, then?" No, the light
  Has never touch'd it, and never can;
It is fashion'd and form'd of night, of night
  Too dark for the eyes of man.

Yet I sometimes think, if my Faith had proved
  As a grain of mustard seed to me,
I could say to this Mountain: "Be thou removed,
  And be thou cast in the sea!"

LIFE AND DEATH

If I had chosen, my tears had all been dews;
  I would have drawn a bird's or blossom's breath,
Nor outmoaned yonder dove. I did not choose —
  And here is Life for me, and there is Death.

Ay, here is Life. Bloom for me, violet;
  Whisper me, Love, all things that are not true;
Sing, nightingale and lark, till I forget —
  For here is Life, and I have need of you.

So, there is Death. Fade, violet, from the land;
  Cease from your singing, nightingale and lark;
Forsake me, Love, for I without your hand
  Can find my way more surely to the dark.

"I WANT IT YESTERDAY"

"Come, take the flower,— it is not dead,
  It stayed all night out in the dew."
"I will not have it now," he said;
  "I want it yesterday, I do."

"It is as red, it is as sweet"—
  With angry tears he turned away,
Then flung it fiercely at his feet,
  And said, "I want it — yesterday."

As sullen and as quick of grief,
  Sometimes a lovelier flower than this
I crush forever, scent and leaf;
  Then scent and leaf forever miss.

It keeps its blush, it keeps its breath,
  It keeps its form unchanged, but I
See in its beauty only death;
  Then drop it in the dust,— and why?

And why? Ah, Hand divine, I know,—
　Forgive my childish pain, I pray,—
Today your flower is fair, but oh!
　I only want it — yesterday!

IN DOUBT

Through dream and dusk a frightened whisper said:
"Lay down the world: the one you love is dead."
　In the near waters, without any cry
　I sank, therefore — glad, oh so glad, to die!

Far on the shore, with sun, and dove, and dew,
And apple-flowers, I suddenly saw you.
　Then — was it kind or cruel that the sea
　Held back my hands, and kissed and clung to me?

SAY THE SWEET WORDS

　Say the sweet words, say them soon;
　　You have said the bitter —
　Changed to tears, by this dim moon
　　You may see them glitter.

　Say the sweet words soon, I pray —
　　Mine is piteous pleading;
　Haste to draw the steel away,
　　Though the wound keep bleeding.

FOR ANOTHER'S SAKE

Sweet, sweet? My child, some sweeter word than sweet,
　Some lovelier word than love, I want for you.
Who says the world is bitter, while your feet
　Are left among the lilies and the dew?

. . . Ah? So some other has, this night, to fold
Such hands as his, and drop some precious head
From off her breast as full of baby-gold?
I, for her grief, will not be comforted.

LITTLE CHRISTIAN'S TROUBLE

His wet cheeks looked as they had worn,
    Each, with its rose, a thorn,

Set there (my boy, you understand?)
    By his own brother's hand:

"Look at my cheek. What shall I do? —
    You know I have but two!"

His mother answered, as she read
    What my Lord Christ had said,

(While tears began to drop like rain:)
    "Go, turn the two again."

MY WEDDING RING

My heart stirr'd with its golden thrill
    And flutter'd closer up to thine,
In that blue morning of the June
    When first it clasp'd thy love and mine.

In it I see the little room,
    Rose-dim and hush'd with lilies still,
Where the old silence of my life
    Turn'd into music with "I will."

Oh, I would have my folded hands
    Take it into the dust with me:
All other little things of mine
    I'd leave in the bright world with thee.

—— TO ——

Sweet World, if you will hear me now:
   I may not own a sounding Lyre
And wear my name upon my brow
   Like some great jewel full of fire.

But let me, singing, sit apart,
   In tender quiet with a few,
And keep my fame upon my heart,
   A little blush-rose wet with dew.

WILLIAM HENRY VENABLE

WILLIAM HENRY VENABLE, son of William and Hannah (Baird) Venable, was born April 29, 1836, in a log house built by his father on a farm not far from Waynesville, Warren County, Ohio. His ancestry, on the paternal side, was English, remotely Norman, while, on the mother's side, it was Scotch-English, with a qualifying strain of Dutch. In the boy's sixth year, his parents with their four children — John, Newell, Henry, and Cynthia — removed to a homestead located near the present "Venable Station," within a short distance of Ridgeville, a hamlet on the Cincinnati and Dayton turnpike, about seven miles north of Lebanon, Ohio.

Stimulated by a home environment of books and culture, Henry early outgrew the limits of learning in the Ridgeville country school, where, however, besides studying the branches commonly taught at the time in rural districts, he gained, under competent guidance, a familiar objective knowledge of physics, botany, and zoology. His reading, even in boyhood, when he assisted on his father's farm in the summer season and went to the district school in the winter, was diverse in character and unusual in amount, ranging, in a desultory fashion, from the Bible and such formidable tomes as Rollin's Ancient History, Plutarch's Lives, Volney's Ruins, the Works of Josephus, and Dick's Christian Philosopher, to Robinson Crusoe, the Arabian Nights, Gulliver's Travels, Don Quixote, and the popular novels of Scott, Bulwer, Dickens, and Cooper. Equally discursive, at this formative period, were his readings in verse, which introduced him to the works of a number of British poets, including Burns, Thomson, Pope, Pollok, Young, Cowper, Byron, Milton, and Shakespeare. Of the American poets, Bryant and Longfellow were his favorites. From Thomson's "The Seasons" he derived his first inspiration to write in metrical form.

WILLIAM HENRY VENABLE

Eager in the pursuit of higher education, young Venable left his rural home to seek the advantages of collegiate training. Under special private instruction, from Dr. Alfred Holbrook, Dr. William Downs Henkle, and others, as well as in the South-Western Normal School, at Lebanon, Ohio, (with which institution he was connected for several years, first as a student and afterwards as a teacher,) he rapidly acquired an academic knowledge of science, language, literature, and history, soon winning distinction by his versatile scholarship. While yet in his teens he was a frequent contributor to local newspapers, and he began those original historical investigations which have since established his reputation as an authority in all that pertains to the literary annals of the Ohio Valley.

In 1864 he received from De Pauw University the honorary degree of Master of Arts, and in 1886, from Ohio University, the degree of Doctor of Laws.

Dr. Venable has spent his entire life, excepting for a single year, in Ohio, where, with tongue and pen, he has devoted himself to the higher interests of his time, working especially to promote the cause of liberal education and literary culture. In addition to his manifold labors as author and lecturer, he has been identified with several public and private schools and with many teachers' institutes and associations. After his experience in the Lebanon Normal School, where he studied and taught, intermittently, from 1855 to 1861, he was called to the principalship of Jennings Academy, Vernon, Indiana, which he conducted for about a year. During his residence in the Hoosier State he took an active part in educational affairs, and was one of the editors of the Indiana School Journal. He was married, on December 30, 1861, in Indianapolis, to Miss Mary Ann Vater, the youngest daughter of Thomas and Eleanor (Palmer) Vater, both of whom were of English parentage and nativity, being born and educated in London, whence in 1832, prompted by a romantic spirit of adventure, they came to America to seek their fortunes in the "Great West." In September, 1862, through the influence of Dr. John Hancock, Mr. Venable was induced to come to Cincinnati, where he entered upon a more extended field of professional work, in the celebrated Chickering Institute, a classical and scientific academy with which he was connected for nearly a quarter of a century, and of which, in 1881, he became the principal and proprietor. Disposing of his interest in this school in 1886, he devoted the next three years to the completion of long-delayed literary undertakings, and to lecturing in many cities and towns in Ohio, Indiana, Pennsylvania, Kentucky, and West Virginia. From 1889 to 1900 he was actively engaged in public educational work in the Queen City, where, in addition to his radical and efficacious reformatory labors as director of the department of English, first in Hughes, and later in Walnut Hills High School, he exercised a far-reaching influence upon educational ideals and methods, through the publication of a volume of trenchant pedagogical essays, entitled "Let Him First Be a Man," and of three unique high school text-books, presenting, respectively, annotated selections from the poetry of Burns, of Byron, and of Wordsworth.

Since his retirement from active professional life in 1900, Mr. Venable has devoted himself exclusively to literature, having produced within this recent period several important works in biography, fiction, and verse.

The author has resided, since 1875, at "Diana Place," a suburban homestead on the highlands of eastern Cincinnati, overlooking the Ohio River. "A very pleasant glimpse of the Venable home, at Mount Tusculum," writes Henry Howe in his Historical Collections of Ohio, 1888, "is given by the Hon. Coates Kinney, the author of the far-famed lyric, 'Rain on the Roof:' 'Just east of Cincinnati, on the Little Miami Railroad, there is a picturesque suburb named (by some admirer of Cicero) Tusculum. Leaving the station, climbing the up-hill street of the town, turning into the wood, passing down through a glen, winding about, and again climbing by stone steps up gentle slopes, across rustic plank bridges, under overhanging trees, you come to the poet's home — a commodious country house almost on top of the hill, looking down over all the landscape óf slopes, and glens, and ravines, and woods that you have just come through. This is the poet's home; and a delightful home it is, full of love and poetry and children. Venable is, in the city, a man of business in the daytime, but a dreamer here on the hills at night. An evening with him there in his cozy library, overlooking the 'brown ravine,' is a rest and refreshment not soon to be forgotten.' "

MY CATBIRD
A Capriccio

Nightingale I never heard,
Nor the skylark, poet's bird;
But there is an æther-winger
So surpasses every singer,
(Though unknown to lyric fame,)
That at morning, or at nooning,
When I hear his pipe a-tuning,
Down I fling Keats, Shelley, Wordsworth,—
What are all their songs of birds worth?
All their soaring
Souls' outpouring?
When my Mimus Carolinensis,
(That's his Latin name,)
When my warbler wild commences
Song's hilarious rhapsody,
Just to please himself and me!

Primo Cantante!
Scherzo! Andante!
Piano, pianissimo!
Presto, prestissimo!
Hark! are there nine birds or ninety and nine?
And now a miraculous gurgling gushes
Like nectar from Hebe's Olympian bottle,
The laughter of tune from a rapturous throttle!
Such melody must be a hermit-thrush's!
But that other caroler, nearer,

Outrivaling rivalry with clearer
Sweetness incredibly fine!
Is it oriole, redbird, or bluebird,
Or some strange, un-Auduboned new bird?
All one, sir, both this bird and that bird,
The whole flight are all the same catbird!
The whole visible and invisible choir you see
On one lithe twig of yon green tree.
Flitting, feathery Blondel!
Listen to his rondel!
To his lay romantical!
To his sacred canticle!
Hear him lilting,
See him tilting
His saucy head and tail, and fluttering
While uttering
All the difficult operas under the sun
Just for fun;
Or in tipsy revelry,
Or at love devilry,
Or, disdaining his divine gift and art,
Like an inimitable poet
Who captivates the world's heart
And don't know it.
Hear him lilt!
See him tilt!

Then suddenly he stops,
Peers about, flirts, hops,
As if looking where he might gather up
The wasted ecstacy just spilt
From the quivering cup
Of his bliss overrun.
Then, as in mockery of all
The tuneful spells that e'er did fall
From vocal pipe, or evermore shall rise,
He snarls, and mews, and flies.

WILLIAM HENRY VENABLE

THE FOUNDERS OF OHIO
April, 1888

The footsteps of a hundred years
   Have echoed since o'er Braddock's Road
Bold Putnam and the Pioneers
   Led History the way they strode.

On wild Monongahela stream
   They launched the Mayflower of the West,
A perfect State their civic dream,
   A new New World their pilgrim quest.

When April robed the Buckeye trees
   Muskingum's bosky shore they trod;
They pitched their tents and to the breeze
   Flung freedom's banner, thanking God.

As glides the Oyo's solemn flood
   So fleeted their eventful years;
Resurgent in their children's blood,
   They still live on — the Pioneers.

Their fame shrinks not to names and dates
   On votive stone, the prey of time: —
Behold where monumental States [1]
   Immortalize their lives sublime!

THE TEACHER'S DREAM

The weary teacher sat alone
   While twilight gathered on;
And not a sound was heard around,
   The boys and girls were gone.

---

[1] The five states formed from the territory north-west of the Ohio River, (known as 'the Ohio Country',) were admitted into the Union in the following order: Ohio, 1803; Indiana 1816; Illinois, 1818; Michigan, 1837; Wisconsin, 1848.

The weary teacher sat alone,
    Unnerved and pale was he;
Bowed by a yoke of care he spoke
    In sad soliloquy:

"Another round, another round
    Of labor thrown away,
Another chain of toil and pain
    Dragged through a tedious day.

"Of no avail is constant zeal,
    Love's sacrifice is loss,
The hopes of morn, so golden, turn,
    Each evening, into dross.

"I squander on a barren field
    My strength, my life, my all;
The seeds I sow will never grow,
    They perish where they fall."

He sighed, and low upon his hands
    His aching brow he prest,
And like a spell upon him fell
    A soothing sense of rest.

Ere long he lifted up his face,
    When, on his startled view,
The room by strange and sudden change
    To vast proportions grew!

It seemed a senate-hall, and one
    Addressed a listening throng;
Each burning word all bosoms stirred,
    Applause rose loud and long.

The wildered teacher thought he knew
    The speaker's voice and look,
"And for his name," said he, "the same
    Is in my record-book."

The stately senate-hall dissolved,
   A church rose in its place,
Wherein there stood a man of God,
   Dispensing words of grace.

And though he heard the solemn voice,
   And saw the beard of gray,
The teacher's thought was strangely wrought:
   "My yearning heart today

"Wept for that youth whose wayward will
   Against persuasion strove,
Compelling force, love's last resource,
   To establish laws of love."

The church, a phantom, vanished soon;
   What apparition then?
In classic gloom of alcoved room
   An author plied his pen.

"My idlest lad!" the teacher said,
   Filled with a new surprise,
"Shall I behold *his* name enrolled
   Among the great and wise?"

The vision of a cottage home
   Was now through tears descried:
A mother's face illumed the place
   Her influence sanctified.

"A miracle! a miracle!
   This matron, well I know,
Was but a wild and careless child
   Not half an hour ago.

"Now, when she to her children speaks
   Of duty's golden rule,
Her lips repeat, in accents sweet,
   My words to her at school."

Dim on the teacher's brain returned
　　The humble school-room old;
Upon the wall did darkness fall,
　　The evening air was cold.

"A dream!" the sleeper, waking, said;
　　Then paced along the floor,
And, whistling slow and soft and low,
　　He locked the school-house door.

His musing heart was reconciled
　　To love's divine delays:
"The bread forth cast returns at last,
　　Lo, after many days!"

1856

NATIONAL SONG

America, my own!
　　Thy spacious grandeurs rise
Faming the proudest zone
　　Pavilioned by the skies;
Day's flying glory breaks
　　Thy vales and mountains o'er,
And gilds thy streams and lakes
　　From ocean shore to shore.

Praised be thy wood and wold,
　　Thy corn and wine and flocks,
The yellow blood of gold
　　Drained from thy cañon rocks;
Thy trains that shake the land,
　　Thy ships that plow the main,
Triumphant cities grand
　　Roaring with noise of gain.

Earth's races look to Thee:
  The peoples of the world
Thy risen splendors see
  And thy wide flag unfurled;
Thy sons, in peace or war,
  That emblem who behold,
Bless every shining star,
  Cheer every streaming fold!

Float high, O gallant flag,
  O'er Carib Isles of Palm,
O'er bleak Alaskan crag,
  O'er far-off, lone Guam;
Where Mauna Loa pours
  Black thunder from the deeps;
O'er Mindanao's shores,
  O'er Luzon's coral steeps.

Float high, and be the sign
  Of love and brotherhood,—
The pledge, by right divine,
  Of Power, to do Good:
For aye and everywhere,
  On continent and wave,
Armipotent to dare,
  Imperial to save!

May, 1899.

AN OLD SPANISH BUGLE

This clarion sounded its final war-warning
  On stormed Santiago's grim day of renown,
When thunders of sea-battle roared through the morning
  And flame-shrouded ships of Cervera went down.

Some artisan wrought it in old Barcelona,
  Whose dark bastions frown on the Mediterrane,

Beyond where the rampires of gray Tarragona
Remember Hamilcar and Cæsar, in Spain.

Perchance its ta-ra-ra has marshaled yare heroes
   In days of the Moor and of proud Ferdinand —
Its blast may have sounded when plumed caballeros
   Of Philip ensanguined the sea and the land.

Perchance Boabdil, on the walls of Granada,
   Defied the far flourish and parl of its note;
Belike that brave Duke of the storm-tost Armada
   Heard fanfares of doom from its clangorous throat!

Lepanto's flotilla whose gonfalons flouted
   Encountering crescents by Moslem upborne,
And squadrons of Alva, in Netherlands routed,
   I trow may have harked yon historial horn.

No more shall it summon hidalgo or vassal,
   To rouse up from slumber and arm for the fray,
Nor city beleaguered nor turreted castle
   Shall fear or rejoice at its challenging bray.

No more by clear Ebro or swift Guadalquivir,
   On coast Caribbean or Philippine shore,
Its signals of wrath shall this bugle deliver,
   Shall madden the charging battalions no more!

Nay, mute let it hang as a trophy and token
   Of conflicts forgotten and war-banners furled,
A sign of the truce that shall never be broken,
   When love, like a baldric, encircles the world.

1909.

WILLIAM HENRY VENABLE

IMMORTAL BIRDSONG

What though mine ear hath never heard
  The wing'd voice of the sky?
Nor listened to the love-lorn bird
  Whose plaints in darkness die?

The poets improvise for me
  Lark-notes that never fail,
And make more sweet than sound can be
  The song of nightingale.

From rapt Alastor's lyric leaves
  Joy's flying carol springs!
On darkling pinion sorrow grieves
  When Adonaïs sings.

I list the lavrock warbling clear
  In birks of bonny Doon;
The bulbul's swooning voice I hear,
  Beneath the Persian moon;

I hear across the centuries
  What Philomela sung,
In Attic groves, to Sophocles,
  When Poesie was young.

SUMMER LOVE

I know 'tis late, but let me stay,
For night is tenderer than day;
Sweet love, dear love, I cannot go,
Dear love, sweet love, I love thee so.
The birds in leafy hiding sleep;
Shrill katydids their vigil keep;
The woodbine breathes a fragrance rare
Upon the dewy languid air;

The fireflies twinkle in the vale,
The river looms in moonshine pale,
And look! a meteor's dreamy light
Streams mystic down the solemn night!
Ah, life glides swift, like that still fire —
How soon our throbbing joys expire;
Who can be sure the present kiss
Is not his last? Make all of this.
I know 'tis late, sweet love, I know,
Dear love, sweet love, I love thee so.

Fantastic mist obscurely fills
The hollows of Kentucky hills;
Heardst thou? I heard or fear I heard
Vague twitters of some wakeful bird;
The wingèd hours are swift indeed!
Why makes the jealous morn such speed?
This rose thou wearst may I not take
For passionate remembrance' sake?
Press with thy lips its crimson heart;
Yes, blushing rose, we must depart;
A rose cannot return a kiss —
I pay its due with this, and this;
The stars grow faint, they soon will die,
But love faints not nor fails.— Good-bye!
Unhappy joy — delicious pain —
We part in love, we meet again!
Good-bye! — the morning dawns — I go;
Dear love, sweet love, I love thee so.

COFFEA ARABICA

More entrancing than aroma
From the Hindu sacred soma,
    Comes a fragrant
    Essence vagrant

WILLIAM HENRY VENABLE

    Floating up
From my quaint Zumpango cup,
    Incense rare,
Evanescent steam ascending,
Curling, wavering, fading, blending,
    Vanishing in viewless air.

Let me sip and dream and sing
Musing many an idle thing,
Let me sing and dream and sip
Making many a fancied trip
  Far away and far away
  Over ocean, gulf and bay
To islands whence the spicy wind
  Breathes languor on the tropic sea,
To sultry strands of teeming Ind,
  To coasts of torrid Araby,
To realms no boreal breath may chill,
    Like rich Brazil,
Or Jabal's clouded hill on hill,
Or warm Bulgosa's valley low,
To zones where summer splendors glow,
Where seasons never come or go,
Where coffee trees perpetual blow.

While I drowse and dream and sip,
Sailing, sailing, slides a ship
  Over the glittering sea,
Measuring leagues of night and day,
  Bearing and bringing to me,
Bringing from far away, away,
  The pale green magical berry,
  The seed of the virtuous cherry,
  The bean of the blossom divine!
Bringing from over the brine,
Bringing from Demerara,
From balsamy San Pará,

Bringing from Trans-Sahara,
  From hoard of the Grand Bashaw,
Or redolent chests of Menelek,
  An Abyssinian cargo
  Richer than freight of Argo,
Treasured in garners under the deck,
Bringing and bearing for me
The gift of the coffee tree!
Better than blood of the Spanish vine,
Or ruddy or amber wine of the Rhine;
  Bearing the bean of the blessed tree!
Better than bousa or sake fine,
  Or sampan loads of oolong tea,
  Souchong, twankay, or bohea,—
Bringing the virtuous bean divine,
    The coffee-tree cherry,
    The magical berry,
More entrancing than aroma
From the Hindu sacred soma.

A WELCOME TO BOZ
Impromptu

In immortal Weller's name,
By Micawber's deathless fame,
By the flogging wreaked on Squeers,
By Job Trotter's fluent tears,
By the beadle Bumble's fate
At the hands of vixen mate,
By the famous Pickwick Club,
By the dream of Gabriel Grub,
In the name of Snodgrass' muse,
Tupman's amorous interviews,
Winkle's ludicrous mishaps,
And the fat boy's countless naps,

WILLIAM HENRY VENABLE

By Ben Allen and Bob Sawyer,
By Miss Sally Brass, the lawyer,
In the name of Newman Noggs,
River Thames and London fogs,
Richard Swiveller's excess,
Feasting with the Marchioness,
By Jack Bunsby's oracles,
By the chime of Christmas bells,
By the cricket on the hearth,
Scrooge's frown and Cratchit's mirth,
By spread tables and good cheer,
Wayside inns and pots of beer,
Hostess plump and jolly host,
Coaches for the country post,
Chambermaid in love with Boots,
Toodles, Traddles, Tapley, Toots,
Jarley, Varden, Mister Dick,
Susan Nipper, Mistress Chick,
Snevellicci, Lilyvick,
Mantalini's predilections
To transfer his "dem" affections,
Podsnap, Pecksniff, Chuzzlewit.
Quilp and Simon Tappertit,
Wegg and Boffin, Smike and Paul,
Nell and Jenny Wren and all,—
Be not Sairey Gamp forgot,—
No, nor Peggotty and Trot,—
By poor Barnaby and Grip,
Flora, Dora, Di and Jip,
Peerybingle, Pinch and Pip—
Welcome, long-expected guest,
Welcome, Dickens, to the West.

1867.

THE POET OF CLOVERNOOK [1]

A poet born, not made,
  By Nature taught, she knew,
And, knowing, still obeyed
  The Beautiful, the True.

Hers was the seeing eye,
  The sympathetic heart,
The subtle art whereby
  Lone genius summons art.

She caught the primal charm
  Of every rural scene,—
Of river, cottage, farm,
  Blue sky, and woodland green.

Baptized in Sorrow's stream,
  She sang, how sweetly well,
Of true Love's tender dream,
  And Death's pale asphodel.

Her pensive muse has fled
  From hill and meadow-brook;
No more her footsteps tread
  Thy paths, fair Clovernook.

No more may she behold
  The dew-crowned summer morn
On wings of sunrise gold
  Fly o'er the bending corn.

No more her mournful gaze
  Shall seek the twilight sky,
When parting autumn days
  Flush hectic ere they die.

---

[1] Read at the celebration of Alice Cary's birthday, to the children of the Public Schools of Cincinnati, April 26, 1880.

Nor note of joyous bird,
  Nor April's fragrant breath,
Nor tear, nor loving word,
  May break the spell of Death.

Sleep on! and take thy rest,
  In Greenwood by the sea!
Dear Poet of the West,
  Thy West remembers thee.

A GENTLE MAN

I knew a gentle Man; —
  Alas! his soul has flown;
Now that his tender heart is still,
  Pale anguish haunts my own.
His eye, in pity's tear,
  Would often saintly swim;
He did to others as he would
  That they should do to him.

He suffered many things,—
  Renounced, forgave, forbore;
And sorrow's crown of thorny stings,
  Like Christ, he meekly wore;
At rural toils he strove;
  In beauty, joy he sought;
His solace was in children's words
  And wise men's pondered thought.

He was both meek and brave,
  Not haughty, and yet proud;
He daily died his soul to save,
  And ne'er to Mammon bowed.
E'en as a little child
  He entered Heaven's Gate;
I caught his parting smile, which said,
  "Be reconciled, and wait."

INVIOLATE

We took a walk in winter woods,
  My little lad and I,—
The hills and hollows all were pearl,
  And sapphire all the sky.

Before guerilla winds we saw
  The scurrying drift retreat;
We thought of budded roots that lay
  Asleep beneath our feet.

We spoke of how, last year, in May,
  One sunny bank we found,
Where wind-flowers stood in fairy crowds,
  To charm the gladdened ground.

A subtle feeling checked the boy,—
  His small hand held me back,
With mute appeal that we should tread
  The wood-path's beaten track.

"My child, 'tis pleasanter to break
  New pathways as we go."
He said, "I do not like to spoil
  The beauty of the snow."

A DIAMOND

Upon the breast of senseless earth
  This immemorial stone,
A jewel of Golconda's worth,
  In sovran beauty shone.

My lady for a moment bore
  The gem upon her brow,
A moment on her bosom wore:—
  'Tis worth the Orient now.

WILLIAM HENRY VENABLE

FROM "FLORIDIAN SONNETS"[1]

"THE GOLDEN TREASURY"

She brought one book to that sequestered Cay
  Rhyme's linkèd sweetness by the voice discrete
  Interpreted with modulation meet:
Melodious Elizabethan lay,
Rare lyric fragrant of Victoria's day,—
  Outrivaling skill of larks and nightingales,—
  Songs from the heights of genius and the dales,
Whose echoes in the haunted memory stay.
From often vesper service to the Muse
  Our hearts, exalted, took a joy secure,
  And drank a spiritual solace pure,
Reviving as to flowers the pensive dews:
  Religion hath a liturgy and shrine,
  And Poesy its ritual divine.

MILTON

Lost Paradise and Paradise Regained,
  Sublime, sonorous, like that seven-fold
  Sphere-music down the crystal heavens rolled
In solemn, epic symphony, deep-strained;
Not these, of lofty argument sustained,
  The strenuous labor of the mighty-souled
  Milton of Cromwell, have the charm to hold
My captive spirit goldenly enchained.
Rather that Milton of a gentler Age,
  Inheriting the selfsame woodland note
  Of him who turned it to the sweet bird's throat:
Not the blind Samson with the world at rage,
  But he, the swain who by smooth-dittied song
  Rescued the Lady from all fear of wrong.

---

[1] By permission of Richard G. Badger.

WORDSWORTH

Poets there be whose passionate verses pour
    E'en as cascading streams that rush along,
    Tumultuous torrential flows of song,
And wake the echoing vales with mellow roar;
And there be bards profound of calmer lore,
    Whose inexhaustive numbers full and strong,
    Like storm-blown, multitudinous billows, throng
And roll in rhythmic thunder on the shore.
The shouting brooks which down the mountains leap,
    Moon-litten lakes that ripple to the breeze,
    Wordsworth! thy joyous hymns resemble these;
Thy grander songs majestically sweep
    Like Amazon or the unfathomed seas,
Deep answering unto harmonious deep.

SURSUM CORDA

Here on this barren fragment unreclaimed
    Of coral reef o'ersurged by tidal brine,
    Shifting each fluctuant hour its border-line,
I did not think to hear, loud-clarion-famed,
Or whispered to my solitude unblamed,
    Rumor of Politics; but o'er the shine
    Of watery waste, and continental fine,
Sounded the Nations and great names were named!
Then I rejoiced with an exceeding awe,
    And the religious rapture patriots know,
    Who in their love of country love the Race,
Enjoining equal privilege and law!
    A Citizen! a Man! how can I go
    Away from Home, beyond my People's place?

WILLIAM HENRY VENABLE

MUTATION

Cult, credo, social orders that pertain
    To human progress, polity and laws;
    Science, philosophy; effect and cause
Of war and wealth or poverty and pain;
Rise and decline of empire; loss and gain
    O' th' whole world; ancient and modern saws
    Of wisdom: these but eddyings and flaws
In the full tide of Time which moves amain
Its fateful course! and what is man? A leaf
    On Igdrasil, that for a season stirs
    With kindred rustling multitudes, then whirs
Into oblivion:— such, our mortal fief!
    How void of worth your proud Opinion, sirs,
Or mine, our term of fluttering so brief.

TO COATES KINNEY

That shrine the sexton told me was thy tomb,
    There where the hills of Wayne slope greenly down
    To willowy Miami, near the pensive Town
Mournful without thee, though its mold consume
Thy consecrated bones, may not inhume
    Genius from proud remembrance; nay, Renown
    Hath woven thy unfading laurel crown,
And o'er thy dust Love's amaranth shall bloom.
Well didst thou rear thy monument, not stone
    Nor votive bronze; no mausoleum wrought
In burnished gold; no obelisk, world-shown,
    To mark where monarch reigned or soldier fought:
My Poet shall to nobler fame be known
    By what he builded of immortal thought.

WILLIAM DEAN HOWELLS

WILLIAM DEAN HOWELLS, novelist, poet, critic, a son of William Cooper Howells and Mary (Dean) Howells, was born at Martin's Ferry, Belmont County, Ohio, March 1, 1837. His preliminary education, he tells us, was largely received in his father's and other Ohio newspaper offices in which he worked as compositor, correspondent, and editor. Early in life he achieved a wide reputation by noteworthy writings in prose and in verse contributed to the Ohio State Journal, the Cincinnati Gazette, the Dial, (edited in Cincinnati, by M. D. Conway,) the New York Saturday Press, and the Atlantic Monthly. In 1860 he brought out, in collaboration with John James Piatt, a volume entitled "Poems of Two Friends," published in Columbus, Ohio. This was followed, in the same year, by a campaign Life of Abraham Lincoln. In 1861 Mr. Howells was appointed United States Consul to Venice, a position which he held until the summer of 1865. He was married, in 1862, in Paris, France, to Miss Elinor G. Mead. After returning to America from his consular service in Italy, he became, successively, editorial writer on the New York Nation; assistant editor and, later, chief editor of the Atlantic Monthly; editorial contributor to Harper's Monthly Magazine; and editor of the Cosmopolitan Magazine; and since 1892 he has conducted with great originality and distinction the "Editor's Easy Chair" department in Harper's Magazine, to which periodical his name adds luster.

In recognition of his eminence as a man of letters, honorary degrees have been conferred on Mr. Howells by Harvard, Yale, Columbia, and Oxford universities, and by Adelbert College.

Mr. Howells holds a distinguished rank among American authors. His versatile genius has given to the world some seventy different volumes, embracing works of biography, history, travel, fiction, drama, essay, criticism, and poetry. But though the Nation claims him as her own, he has never failed to render a loyal tribute of gratitude to his native State; and several of his books, among which may be mentioned those entitled "Life of Rutherford B. Hayes," "Ohio Stories," "My Year in a Log Cabin," and "A Boy's Town," derive much of their absorbing interest from his familiar knowledge of Ohio.

A consummate master of elegant prose, a profound and subtle critic whose literary judgments are respected wherever English is read, a novelist of extraordinary penetration and power, William Dean Howells is also an artist of rare skill and surprising invention in the province of poetry. To few American authors whose reputation mainly rests upon the intrinsic excellence of their works in prose, has it been given to contribute so much that is of enduring merit to the poetical literature of the Nation. His early poems are distinguished for melodious cadence and exquisite touches of descriptive beauty, while his more recent achievement in verse, fairly represented in the volume, Stops of Various Quills, shows the ripe thought and imagination of a philosophic poet who, in the spirit of noble altruism, has sympathetically studied human nature and human society, and who has pondered deeply the ultimate problems of life.

THE MOVERS

Parting was over at last, and all the good-byes had been spoken.
Up the long hill-side the white-tented wagon moved slowly,
Bearing the mother and children, while onward before them the
        father
Trudged with his gun on his arm, and the faithful house-dog
        beside him,
Grave and sedate, as if knowing the sorrowful thoughts of his
        master.

April was in her prime, and the day in its dewy awaking;
Like a great flower, afar on the crest of the eastern woodland,
Goldenly bloomed the sun, and over the beautiful valley,
Dim with its dew and its shadow, and bright with its dream of a river,
Looked to the western hills, and shone on the humble procession,
Paining with splendor the children's eyes, and the heart of the mother.

Beauty, and fragrance, and song filled the air like a palpable presence.
Sweet was the smell of the dewy leaves and the flowers in the wildwood,
Fair the long reaches of sun and shade in the aisles of the forest.
Glad of the spring, and of love, and of morning, the wild birds were singing;
Jays to each other called harshly, then mellowly fluted together;
Sang the oriole songs as golden and gay as his plumage;
Pensively piped the querulous quails their greetings unfrequent,
While, on the meadow-elm, the meadow-lark gushed forth in music,
Rapt, exultant and shaken, with the great joy of his singing;
Over the river, loud-chattering, aloft in the air, the king-fisher,
Hung ere he dropped like a bolt into the water beneath him;
Gossiping, out of the bank, flew myriad twittering swallows;
And in the boughs of the sycamore quarreled and clamored the blackbirds.

Never for these things a moment halted the movers, but onward
Up the long hill-side the white-tented wagon moved slowly,
Till, on the summit, that overlooked all the beautiful valley,
Trembling and spent, the horses came to a standstill unbidden;
Then from the wagon the mother in silence got down with her children,
Came and stood by the father, and rested her hand on his shoulder.

Long together they gazed on the beautiful valley before them;
Looked on the well-known fields that stretched away to the wood-lands,
Where, in the dark lines of green, showed the milk-white crest of the dogwood,
Snow of wild plums in bloom, and crimson tints of the redbud;
Looked on the pasture fields where the cattle were lazily grazing—
Softly, and sweet, and thin, came the faint, far notes of the cow-bell;
Looked on the oft-trodden lanes, with their elder and blackberry borders,
Looked on the orchard, a bloomy sea, with its billows of blossoms.
Fair was the scene, yet suddenly strange and all unfamiliar,
Like as the faces of friends, when the word of farewell has been spoken.
Long together they gazed; then at last on the little log-cabin —
Home for so many years, now home no longer forever —
Rested their tearless eyes in the silent rapture of anguish.
Up on the morning air, no column of smoke from the chimney
Wavering, silver and azure, rose, fading and brightening ever;
Shut was the door where yesterday morning the children were playing,
Lit with a gleam of the sun, the window stared at them blindly,
Cold was the hearth-stone now, and the place was forsaken and empty.
Empty? Ah no! but haunted by thronging and tenderest fancies,
Sad recollections of all that had ever been, of sorrow or gladness.

Once more they sat in the glow of the wide red fire in the winter,
Once more they sat by the door in the cool of the still summer evening,
Once more the mother seemed to be singing her babe there to slumber,
Once more the father beheld her weep o'er the child that was dying,

Once more the place was peopled by all the Past's sorrow and gladness!
Neither might speak for the thoughts that came crowding their hearts so,
Till, in their ignorant sorrow, aloud the children lamented;
Then was the spell of silence dissolved, and the father and mother
Burst into tears, and embraced, and turned their dim eyes to the westward.

From Coggeshall's The Poets and Poetry of the West, 1860.

FORLORN

Red roses, in the slender vases burning,
    Breathed all upon the air,—
The passion and the tenderness and yearning,
    The waiting and the doubting and despair.

Still with the music of her voice was haunted,
    Through all its charmèd rhymes,
The open book of such a one as chanted
    The things he dreamed in old, old summer-times.

The silvern chords of the piano trembled
    Still with the music wrung
From them; the silence of the room dissembled
    The closes of the songs that she had sung.

The languor of the crimson shawl's abasement,—
    Lying without a stir
Upon the floor,— the absence at the casement,
    The solitude and hush were full of her.

Without, and going from the room, and never
    Departing, did depart
Her steps; and one that came too late forever
    Felt them go heavy o'er his broken heart.

And, sitting in the house's desolation,
  He could not bear the gloom,
The vanishing encounter and evasion
  Of things that were and were not in the room.

Through midnight streets he followed fleeting visions
  Of faces and of forms;
He heard old tendernesses and derisions
  Amid the sobs and cries of midnight storms.

By midnight lamps, and from the darkness under
  That lamps made at their feet,
He saw sweet eyes peer out in innocent wonder,
  And sadly follow after him down the street.

The noonday crowds their restlessness obtruded
  Between him and his quest;
At unseen corners jostled and eluded,
  Against his hand her silken robes were pressed.

Doors closed upon her; out of garret casements
  He knew she looked at him;
In splendid mansions and in squalid basements,
  Upon the walls he saw her shadow swim.

From rapid carriages she gleamed upon him,
  Whirling away from sight;
From all the hopelessness of search she won him
  Back to the dull and lonesome house at night.

Full early into dark the twilights saddened
  Within its closèd doors;
The echoes, with the clock's monotony maddened,
  Leaped loud in welcome from the hollow floors;

But gusts that blew all day with solemn laughter
  From wide-mouthed chimney-places,
And the strange noises between roof and rafter,
  The wainscot clamor, and the scampering races

Of mice that chased each other through the chambers,
    And up and down the stair,
And rioted among the ashen embers,
    And left their frolic footprints everywhere,—

Were hushed to hear his heavy tread ascending
    The broad steps, one by one,
And toward the solitary chamber tending,
    Where the dim phantom of his hope alone

Rose up to meet him, with his growing nearer,
    Eager for his embrace,
And moved, and melted into the white mirror,
    And stared at him with his own haggard face.

But, turning, he was 'ware *her* looks beheld him
    Out of the mirror white;
And at the window yearning arms she held him,
    Out of the vague and sombre fold of night.

Sometimes she stood behind him, looking over
    His shoulder as he read;
Sometimes he felt her shadowy presence hover
    Above his dreamful sleep, beside his bed;

And rising from his sleep, her shadowy presence
    Followed his light descent
Of the long stair; her shadowy evanescence
    Through all the whispering rooms before him went

Upon the earthy draught of cellars blowing
    His shivering lamp-flame blue,
Amid the damp and chill, he felt her flowing
    Around him from the doors he entered through.

The spiders wove their webs upon the ceiling;
    The bat clung to the wall;
The dry leaves through the open transom stealing,
    Skated and danced adown the empty hall.

About him closed the utter desolation,
  About him closed the gloom;
The vanishing encounter and evasion
  Of things that were and were not in the room

Vexed him forever; and his life forever
  Immured and desolate,
Beating itself, with desperate endeavor,
  But bruised itself, against the round of fate.

The roses, in their slender vases burning,
  Were quenchèd long before;
A dust was on the rhymes of love and yearning;
  The shawl was like a shroud upon the floor.

Her music from the thrilling chords had perished;
  The stillness was not moved
With memories of cadences long cherished,
  The closes of the songs that she had loved.

But not the less he felt her presence never
  Out of the room depart;
Over the threshold, not the less, forever
  He felt her going on his broken heart.

IN EARLIEST SPRING

Tossing his mane of snows in wildest eddies and tangles,
  Lion-like, March cometh in, hoarse, with tempestuous breath,
Through all the moaning chimneys, and thwart all the hollows and angles
  Round the shuddering house, threating of winter and death.

But in my heart I feel the life of the wood and the meadow
  Thrilling the pulses that own kindred with fibres that lift
Bud and blade to the sunward, within the inscrutable shadow,
  Deep in the oak's chill core, under the gathering drift.

Nay, to earth's life in mine, some prescience, or dream, or desire
  (How shall I name it aright?) comes for a moment and goes,—
Rapture of life ineffable, perfect,— as if in the brier,
  Leafless there by my door, trembled a sense of the rose.

DEAD

I

Something lies in the room
  Over against my own;
The windows are lit with a ghastly bloom
  Of candles, burning alone,—
Untrimmed, and all aflare
In the ghastly silence there!

II

People go by the door,
  Tiptoe, holding their breath,
And hush the talk that they held before,
  Lest they should waken Death,
That is awake all night
There in the candlelight!

III

The cat upon the stairs
  Watches with flamy eye
For the sleepy one who shall unawares
  Let her go stealing by.
She softly, softly purrs,
And claws at the banisters.

IV

The bird from out its dream
  Breaks with a sudden song,
That stabs the sense like a sudden scream;
  The hound the whole night long
Howls to the moonless sky,
So far, and starry, and high.

WILLIAM DEAN HOWELLS

SOCIETY

I looked and saw a splendid pageantry
    Of beautiful women and of lordly men,
    Taking their pleasure in a flowery plain,
Where poppies and the red anemone,
And many another leaf of cramoisy,
    Flickered about their feet, and gave their stain
    To heels of iron or satin, and the grain
Of silken garments floating far and free,
As in the dance they wove themselves, or strayed
    By twos together, or lightly smiled and bowed,
Or curtseyed to each other, or else played
At games of mirth and pastime, unafraid
    In their delight; and all so high and proud
    They seemed scarce of the earth whereon they trod.

I looked again and saw that flowery space
    Stirring, as if alive, beneath the tread
    That rested now upon an old man's head
And now upon a baby's gasping face,
Or mother's bosom, or the rounded grace
    Of a girl's throat; and what had seemed the red
    Of flowers was blood, in gouts and gushes shed
From hearts that broke under that frolic pace.
And now and then from out the dreadful floor
    An arm or brow was lifted from the rest,
As if to strike in madness, or implore
    For mercy; and anon some suffering breast
    Heaved from the mass and sank; and as before
The revellers above them thronged and prest.

---

[1] Copyright, 1895, by Harper & Brothers.

RESPITE [1]

Drowsing, the other afternoon, I lay
  In that sweet interlude that falls between
  Waking and sleeping, when all being is seen
Of one complexion, and the vague dreams play
Among the thoughts, and the thoughts go astray
  Among the dreams. My mother, who has been
  Dead almost half my life, appeared to lean
Above me, a boy, in a house far away,
That once was home, and all the troubled years
  That have been since were as if they were not.
The voices that are hushed were in my ears,
  The looks and motions that I had forgot
Were in my eyes; and they disowned the tears
  That now again beneath their lids are hot.

---

[1] Copyright, 1895, by Harper & Brothers.

DENTON JAQUES SNIDER

DENTON JAQUES SNIDER was born at Mount Gilead, Morrow County, Ohio, January 9, 1841. He graduated from Oberlin College in 1862, after which he engaged in teaching, and in varied and protracted studies chiefly of a philosophical character. For many years he has devoted himself exclusively to authorship, and to the elucidation, from the lecture-platform, of his speculative doctrines. Mr. Snider was one of the lecturers in the Concord School of Philosophy, at Concord, Mass. He is a man of profound erudition and strikingly original thought, his "Commentaries on the Literary Bibles" being regarded by an authority no less eminent than Dr. William T. Harris, editor of the Journal of Speculative Philosophy, as of unique and permanent value as a critical interpretation of the ethical significance of Goethe, Shakespeare, Dante, and Homer.

The poetical work of Denton Jaques Snider is comprised in five volumes: Delphic Days (1878); Agamemnon's Daughter (1885); Prorsus Retrorsus (1890); Homer in Chios (1891); and Johnny Appleseed's Rhymes (1894). It is impossible by detached quotation to convey any adequate conception of the scope and purport of the author's later volumes of verse; and the selections here given are therefore limited to illustrative extracts from "Delphic Days," an excursive pastoral, the idyllic beauty and invigorating atmosphere of which must commend it to every lover of Hellas and the Castalian muse.

DELPHIC DAYS
(Extracts)

ELPINIKE

In these verses I wish to build a new temple of Fortune,
    For the Goddess to-day showed me a favor divine;
I shall raise her a temple and deck it with friezes of marble
    Which will emblazon her deed worthy of glorious Gods.
For she led me direct to the house where dwells Elpinike,
    Whom to behold I had wished all the long day of unrest.
Just at dusk I sauntered around through the lanes of the village,
    With a sweet image in mind ta'en from a maid I had seen
Watering her horse at the gush of a fountain early this morning:
    Lorn and unhappy I strayed in a delicious still pain,
When a door that stood right before me was oped and the image
    Flew into body at once, with transformation divine.
Such is always the brightest Olympian present of Fortune,
    When the dear shadow she turns into fresh life at her touch;
So I beheld the pale lines of my fancy to color transmuted,
    Till my soul became eye — then too mine eye became soul.

* * * *

To the house I came where dwelleth the fair Elpinike;
    We sat down by the fire that in the chimney was lit;
On the hearth the twigs of the oak and the olive were sparkling,
    There on the mats we sat down round the bright blaze of the fire.
Large was the company—youthful and old—about her assembled,
    Crowds of suitors and guests who find delight in her look.
Many a story was told of the time of the Great Revolution,
    How Palicaris so bold slew then the barbarous Turk.
Next they sang, sang gaily of wine and of certain three maidens
    Who dispensed to the guests liquid of poesy's flame.
But to me Elpinike came with a jar full of sweetmeats,
    Bade me to eat of the fruit — citrons from Chios they were,

Made by her hand of deep skill and then laid away for occasion,
  Till the right one should come who could enjoy her sweet art.
Long she stood there before me, pretending to hold me the server,
  Longer I caused her to stand uttering words for delay
Sweeter than citrons — words that were sweetened by Eros
  With the glance of the eye and the soft touch of the hand.
Then she reached me a beaker that brimmed with Castalia's pure water
  Just from the spring by the rock, redolent with a new song
Fresh from the Muse; with her face in each drop I drank off the crystal —
  Draughts that reached to the soul, quenching its thirst by the hymn.
Now all the day I but eat of the junkets of fair Elpinike,
  With them I drink of the brook, limpid Castalia's stream.

* * * * *

When I go now on my walk through Delphi, every one knows me,
  Gives a familiar salute with a fair word or a nod,
And they call me Didaskali — that is, the Master or Teacher,
  With a strange guess at my life, hinted perchance in my face.
I accept the kind title and always return friendly greeting
  To every nod of the head, to every smile of the eye.
Even the children no longer laugh at the foreigner's costume,
  But they will follow my steps, gently take me by the hand,
Babbling their little delights in many a word of old Homer,
  And these words too I greet like the dear faces of friends.
Also the mother will stop the full sweep of her loom to salute me,
  As she sits weaving the threads for the phoustána's white folds.
With the Papás too, the priest, I oft take a stroll up the mountain —
  Dark-haired, long-robed priest, with his hair parted like Christ's
Just in the middle, and falling loosely over his shoulders;
  Kindly and good is the man, with not a stain on his soul.
Hours pass unnoticed as over the valley we look from the summit,

Talking of things far away on the wide world's other half
Where is my home by the River. But to Elpinike I play now
  Teacher all the day long, teaching her mouth-wrenching words
Ta'en from my language — words that before never flowed from
    her tongue-tip:
Willing the Master doth work, willing too seemeth the maid;—
For she keeps asking: What is the name of this thing in English?
  So I utter the sounds which she attempts to repeat;
O'er the rough vocables then she skips like a brook over
    boulders —
Still her stammer I love, for it is fair as herself,
Even new beauty reveals, for she always resembles Castalia
  When a rock may be cast into the flow of its stream:
For it will ripple and warble around the ugly intruder,
  Making a melody new sung from the rill of the Muse;
Were there naught in the way of the stream, the beautiful water
  Onward would flow in its course, lisping not even a note,
But with the babble and dash of its drops now a hymn it is
    singing
In the struggle it makes for its own happy repose.
Often merely a pebble thrown into pearly Castalia
  Tunes her to sweetest of notes which she before never sang.
So in that streamlet I throw a large stone or perchance a small
    pebble,
Which the clear waters embrace with a pellucid soft throb.
Such is the way that I teach Elpinike the words of my language,
  Which with her musical breath she doth convert to a song.
Sweet are all her mistakes, for they drip with melodious honey,
  Sweeter by far is her mouth twisted to utter my words,
And the rude sounds of my voice that through her soft lips are
    but spoken
  Changed are at once to a strain that hath the breath of the
    Muse.

* * * * *

Here in this alley there lies the fragment of some ancient column,
  Half imbedded in soil, tipped to one side in its fall;

See the shape of the flower there sculptured in happiest outline,
   Just in the bloom of its growth with all the leaves on the stalk.
Even in marble it has a fresh look as if blowing in springtide,
   Though rude handfuls of Time long have been flung on its form;
Gently it clings to the stone and lovingly winds round the pillar,
   Yet it turns to my glance with a soft smile in its eye.
So art thou, divine Elpinike, the flower of Delphi,
   Ancient thou art, I should say, just in the bud of thy youth;
For if the Delphian priestess now were alive in her beauty,
   She thy form would assume, robed in the waves of white folds.
But though so young, thou art hid, methinks in the ages of Delphi,
   Beautiful flower in stone sprung from a fancy of old.
Note but this leaf, how graceful it lies in the curve of the marble;
   Then another succeeds — half of it only you see;
Then still further below is beheld the mere tip of a leaflet,
   All the others are hid in the dark tomb of the ground.
But the day will come when the leaves shall leap from their cover,
   And the day will come when Elpinike shall bloom.
Now I am going to dig from the rubbish this column of flowers,
   Piece together its parts, cleanse from the dirt every line,
Set up the column in light that again it may sun itself proudly:
   Then what a fragrance will rise out of that flowery shaft!

      *   *   *   *   *

I was down in the valley where sports the orchard of Olives,
   Elpinike was there — stood at my side as I looked,
And she lent me her beautiful eyes, her soul too she lent me,
   Bade me upward to glance where was the Delphian town;
Through a long verdant view enchased by the weft of the branches
   The old temple I saw rise once again in its pride;
Thither the leaves made a framework of gracefullest lines for its splendor,
   Through them the marble upsprang gleaming anew from the hill,

Just as fair Elpinike began in her smiles to enwrap me,
  And as I felt her mild breath freighted with words from her soul,
I looked up through the twigs and the leaves and beheld ancient Delphi
  Filled with beauty and light, moving to measures of hymns.

* * * * *

Out on the slant of the hill-side lies the old Delphian graveyard:
  By it oft I must pass when to the Olives I go;
Ancient coffins of stone through the fields in disorder are scattered:
  Some are just broken in twain smote by a single rude blow,
Others have had many blows from the ages and crumbled to fragments,
  Still a few have remained whole in the tempest of time.
But they all are now empty where once were laid the dear bodies,
  Laid with many a tear in the thick casket of rock,
Strong enough to preserve what it held in its chamber forever:
  But not e'en ashes are here speaking of life and its sleep.
How I would like to behold some one of the shapes in its splendor
  Rise now out of this stone, in a new Delphian birth,
And with the flow of the folds sweep there through the Halls of Apollo,
  Mid the high columns that shine as in the days of the God!
But the fair body has perished in spite of the strength of the fortress:
  So Elpinike thou too must by dark Death be entombed.
But let us fly from the thought — let us hurry away to the Olives:
  There cheerless Acheron's stream dries in the sheen of the leaves,
There are the happy domains of our Eros illumed by the sunbeams,

There let us know what is love, yielding to honeyed caress,
　　While the Hours still lend us their wings and bedew the sweet senses:
For I feel sorely afraid, love may not be after death;
　　Eros, the gladsome, flees from the gloomy regard of grim Pluto,
But the Olives he seeks, sporting his wings in the trees;
　　Nor will Apollo, the light-darter, descend to the realm of Hades,
Only over the Earth hovers his gold-dropping car.

　　　　　*　　*　　*　　*　　*

Seasons depart and return with delight to the Delphian hill-side,
　　Disappear for a time but are restored with new birth;
High Parnassus, propped on its pillars, knows no mutation,
　　Though for the summer it change merely its vestment of snow;
Ever green are the pines that slope down the sides of the mountain,
　　While the leaf of the bush hints, when it falls, the new bud;
Still too Castalia is here — the perennial musical runnel,
　　Singing the same happy strain heard by the poets of old;
But, ah youth, the fairest, supremest blossom of Nature
　　Passes away at its bloom by irreversible law;
Man, the top of creation, decays, and soon drops into ashes —
　　Flung by time on the earth as a mere handful of dust.
What is fairest must die, its place is soon filled by another,
　　While there endures the rude rock ages on ages the same.

SARAH CHAUNCEY WOOLSEY

SARAH CHAUNCEY WOOLSEY ("Susan Coolidge") was born in Cleveland, Ohio, January 29, 1845. She was a daughter of John Mumford and Jane (Andrews) Woolsey, and a niece of Dr. Theodore Woolsey, ex-president of Yale College. Inheriting from her forebears a decided literary proclivity, she early won distinction as a writer of poems and prose sketches, many of which she contributed, under her pen-name, to newspapers and magazines. In 1874 Miss Woolsey removed to Newport, R. I., where she resided until the date of her death, April 9, 1905.

In a brief characterization of the author and her work, the editor of The Outlook writes: "Her personality was unusually interesting. She had a marked individuality, delightful humor, conversational ability of a rare order, and many intellectual resources. She came of a family distinguished for generations by dignity of character and cultivation of mind; her own education was exceptionally careful and thorough. Her interests were manifold. She wrote with great ease, and her work, both in verse and prose, had a very delightful quality."

GULF-STREAM [1]

Lonely and cold and fierce I keep my way,
    Scourge of the lands, companioned by the storm,
Tossing to heaven my frontlet, wild and gray,
    Mateless, yet conscious ever of a warm
And brooding presence close to mine all day.

What is this alien thing, so near, so far,
    Close to my life always, but blending never?

---

[1] Copyrighted by Little, Brown & Company.

Hemmed in by walls whose crystal gates unbar
  Not at the instance of my strong endeavor
To pierce the stronghold where their secrets are?

Buoyant, impalpable, relentless, thin,
  Rise the clear, mocking walls. I strive in vain
To reach the pulsing heart that beats within,
  Or with persistence of a cold disdain,
To quell the gladness which I may not win.

Forever sundered and forever one,
  Linked by a bond whose spell I may not guess,
Our hostile, yet embracing currents run;
  Such wedlock lonelier is than loneliness.
Baffled, withheld, I clasp the bride I shun.

Yet even in my wrath a wild regret
  Mingles; a bitterness of jealous strife
Tinges my fury as I foam and fret
  Against the borders of that calmer life,
Beside whose course my wrathful course is set.

But all my anger, all my pain and woe,
  Are vain to daunt her gladness; all the while
She goes rejoicing, and I do not know,
  Catching the soft irradiance of her smile,
If I am most her lover or her foe.

GOOD-BYE [1]

The interlacing verdurous screen
Of the stanch woodbine still is green,
And thickly set with milk-white blooms
Gold-anthered, breathing out perfumes;
The clematis on trellis bars
Still flaunts with white and purple stars;

---

[1] Copyrighted by Little, Brown & Company.

No missing leaf has thinner made
The obelisks of maple shade;
Fresh beech boughs flutter in the breeze
Which, warm as summer, stirs the trees;
The sun is clear, the skies are blue:
But still a sadness filters through
The beauty and the bloom; and we,
Touched by some mournful prophecy,
Whisper each day: "Delay, delay!
Make not such haste to fly away!"
And they, with silent lips, reply:
"Summer is gone; we may not stay.
Summer is gone. Good-bye! good-bye!"

Roses may be as fragrant air
As in the sweet June days they were;
No hint of frost may daunt as yet
The clustering brown mignonette,
Nor chilly wind forbid to ope
The odorous, fragile heliotrope;
The sun may be as warm as May,
The night forbear to chase the day,
And hushed in false security
All the sweet realm of Nature be:
But the South-loving birds have fled,
By their mysterious instinct led;
The butterflies their nests have spun,
And donned their silken shrouds each one;
The bees have hived them fast, while we
Whisper each day: "Delay, delay!
Make not such haste to fly away!"
And all, with pitying looks, reply:
"Summer is fled; we may not stay.
Summer is gone. Good-bye! good-bye!"

SARAH CHAUNCEY WOOLSEY

BEREAVED [1]

When Lazarus from his three days' tomb
    Fronted with dazzled eyes the day,
And all the amazèd crowd made room,
    As, wrapped in shroud, he went his way,
His sisters daring scarce to touch
His hand, their wonderment was such;

When friends and kindred met at meat,
    And in the midst the man just dead
Sat in his old-time wonted seat,
    And poured the wine, and shared the bread
With the old gesture that they knew,—
Were they all glad, those sisters two?

Did they not guess a hidden pain
    In the veiled eyes which shunned their gaze;
A dim reproach, a pale disdain
    For human joys and human ways;
A loneliness too deep for speech,
Which all their love might never reach?

And as the slowly ebbing days
    Went by, and Lazarus went and came
Still with the same estrangèd gaze,
    His loneliness and loss the same,
Did they not whisper as they grieved,
"We are consoled — and he bereaved"?

Oh, weeper by a new-heaped mound,
    Who vexes Heaven with outcries vain,
That, if but for one short hour's round,
    Thy heart's desire might come again,—
The buried form, the vanished face,
The silent voice, the dear embrace,—

[1] Copyrighted by Little, Brown & Company.

Think if he came, as Lazarus did,
  But came reluctant, with surprise,
And sat familiar things amid
  With a new distance in his eyes,
A distance death had failed to set,—
If hearts met not when bodies met!

If when you smiled you heard him sigh,
  And when you spoke he only heard
As men absorbed hear absently
  The idle chirping of a bird,
As, rapt in thoughts surpassing speech,
His mind moved on beyond your reach;

And still your joy was made his pain,
  And still the distance wider grew,
His daily loss your daily gain,
  Himself become more strange to you
Than when your following soul sought his
In the vast secret distances;—

If, death once tasted, life seemed vain
  To please or tempt or satisfy,
And all his longing was again
  To be released and free to die,
To get back to scarce-tasted bliss,—
What grief could be so sharp as this?

ASHES [1]

I saw the gardener bring and strow
  Gray ashes where blush roses grew.
The fair, still roses bent them low,
  Their pink cheeks dimpled all with dew,
And seemed to view with pitying air
The dim gray atoms lying there.

---

[1] Copyrighted by Little, Brown & Company.

Ah, bonny rose, all fragrances,
And life and hope and quick desires,
   What can you need or gain from these
Poor ghosts of long-forgotten fires?
   The rose-tree leans, the rose-tree sighs,
   And wafts this answer subtly wise:
"All death, all life are mixed and blent,
Out of dead lives fresh life is sent,
   Sorrow to these is growth for me,
   And who shall question God's decree?"

Ah, dreary life, whose gladsome spark
   No longer leaps in song and fire,
But lies in ashes gray and stark,
   Defeated hopes and dead desire,
Useless and dull and all bereft,—
Take courage, this one thing is left:
   Some happier life may use thee so,
Some flower bloom fairer on its tree,
   Some sweet or tender thing may grow
To stronger life because of thee;
   Content to play a humble part,
   Give of the ashes of thy heart,
And haply God, whose dear decrees
Taketh from those to give to these,
   Who draws the snow-drop from the snows,
   May from those ashes feed a rose.

THORNS [1]

Roses have thorns, and love is thorny too;
   And this is love's sharp thorn which guards its flower,
   That our belovèd have the cruel power
To hurt us deeper than all others do.

---
[1] Copyrighted by Little, Brown & Company.

The heart attuned to our heart like a charm,
   Beat answering beat, as echo answers song,
   If the throb falter, or the pulse beat wrong,
How shall it fail to grieve us or to harm?

The taunt which, uttered by a stranger's lips,
   Scarce heard, scarce minded, passed us like the wind,
   Breathed by a dear voice, which has grown unkind,
Turns sweet to bitter, sunshine to eclipse.

The instinct of a change we cannot prove,
   The pitiful tenderness, the sad too-much,
   The sad too-little, shown in look or touch,—
All these are wounding thorns of thorny love.

Ah, sweetest rose which earthly gardens bear,
   Fought for, desired, life's guerdon and life's end,
   Although your thorns may slay and wound and rend,
Still men must snatch you; for you are so fair.

ALICE WILLIAMS BROTHERTON

ALICE WILLIAMS BROTHERTON, daughter of Alfred Baldwin Williams and Ruth Hoge (Johnson) Williams, was born in Cambridge, Ind. In her girlhood she accompanied her parents to Cincinnati, Ohio, where, except for short periods of residence in her native State and in St. Louis, Mo., she has lived ever since, her present home being on Locust Street, Walnut Hills. Her education was received mainly in Cincinnati, where she attended Woodward High School, graduating from that institution in 1870. She was married, October 18, 1876, to Mr. William Ernest Brotherton, of Cincinnati. As early as the year 1872 she began to write for the press, and in recent years she has been a contributor to various leading periodicals, including the Century, Scribner's, the Atlantic Monthly, St. Nicholas, Poet-Lore, and the New York Independent. She is the author of three published volumes: Beyond the Veil (poems, 1886); The Sailing of King Olaf, and Other Poems, (1887); and What the Wind Told the Tree-Tops (prose and verse, 1888). A number of her lyrics, among which are those entitled "Rosenlied," "The Song of Fleeting Love," "The Fisher-Wife's Lullabye," "Unawares," "Boys, Keep the Colors Up," "God Knows," and "June Roses," have been set to music.

For many years Mrs. Brotherton has been an efficient and valued member of the Cincinnati Woman's Club and a leading spirit of the Cincinnati Woman's Press Club, of which latter organization she was several times chosen the president. Since 1892 the author has devoted much of her thought and energy to the preparation of critical essays and addresses on Shakespeare, the drama, and other literary topics; and she has delivered numerous lectures before study-clubs, women's clubs, and dramatic schools.

THE BLAZING HEART [1]

Who are ye, spirits, that stand
  In the outer gloom,
Each with a blazing heart in hand,
Which lighteth the dark beyond the tomb?

"Oh, we be souls that loved
  Too well, too well!
Yet, for that love, though sore reproved,
(Oh, sore reproved!) have we 'scaped hell.

"'Scaped hell, but gained not heaven.
  Woe, woe and alas!
Only — to us this grace is given,
To light the dark where the dead must pass.

"Behind us the shadows throng,
  And the mists are gray;
But our blazing hearts light the soul along
From grave to yon gate that hides the day."

Who may this lady be
  At my right hand?
"This is the heart which for Antony
Changed from soft flesh to a burning brand."

"This for Aeneas glowed,
  Is glowing still."
"This kindled for Phaon; the flame it showed
No waters of ocean could quench or kill."

This shape, with the flowing hair?
  "She loved so much
That even the Sinless heard her prayer,
Pitied her pangs, and suffered her touch."

[1] From the Atlantic Monthly.

Bid the sounds of crackling cease!
"They blaze, they burn!"
Let me flee back to my coffined peace!
"Pass on (they beckon); there's no return."

Spirits, why press ye close?
I am faint with fear!
"Already *thy* heart like an ember glows;
Pluck it forth from thy bosom, thy place is here."

Happy Francesca! thine
Is the fairer lot.
Better with him in hell to pine
Than stand in cool shadows by him forgot!

ROSENLIED [1]

I

I said to the rose, "O rose!
What was it the nightingale sang?
For all night beneath my lattice
In the dusk his clear notes rang."

Then the hue of the crimson rose
Was dyed a lovelier red,
And she trembled with passionate longing,
And drooped her gentle head.

"Last night beside the lattice,
Before the white moon set,
Two stood within the shadow —
O heart! dost thou forget?

"A kiss; and two hands close clinging
In a silent, long troth-plight, —
O heart, O heart, thou knowest
What the nightingale sang all night!"

---
[1] From the Atlantic Monthly.

ROSENLIED [1]
II

The nightingale sang to the rose
  Through the livelong night,
Till its hue from a ruby-red
  Turned wan and white.
All night it rose and fell —
  That silvery strain,
And the heart of the red rose throbbed
  With divinest pain:

"O love, O love!" (it rang),
  "I love but thee.
Thou art queen of all flowers," (he sang),
  "And queen of me!
O love, *my* love!" he said.
  Before the dawn
The rose on its stalk hung dead.
  The bird was gone.

THE POISON FLASK
[*Temp.* Louis XV.]

A crystal flasket: one drop (ay, that's all)
  Of its clear contents well administered —
Dripped in the succory water, say,— she'll fall
  Dead in a flash, with no accusing word.
Not that I mean to do it! Nay, the nerve
  Is scarce mine. Something, though, it is, to hold
Here in my hand the subtle spell might serve
  To stretch that supple body stiff and cold!

Gods, how I hate her!— with those sleepy eyes
  Like two gray agates filled with lambent light! —

---

[1] From the Century Magazine.

ALICE WILLIAMS BROTHERTON

Hate that full bosom's lazy fall and rise,
  The red ripe lips, the cheek's vermeil and white!
I loathe your lush blonde beauties. I am dark —
  Small and so dark — eyes, brows and dusky hair,
My skin's a clearer white than hers, though, mark,—
  If she were gone the king would find me fair.

If she were gone.—This liqueur has the hue
  Of liquid diamonds. What a flash that was!
This gold top's chasing, now, is curious, too:
  How clear the crystal is and free from flaws.
Venetian? — fit to hold (the chymist said)
  These Medicean drops — the very same
That Catherine used to mingle with the red
  Wine draught of certain friends who crossed her game.

If Artemise were gone. A better way
  Might be — to spoil her beauty by the art
Of some infernal wash, some acid, say,
  In her cosmetics, to eat, scar, and smart.
That is a wild dream only! What I seek
  Is something quick and final.— Not a trace
Left of the method.— Dead folks never speak,
  Even if they return to haunt the place.

A poisoned ring would be at once suspect,
  That's such an old device; and the bouquet,
And gloves with poisoned perfumes, all reject
  Save the mere novice. If — mind *if,* I say,—
The deed were done with this, there is no clue
  Whereby Justice the author could divine.
She lives but at my will! And I — I know
  If she were gone the king — the *king* were mine!

How small the flask is. Small enough to swing
  Here at my girdle with the silver keys
Held by the chatelaine. I'll wear the thing
  Just so upon the chain; and if she sees

And wonders at the bauble, I reply
   It is —'tis my scent flasket, vinaigrette! —
No, no! I'll wear it not! I'll put it by
   In the carved casket there with jewels set.

So, then, I turn the key upon the flask
   Of liquid death. I shall not use it — No.
But it is sweet to feel how slight a task
   'Twould be to bring her insolent beauty low.
I'll keep it then; sometimes, perhaps, unlock
   The casket's secret drawer, hang gloating o'er
My deadly treasure.— Ha! Was that a knock?
   Some one is standing just without the door.

'Tis Artemise herself. "Yes! Enter, straight."
   What means the look of triumph in her eye?
"How radiant, sweet! — robed as for some grand fete!
   What lovely pearls! — a queen for such might sigh.
Ah — How? You dine tonight, love, with the king?
   You happy girl! Nay, wait one moment yet.
I'll scarce ten seconds keep you tarrying.
   See! I but fasten on — my vinaigrette."

MY ENEMY [1]

I

My foe was dark, and stern, and grim,
I lived my life in fear of him.
I passed no secret, darkened nook
Without a shuddering, furtive look,
Lest he should take me unawares
In some one of his subtle snares.
Even in broad noon the thought of him
Turned all the blessèd sunlight dim,
Stole the rich color from the rose,
The perfume from the elder-blows.

---

[1] From the Century Magazine.

I saw him not, I heard no sound;
But traces everywhere I found
Of his fell plotting. Now, the flower
Most prized lay blasted by his power;
From the locked casket, rent apart,
The jewel dearest to my heart
Was stolen; or, from out the dark,
Some swift blow made my heart its mark.

Sweet eyes I loved grew glazed and dim
That had but caught a glimpse of him;
And ears, were wont to hear each sigh
Of mine, were deafened utterly,
Even to my shrieks; and lips I pressed,
Struck a cold horror to my breast.
   This hath he done, my enemy.
   From him, O God, deliver me!

II

I reached but now this place of gloom
Through yon small gateway, where is room
For only one to pass. This calm
Is healing as a Sabbath psalm.
A sound, as if the hard earth slid
Down-rattling on a coffin-lid,
Was in mine ears. Now all is still,
And I am free to fare at will —
Whither? I seem but tarrying
For one who doth a message bring.

Who meets me in the way, whose face
Is radiant with an angel's grace?
Smiling, he saith in underbreath:
"I am thy foe long dreaded,— Death."
"O Death, sweet Death, and is it *thou*
I called mine enemy but now?"

I place my trusting palms in his,
And lift my chill lips for his kiss.
"Press close, be near me to the end,
When all are fled, my one true friend!"

"Yea, *friend*," he answereth. "All, and more
Than all I took, do I restore —
Blossom and jewel, youth and hope;
And see, this little key doth ope
The shining portal that we see,
Beyond which — *love* awaiteth thee."
  "O blinded eyes! Ah, foolish heart!
    Adieu, dear Death — one kiss! We part."

THE LIVING PAST

"Let us bury the dead past." Ay,
Let us bury it close and deep.
But what if it stir in its grave and cry?
What if it rise to haunt our sleep?
Rend from its features the cerement bands;
With grinning skull instead of a head
Stand by our side and wring its hands?
Ah, what — if the past *be not dead?*"

The heart of man is a living thing.
You think to slay it and lay it to rest;
But, on a day, it will rise and fling
The grave-cloths off from face and breast.
You think to gloss with a glaze of ice
The waters that lie so darkly still:
The tide will rise till it dare the skies,
The ocean laughs at your puny will.

The past, we say; but there is no past —
The past is the present and future too.
It is only a lie that does not last;
The truth *is life,* and it springs anew,

Though you bury it deep and stamp it down.
A deed that is done is a stubborn thing:
When the mould is turned and the seed is sown,
Can we change the harvest for sorrowing?

Deeds are the letters with which we spell
God's meaning out, in this world of ours.
Dare we change His text? One stroke expel,
The storm of His wrath that instant lowers.
Facts are stern, and hard, and grim —
They change not; but — if we read them right —
Some day the message they hold from Him
Gleams forth in letters of living light.

A PERSIAN FABLE

Before the close-barred gate of Paradise
  A poor man watched a thousand years; then dozed
One little instant only, with dulled eyes:
  That instant open swung the gate — and closed.

CAMPION [1]

I placed a scarlet campion flower
  In the wreathed tresses of my head.
"No damosel in hall or bower
  Is fairer than my love," he said.

Years after in a folded book
  I found a withered campion flower;
And paled, with that swift backward look
  That ghost-seers have at twilight hour.

O withered heart, O love long dead!
  "Poor faded flower that shone so fair,
Well suits thy phantom bloom" (I said)
  "With the white tresses of my hair."

---
[1] From the Century Magazine.

THE SPINNER
From the German of Voss

I sat and spun before my door:
    A youth along the road came straying,
His hazel eyes a deep smile wore,
    And blushes on his cheek were playing;
My glance was from the distaff won,
I sat abashed, and spun and spun.

In friendly tones, "Good day!" he spoke,
    With timid grace approaching nigher:
Startled was I, the thread it broke,
    My foolish heart leapt high and higher.
The thread once more I fastened on,
And sat abashed, and spun and spun.

He clasped, with tender touch, my hand,
    And vowed none could with it compare —
The very loveliest in the land,
    So swan-white, plump and dainty fair!
As with his praise my heart he won
I sat abashed, and spun and spun.

Upon my chair he laid his arm,
    And praised the finely-wroughten thread.
So near his mouth, so red and warm,
    How gently: "Sweetest maid!" it said!
The while he gazed my face upon
I sat abashed, and spun and spun.

His handsome face toward my own
    Meantime he bent with glances winning;
It touched, by some odd chance unknown,
    My head that nodded in the spinning:
He kissed me, this audacious one! —
I sat abashed, and spun and spun.

I turned, reproof in earnest tone
   Upon his forwardness bestowing;
He clasped me close and, bolder grown,
   He kissed my face with blushes glowing.
O tell me sisters — every one!
Is 't strange that now no more I spun?

SHAKESPEARE [1]

Working as erst by law, not miracle,
   By genius God doth lift a common soul
   To some still spot where it may glimpse the goal;
Bidding it on the mountain heights to dwell,
Yet not so far apart but it may tell
   To toilers in the plain below the whole
   Of the vision. Master, still the organ-roll
Of thy deep music vibrates, and its spell
Aids the uplift that stirs our grosser clay
   To rise and seek the heights. O soul God set
   A little lower than his white angels, yet
A round for man to climb the starward way
   Thou art. One palm with angels' long since met,
The other warm in man's grasp still doth stay.

WOMAN AND ARTIST
To E. W. T.

If she neglected one especial gift
And turned from laurel crowns she might have won,
From the high tasks that genius might have done,
Dropping the pencil or the brush to lift
Wee baby feet across the stones, to sift
Meanings from childish prattle, and to croon
Low, tender, cradle-songs in dreamy tone;
Catching from baby eyes, as through a rift

---
[1] Copyright, 1890, by Charles H. Crandall.

In clouds, the light of heaven.— Is this a lot
To be deplored? Nay, would she if she could
Exchange? First, *woman* — after, poet — what
You will! Her soul has seized the greater good:
The dizzy heights of Fame were well forgot
To sound the wondrous depths of Motherhood.

EDITH MATILDA THOMAS

EDITH MATILDA THOMAS was born in the village of Chatham, Medina County, Ohio, August 12, 1854. Her parents, Frederick J. Thomas and Jane Louisa (Sturges) Thomas, the former of whom was of Welsh, and the latter, of English ancestry, were both natives of New England, and her mother's grandfather was a patriotic soldier in the Revolutionary War. In Edith's infancy the family moved to Kenton, Ohio, and in the year 1859, to Bowling Green, where her father, a prominent teacher, died in 1861. Soon thereafter the widowed mother and her three daughters removed to Geneva, Ohio, where the subject of this sketch received her academic education, at the Normal Institute, from which she graduated in 1872, at the age of eighteen.

After a brief experience as a teacher, in Geneva, Ohio, Miss Thomas resolved to make the pursuit of literature a profession. Her career as an author may be said to have begun in early childhood, when, in her first efforts at composition, she displayed a precocious ability which was observed by her parents and teachers, from whom, in the formative years of her girlhood, she received judicious encouragement. "While a student," we are told, "she had contributed verses to various newspapers, and these had been widely copied, the marks of inspiration they bore being quickly recognized by lovers of genuine poetry. The freshness of expression, the buoyant tone, and the exquisite finish of her lines, set them in strong contrast to those produced by most writers of the time; and the first to call attention to these qualities and to give the new singer a welcome, was Helen Hunt Jackson, who introduced her to the editors of the Atlantic Monthly and the Century, and thus to

---

[1] National Cyclopædia of American Biography.

a larger circle of readers than she had yet addressed."[1] In 1888, the year following that of her mother's death, Miss Thomas removed from Geneva, Ohio, to New York City, where, at her home in West New Brighton, on Staten Island, she has ever since devoted herself to literature, being a frequent contributor to the Century, the Atlantic Monthly, Scribner's, and other leading magazines.

The originality, beauty, and power of her lyrical productions have won for Miss Thomas the universal admiration and applause of critics. By a recent Ohio historian, in a review of the literature of the State, she is extolled as "a divinely favored poet,— one who has 'slept on the Mountain of Song,' and brought home pure Parnassian dews;" and Edmund Clarence Stedman, in his American Anthology, after commenting on the strength, the delicacy, and the exquisite classicism of her verse, declares of the author that "her place is secure among the truest living poets of our English tongue." It may further be asserted, confidently, that Miss Thomas, in her peculiar domain of lyric art, is unrivaled; and that for originality and breadth of conception, depth of feeling, classic dignity and finish, haunting melody, and ease of execution, her best poems have rarely been equaled by any writer of her sex on either side of the Atlantic. As a master of the sonnet form she has few compeers.

DEAD LOW TIDE

It is dead low tide, and the wasted sea beats far;
  Up from the caves of the underworld slowly climb
  Night and her shadows unconquered from eldest time!
The cry of the sea-bird is hushed on the glimmering bar,
And the beach, with its strewing of dulse, is lonely and wide:
    It is dead low tide.

The rocks are divulged, that hidden and cruel lie,
  Under the waves in wait, as the beast in its lair!
  Huge and harmless they shoulder the dusk night air;
A lighthouse gleams — they are charmed by its sorcerous eye!

---

[1] National Cyclopædia of American Biography.

The rocks are uncovered, and many a wreck beside:
    It is dead low tide.

Not now shall the willing keel slip down to the sea,
  Not now shall the home-desiring bark come home;
  The rocking surge is a dream, and the flying foam,
  And the sails that over the windy billows roam —
A dream! for the sea is gone, and the wind has died:
    It is dead low tide.

There is rest from motion, from toil; yet it is not rest!
  The sounds of the land and the sea-sounds falter and cease;
  The wave is at peace with the shore; yet it is not peace!
As the soldier at truce, as the pilgrim detained on his quest,
Baffled and silent, yet watchful, all things abide
    The turn of the tide.

I too abide. To the spirit within responds
  The baffled yet watchful spirit of all things without.
  "Shall I rest forever, beleaguered by sloth and doubt?"
"Not so; thou shalt rise and break the enchanted bonds,
And the limit that mocked thee with laughter shalt override
    At turn of the tide!"

Still higher the Night ascends, and star upon star
  Arises by low-lying isle, and by headland steep,
  And fathoms with silver light the slumbering deep. . . .
Hark! was it a lapsing ripple along the bar?
Hark! was it the wind that awoke, remembered, and sighed?
    Is it turn of the tide?

THEFTS OF THE MORNING

  Bind us the Morning, mother of the stars
  And of the winds that usher in the day!
  Ere her light fingers slide the eastern bars,
  A netted snare before her footsteps lay;
  Ere the pale roses of the mist be strown,
  Bind us the Morning, and restore our own!

With her have passed all things we held most dear,
Most subtly guarded from her amorous stealth;
We nothing gathered, toiling year by year,
But she hath claimed it for increase of wealth;
Our gems make bright her crown, incrust her throne:
Bind us the Morning, and restore our own!

Where are they gone, who round our myrtles played,
Or bent the vines' rich fruitage to our hands,
Or breathed deep song from out the laurels' shade?
She drew them to her; who can slack the bands?
What lure she used, what toils, was never known:
Bind us the Morning, and restore our own!

Enough that for her sake Orion died,
Slain by the silver Archer of the sky —
That Ilion's prince amid her splendors wide
Lies chained by age, nor wins his prayer to die;
Enough! but hark! our captive loves make moan:
Bind us the Morning, and restore our own!

We have beheld them whom we lost of old,
Among her choiring Hours, in sorrow bowed.
A moment gleam their faces, faint and cold,
Through some high oriel window wreathed with cloud,
Or on the wind before her they are blown:
Bind us the Morning, and restore our own!

They do her service at the noiseless looms
That weave the misty vesture of the hills;
Their tears are drink to thirsting grass and blooms,
Their breath the darkling wood-bird wakes and thrills;
Us too they seek, but far adrift are thrown:
Bind us the Morning, and restore our own!

Yea, cry her *Thief!* from where the light doth break
To where it merges in the western deep!

If aught of ours she, startled, should forsake,
Such waifs the waiting Night for us will keep.
But stay not; still pursue her, falsely flown:
Bind us the Morning, and restore our own!

WILD HONEY

If I follow the wild bee home,
  And fell with a ringing stroke
  The populous shaft of the oak,
What shall I taste in the comb
And the honey that fills the comb?

From tables flush Nature prepares;
  From hillside and hollow, and copse,
  And blossoming forest-tops;
From fallows the husbandman spares,
Are borne to me flavorous airs.

I shall taste the months and the days
  Of the season that now is done;
  I shall warm with the wine of the sun,
Stored, in mysterious ways,
In this secret-builded maze!

Then will I, tasting, say,—
  This is arbutus' gift,
  Reached from the leafy drift,
On a glistening April day;
And this is the spirit of May.

This, which o'erbubbles the brim,
  Is naught but the essence of June;
  And this is July's rich boon;
And this, in which visions swim,
Is August, heated and dim.

In these amber wards repose
  The life of the summer hours
  And the coinèd wealth of flowers:
The breath of the mint and wild rose
May sweeten the winter snows!

Ye that embalm the year
  With spices and cerements meet,
  Drop on my lips such sweet
As fell on the mouth severe
Of the Theban poet-seer:

Then, with a mellow tongue,
  In words that have caught the charm
Of a hidden and murmuring swarm,
I will utter some notes, unsung
Since time and the world were young!

SYRINX[1]

Come forth, too timid spirit of the reed!
  Leave thy plashed coverts and elusions shy,
And find delight at large in grove and mead.
  No ambushed harm, no wanton peering eye;
The shepherd's uncouth god thou need'st not fear,—
Pan has not passed this way for many a year.

'Tis but the vagrant wind that makes thee start,—
  The pleasure-loving south, the freshening west:
The willow's woven veil they softly part,
  To fan the lily on the stream's warm breast:
No ruder stir, no footsteps pressing near,—
Pan has not passed this way for many a year.

Whether he lies in some mossed wood, asleep,
  And heeds not how the acorns drop around,

---

[1] **Syrinx.** In Greek mythology, a nymph who was changed by Pan into a reed.

EDITH MATILDA THOMAS

Or in some shelly cavern near the deep,
  Lulled by its pulses of eternal sound,
He wakes not, answers not our sylvan cheer,—
Pan has been gone this many a silent year.

Else we had seen him, through the mists of morn,
  To upland pasture lead his bleating charge:
There is no shag upon the stunted thorn,
  No hoof-print on the river's silver marge;
Nor broken branch of pine, nor ivied spear,—
Pan has not passed that way for many a year.

O tremulous elf, reach me a hollow pipe,
  The best and smoothest of thy mellow store!
Now I may blow till Time be hoary ripe,
  And listening streams forsake the paths they wore:
Pan loved the sound, but now will never hear,—
Pan has not trimmed a reed this many a year!

And so, come freely forth, and through the sedge
  Lift up a dimpled, warm, Arcadian face,
As on that day when fear thy feet did fledge,
  And thou didst safely win the breathless race. . . .
I am deceived: nor Pan nor thou art here,—
Pan has been gone this many a silent year!

AVALON — FAIR AVALON[1]

Now, while the leaf-flocks rise upon the wind,
  Now, while the grass-blade blanches with the frost,
Find we that Isle (of yore not hard to find)—
  Refuge of all sweet things in old time lost!
    Out of a world that grows austere and bleak,
    'Tis Avalon — fair Avalon I seek!

---

[1] From "Cassia, and Other Verse." Copyright, 1905, by Richard G. Badger.

Thou wilt not trust that such a realm may be?
  In the mid-rapture of her Perfect Day,
Did summer never whisper unto thee:
  "Follow where undivided is my sway!"
    Thus, to my spirit did the Summer speak —
    And Avalon — fair Avalon I seek!

I heard the farewell vesper of the thrush,
  The meadow-haunting plover's last *good-night;*
The floating call, amid the twilight hush,
  Of wild fowl, that would thither wing their flight:
    Weak, though they be, their courage is not weak;
    And I — fair Avalon I, also, seek!

Why cling to unleafed grove and leafless field?
  Why linger till the dearth of wintry hours?
Why bear the wound that may be closed and healed
  With balm nepenthean pressed from wizard flowers,
    While thornless roses pillow thy pale cheek?
    'Tis Avalon — fair Avalon I seek!

There be so many there of dear esteem —
  There be so many there that were storm-tossed,
That ventured all for sake of some great Dream;
  And there they found what they had deemed was lost!
    O Isle of all desire, from days antique —
    'Tis Avalon — fair Avalon I seek!

AT LETHE'S BRINK [1]

I

Ye souls, of life too fond,
Why seek to carry memory to the shades, —
Those blessèd seats in the deep meads and glades?
  For me, I have been bond

---

[1] From "Cassia, and Other Verse." Copyright, 1905, by Richard G. Badger.

To griefs too many, and to joys too fierce:
Let neither with remembrance longer pierce!
      Lead me, Caducean wand,
Where the green turf with Lethe-dew is wet;
There, my burnt, throbbing temples will I steep;
      I would forget . . .
Oh, let me sink in the Great Deep of Sleep!

II

      Why would ye beckon dreams?
To set the thorn, where never grew the thorn?
To make sweet rest a mockery forlorn?
      To give the silent streams
Of this fair, twilight Country, where we go,
The burden of the song we too well know?
      To feign the hot noon beams
Strike the bow'd head (where noon came never yet)?
Far, far from me the soothless dream-throng keep!
      I would forget . . .
Oh, let me sink in the Great Deep of Sleep!

III

      Ay, bid adieu to all;
Nor grieve that one, the sweetest, stays behind.
Be deaf unto his cries; and be ye blind
      To looks that would enthrall;
For Love, most far of all the clamant throng
That held the fevered hands of Life so long,
      Follows with haunting call:
Hence, most of all, to him the bound be set —
Between us, thrice the lustral waters creep!
      I must forget . . .
Oh, let me sink in the Great Deep of Sleep!

IV

      But ye; why doubt to drink,—
Ye spirits that from many a land and zone

Of the wide earth, with me are hither blown,—
      Why stand ye at the brink
A timorous throng, who, erewhiles, have besought
That ye might cease from toils, from strife, from thought?
      Why, therefore, do ye shrink?
Follow, and quaff with closèd eye; and let
The sight draw inward, while the shadows sweep. . . .
      I would forget . . .
And now . . . I sink in the Great Deep of Sleep.

VERTUMNUS [1]

I took a day, and sought for him
Through bosky aisles untracked and dim,
Through cultured field and orchard sweet:—
Did I o'ertake his flying feet?

Once, as I crossed a sylvan glade,
My step the green-brier would have stayed;
The violet looked as it would speak,
And the wild-service, white and meek,
Against my face its coolness laid;
And once the dew on blended blade
Turned towards the sun a sparkling eye,
As flushed and eager I sped by.

As I sped by, as I sped by,—
And fervid noon was in the sky,
And sickles rested on the swath,—
One bearded stalk awoke from sloth,
And lightly swayed it to and fro
Till all its fellows swayed arow;
And where no breathèd sound had been
Went bickering whispers fine and thin.

---

[1] **Vertumnus.** In Roman mythology, "god of the changing year."

As I ran on, as I ran on,—
Some boughs grown bright and some grown wan,
And creeping leafy fires wide spread,—
All suddenly the hazel shed
Before my feet its umbered mast,
The oak a shower of acorns cast,
The vine swung low its clusters blue,
The star-flower elvish glances threw.

Morn was I when the chase began;
Close on the evening-bound I ran;
And, counting but a rounded day,
Lo, seasons three had slipped away!
An hundred times the clue I missed,
Too rapt to pause, to look, and list,—
An hundred times, unweeting, trod
Straight past the merry, masking god.

A RAINBOW

Large glistening drops stood in her eyes,
  But yet could win no leave to flow;
And I, not willing to surprise
  The tears she would not show,—
    I looked another way.
Some smiling words, at last, she spake;
  Then down the tears dropped unconfined.
This sun and shower conspired to make
  A rainbow in my mind,
    That lingers to this day.

MIGRATION

The cagèd bird, that all the autumn day
In quiet dwells, when falls the autumn eve
Seeks how its liberty it may achieve,
Beats at the wires and its poor wings doth fray:

For now desire of migrant change holds sway;
This summer-vacant land it longs to leave,
While its free peers on tireless pinions cleave
The haunted twilight, speeding south their way.
Not otherwise than as the prisoned bird,
We here dwell careless of our captive state
Until light dwindles, and the year grows late,
And answering note to note no more is heard;
Then, our loved fellows flown, the soul is stirred
To follow them where summer has no date.

"OFT HAVE I WAKENED"

Oft have I wakened ere the spring of day
And from my window looking forth have found
All dim and strange the long-familiar ground.
But soon I saw the mist glide slow away,
And leave the hills in wonted green array,
While from the stream-sides and the fields around
Rose many a pensive day-entreating sound,
And the deep-breasted woodlands seemed to pray.
Will it be even so when first we wake
Beyond the Night in which are merged all nights,—
The soul sleep-heavy and forlorn will ache,
Deeming herself midst alien sounds and sights?
Then will the gradual Day with comfort break
Along the old deeps of being, the old heights?

THOMAS EMMETT MOORE

IN a free and genial characterization contributed to the Washington Post, Mr. Willard Holcomb, playwright, journalist, and author, writing of the subject of this sketch, says: "Once in a while one runs across a country editor with a highly original streak. Such a man is Thomas Emmett Moore. The fame of this editor's paper is due to his personality. He talks with a drawl that rivals Mark Twain's. Whether this is an indication or a concomitant of humor, may be a matter for conjecture, but certainly Mr. Moore shows in his work plenty of humor. His verses,— for he follows, in the poetic line, the distinguished son of Erin whose name he bears,— range from grave to gay, with a preponderance in favor of the latter. His writings show him to be widely read, both in the ancient classics and in standard English literature; in fact, this particular country editor is college-bred, after the fashion of the hero of 'The Gentleman from Indiana.'"

Thomas Emmett Moore, son of Hon. John Towner Moore and Della L. Moore, was born at Piketon, Pike County, Ohio, March 1, 1861. In his early boyhood his parents moved to Jackson, Ohio, where Thomas received his education. Graduating from the High School at the age of eighteen, he immediately began the study of law, and in 1881 he was admitted to the bar. After several years of legal practice in partnership with his father, he became the proprietor and managing editor, successively, of the Jackson Sun, the Jackson Herald, and the Wellston Daily Sentinel. On January 30, 1881, Mr. Moore was married to Miss Mary L. Tripp, in Jackson, where he continued to reside until the year 1891, when he removed with his family to Wellston, Ohio, his present home.

Mr. Moore is the author of but one published volume, an historical romance, My Lord Farquhar, issued in New York, by the Abbey Press, in 1902. It is understood that he has in preparation a collection of his best poems, and that he has completed a new novel entitled "King Saul," dealing with Oriental life and customs.

SOUL SONG
(Extract)

I am the song of bosom to bosom and lip to lip,
And the wooing breath of the world's sweet kisses!
Hark! to the music of sunlight and shadow —
To youths and maidens singing in the vineyards,
Where the grapes are clustered and painted by the hand of Him
    who loves! —
I am one with Shiraz and Engedi;
I am the spirit of the rose, and the song of the nightingale;
I am the lisp of the wind, and the sob of sorrow;
Yea, I am the melody that outlasts the æons of the far white
    stars!

On the keys of my being God presses,
And joy, and sadness, hope, fear, wrath, defiance and love
Eddy and sweep, and float, and rise, and fall, and rise again,
Desolate, despairing, triumphant, immortal!
Hark! comes the Dies Irae! Hark to the Soul's eternal victory!
O sad, O sweet, O solemn, O joyful, is the chanson of the
    centuries!
Listen! the full diapason of the Song Triumphant:
The panomphean runes of the limitless oceans,
The twilight whispers that sigh through the leaves of the forests,
The wild, free voices of the flying Heralds of Heaven,
The lowing of cattle on a thousand hills,
And the hum of the bees in the clover!
Oh, bend thine ear to the faint, unheeded piping of the things
    that breed
In microscopic myriads; to the ripple of sap gurgling upward in
    Spring;
To the lay of the bursting bloom!

LIGHT

One with a saddened heart to Buddha bowed,
  And in the darkness waited for a sign;
While one who suffered much to Allah vowed,
  And one knelt, tearful, at the Savior's shrine.

Was there no light for these that lowly prayed —
  These brothers, seeking truth, who, trusting, came
In the white garments of pure faith arrayed?
  Yea; in each soul there dawned a Light — the same!

THE PALMER

There came a Palmer with his staff,
  Age-furrowed brow, and eye grown dim,
Who pointed onward as he passed,
  And I rose up and followed him.

"Whence comest thou, O Pilgrim, gray?
  And whither must this journey tend?"
He paused, and smiling gently, said:
  "From God. Our journey hath no end!"

HENRY HOLCOMB BENNETT

HENRY HOLCOMB BENNETT, son of John Briscoe Henry and Eliza (McClintock) Bennett, and elder brother of John Bennett, was born in Chillicothe, Ohio, December 5, 1863. He was educated in the public schools of his native city, and in Kenyon College, class of '86. After leaving college he devoted himself, for a period, to various lines of business, chiefly railroading, in the West, where he lived five or six years. Returning to Chilliocothe, he became a reporter for, and, later, city editor of, the Scioto Gazette. Mr. Bennett withdrew from journalism in the autumn of 1897, since which time he has given his energy chiefly to writing stories of army life and articles on ornithology, the latter illustrated by his own drawings. He has been an occasional contributor to several leading periodicals of the day, including Munsey's, McClure's, the Century, and Lippincott's; and in the last-named magazine appeared (1898-9) a series of his sketches on the National Guard.

This versatile writer is a thorough student of American history, and a specialist of recognized authority on matters pertaining to the annals of Ohio, especially in the territorial period and the period of early statehood. He was secretary of the committee in charge of the "Constitutional" Centennial of Ohio, held in 1902, and chairman of the committee on decoration, of the Ohio Centennial of 1903; and it was he who, in 1902, designed the large bronze tablet erected to mark the site of the old Capitol at Chillicothe, the first state-house in America.

As a landscape-painter, Mr. Bennett has studied under some of the best American artists, and his work in water-color and in book-illustration has secured for him a reputation which keeps his talents increasingly in demand. Though he has not yet published any book of verse, he is well known as a poet, owing to the universal popularity of his patriotic lyric, "The Flag Goes By." Poems from his pen have appeared in the Century Magazine, the Youth's Companion, and the New York Independent.

THE FLAG GOES BY [1]

Hats off!
Along the street there comes
A blare of bugles, a ruffle of drums,
A flash of color beneath the sky:
Hats off!
The flag is passing by!

Blue and crimson and white it shines,
Over the steel-tipped, ordered lines.
Hats off!
The colors before us fly;
But more than the flag is passing by.

Sea-fights and land-fights, grim and great,
Fought to make and to save the State:
Weary marches and sinking ships;
Cheers of victory on dying lips;

Days of plenty and years of peace;
March of a strong land's swift increase;
Equal justice, right and law;
Stately honor and reverend awe;

Sign of a nation, great and strong
To ward her people from foreign wrong:
Pride and glory and honor,— all
Live in the colors to stand or fall.

---

[1] From the Youth's Companion.

Hats off!
Along the street there comes
A blare of bugles, a ruffle of drums;
And loyal hearts are beating high:
Hats off!
The flag is passing by!

THE REDBIRD'S MATINS[1]

I cling
And swing,
High in the budding maple trees;
And out on the perfumed air I fling
A message of song to the herald breeze,
To be carried down to the golden bees
Where they gossip over their garnering.
Clear, long,
And strong
I make my song,
That all the wakening world may hear
The tidings sweet that I repeat,—
This is the joy-time of the year!
Be glad! Be glad! and have no fear,—
This is the joy-time of the year!

The merry note
From out my throat
Is borne afar on wings of air,
And through the woodland ways remote
The quivering echoes rise and float;
And every one the tidings bear,—
Be glad! Be glad! The spring is here!
This is the joy-time of the year.

---

[1] From St. Nicholas.

Cheer up! Cheer up!
The blossomed cup
Is filled for all the bees to sup.
The waters run
Beneath the sun
Like strands of silver through the grass;
And all the bees
Among the trees
Make love to every flower they pass.
Oh, hear! Oh, hear!
How loud and clear
I sing to the listening world below;
How joyously comes my word of cheer,—
This is the joy-time of the year,
When blossoming wind-flowers bend and blow,
When the sun shines warm and waters flow:
Be glad! Be glad! The spring is here;
This is the joy-time of the year!

JOHN BENNETT

JOHN BENNETT, son of John Briscoe Henry, and Eliza (McClintock) Bennett, and younger brother of Henry Holcomb Bennett, was born in Chillicothe, Ohio, May 17, 1865. His parents, both of whom were Virginians, descended from Scotch, Scotch-Irish, Dutch, English, and French ancestors, transmitted to their sons traits and tendencies of imagination, sentiment, and adventure, which afforded a potential equipment for romantic authorship and for pictorial art. "From my earliest recollection," writes Mr. Bennett, "I have been a teller of stories, and I was a reciter of gigantic romances of travel to other children on the neighboring horse-blocks, in the long summer evenings of this beautiful Scioto Valley. My boyhood was spent in roaming over the hills of Ross County, trudging through their enchanted woods, and traversing the river with a comrade." John's father cultivated in him an observant love of natural beauty, and of small things and creatures, and fostered in him a strong inherited gift for drawing. Among books, the boy's "prime favorites" were "the British dramatists, the English classics, and the poetry of Burns."

Mr. Bennett received his education in the public schools of Chillicothe. Though denied the advantages of higher collegiate training, he early won distinction by his scholarly attainments, having been from childhood a precocious student and an omnivorous reader of biography, fiction, and English history. In 1883 he entered the Art Students' League, in Cincinnati, where he began those artistic pursuits which soon gained for him public recognition, and which, later in life, he continued in the Art Students' League of New York. For a period of about fourteen years he was employed, by turns, as newspaper-correspondent, as reporter for and editor of the Chillicothe Daily News, as caricaturist, and as paragrapher, publishing miscellaneous verse and prose in the Cincinnati Commercial-Gazette, in St. Nicholas, and elsewhere. Mr. Bennett's first book, Master Skylark, issued in 1897, by The Century Company, has been translated into both Dutch and German. This delightful story of the Elizabethan stage was followed, in 1900, by Barnaby Lee, an American colonial romance, and in 1906, by The Treasure of Peyre Gaillard, a romance of the Santee Swamps.

In 1898, on account of ill health, Mr. Bennett removed to Charleston, South Carolina, where he has since had his residence, and where, in 1902, he was married to Miss Susan Adger Smythe. Of late years he has devoted himself mainly to authorship. As an adjunct to his literary labors in the South, however, he makes an avocation of lecturing, on such subjects as: "Plantation Folk Music;" "Primitive African Communal Balladry in America;" and "The Growth of Music, Illustrated by Southern Negro Songs."

THE MERRY SPRINGTIME
(From "Master Skylark")

Hey, laddie, hark to the merry, merry lark!
   How high he singeth clear:
"Oh, a morn in spring is the sweetest thing
   That cometh in all the year!
Oh, a morn in spring is the sweetest thing
   That cometh in all the year!"

Ring, ting! it is the merry springtime;
   How full of heart a body feels!
Sing hey, trolly-lolly! oh, to live is to be jolly,
   When springtime cometh with the summer at her heels!

God save us all, my jolly gentlemen,
   We'll merry be to-day;
For the cuckoo sings till the greenwood rings,
   And it is the month of May!
For the cuckoo sings till the greenwood rings,
   And it is the month of May!

SONG OF THE HUNT
(From "Master Skylark")

The hunt is up, the hunt is up,
Sing merily we, the hunt is up!
  The wild birds sing,
  The dun deer fling,
  The forest aisles with music ring!
    Tantara, tantara, tantara!

Then ride along, ride along,
Stout and strong!
  Farewell to grief and care;
With a rollicking cheer
For the high dun deer
  And a life in the open air!
    Tantara, the hunt is up, lads;
    Tantara, the bugles bray!
    Tantara, tantara, tantara,
      Hio, hark away!

SONG OF THE DUTCH CANNONEERS

Boom, pouf, boom! Awake! I hear the captain calling;
  The culverins are speaking; the battle has begun;
A soldier's death and glory through the stricken field are seeking
  For the boldest and the bravest. Up to meet them, every one!
    The man who holds his life too good
      To risk at glory's call
    Deserves to take his daily food
      Behind a prison-wall!

But where, through choke and sulphur-smoke, the hungry cannon
    bellow,
  The hero's cry rings through the sky! Ho, comrades, every
    one!
'Tis courage makes the soldier, slinking cowardice the fellow;
  And the brave wear glory's garlands at the setting of the sun!

Boom, pouf, boom! Awake! It is the cannon's bellow.
Boom, boom, boom! To arms! The battle has begun.
If courage makes the soldier, and cowardice the fellow,
We will all wear glory's garlands at the setting of the sun!

TO THE ROBIN THAT SINGS AT MY WINDOW

Robin, a-bob in the top of the sycamore,
Swinging and singing and flinging your song
    Out on the April breeze
    Over the maple trees,
Like a gay cavalier lilting along
Over the hills to the valleys of Arcady,
Through dewy dells where the spring blossoms blow,
    Out of gray shadow-lands
    Into May meadow-lands
Starry with wind-flowers whiter than snow. . . .
Oh, let me ride with you, Robin, to Arcady,
A-spur through the cool of the dew and the dawn!
    Oh, let me sing with you,
    Make the road ring with you,
Gaily and gallantly galloping on!

Sing, Robin, sing a wild ballad of Arcady,
Fresh as the wind and the dew of the dawn!
    Sing as I ride with you,
    Sing side by side with you,
While we go galloping, galloping on!
Sing of the deeds that were done while the world was young;
Sing of brave stories that never were told;
    Sing of the olden time;
    Sing of the golden time;
Sing of the glory that never grows old.
Sing the grand hymn in the throat of the summer hills;
Sing the wind's song and the rush of the rain;
    Sing of the mystery
    Older than history
Sung by the seed in the growth of the grain.

Sing me the song of the sun and the summer-time;
Sing me the song that the bumblebee drones
    As he goes blundering
    Home from his plundering
Deep down in orchards that nobody owns.
Flute-throated herald of June and of hollyhocks,
Ripple-tongued singer of roses and rain,
    Earliest, merriest,
    Bravest and veriest
Promise of summer and sunshine again:
Come, let me ride with you, Robin, to Arcady,
Over the hills in the dawn of the day,
    Out of the shadow-lands
    Into the meadow-lands
Where it is summer forever and aye!

THE HILLS OF ROSS

The bold old sandstone hills of Ross
Swing up and down the land
Like burly giants roystering
Together, hand-in-hand;
And over hill and over dale
The clouds go rolling free
Like great gold-laden galleons
Across a summer sea;
And high along the windy sky
The buzzards wheel and wing;
About, about, now in, now out,
They reel and sweep and swing
Until one's head goes round and round
With every dizzy ring.

Across the knurly hills of Ross
'Bold Summer blew his horn;
It stirred a thousand dreaming dales
And waked the sleeping corn;

So high, so far, so clear it rang
Through all the drowsy world,
The wild-flower host wide open sprang,
The blind brown ferns uncurled.
It roused a myriad untaught notes
In hedge and bush and tree;
It set the wild-wood echoing
With bubble-throated glee;
And sent a sudden, laughing thrill
All through the heart of me.

Along the brawny hills of Ross
The west wind whirls the rain,
Across the murky chimney-pots,
Adown the dusty pane;
And, oh, that wind is calling me
From out the dusty town,
'Out to the misty meadow-land,
Out to the dewy down,
Out to the wind-blown hills of Ross,
Into the summer shower,
To be a fellow to the field,
A brother to the flower,
And part of the midsummer day,
If only for an hour.

OBSTINACY
(From "Barnaby Lee")

There dwelt a man in Amsterdam, so obstinate, they say,
That the ocean could not move him, though it washed the dikes away;
So when the world was ended and he would not move his chair,
They had to roll the world away and leave him sitting there.

FRANCES NEWTON SYMMES

FRANCES NEWTON SYMMES, daughter of John H. and Hallie (Smith) Newton, was born April 16, 1865, at "Rosebank," an old colonial homestead in St. Louis, Missouri. Mr. Newton died in 1869, and five years later his widow was married to Mr. A. L. Symmes, who, in 1874, brought his wife, with the nine-year-old child, to his home in Clifton, Cincinnati. Frances, in her early womanhood, adopted the surname of her stepfather. At the time of her coming to the Queen City, Miss Symmes "had not seen the inside of a school, nor learned a compulsory lesson." She received her first tuition as a pupil in the Sacred Heart Convent, on Walnut Hills, and later she became a student in the Bartholomew English and Classical School, of which institution she is a graduate. Her higher academic education was received at Smith College, Northampton, Mass., where she pursued her studies with the special object of fitting herself for the teacher's profession. After her return from Northampton, Miss Symmes soon attracted attention by her ability and scholarship, as one of the instructors in Madam Fredin's private school, Walnut Hills, with which academy she was connected until her change of residence to Chicago, Ill., where she entered upon a wider field of usefulness as teacher of English in the Kenwood Institute. In the autumn of 1906, she removed to Providence, Rhode Island, where she still resides, devoting her talents to educational work in Miss Wheeler's School, a leading female seminary of that city.

The only book thus far published, from the pen of Miss Symmes, is a small collection of poems entitled "Brier Bloom," issued in Cincinnati in 1893.

FRANCES NEWTON SYMMES

HEART STIRRINGS

Like little spring birds in the hedges,
   Stir the songs in my heart.
In a tangle of follies and fancies,
In a network of dreams and romances;
As the fluttering thrush in the snow of the briers,
Or the robin a-swing in the peach-blossom fires,
   Stir the songs in my heart.

Like the timid spring-flowers in the meadow,
   Stir the songs in my heart.
'Neath the mosses of memory sleeping,
'Twixt the leaves of remembrance peeping;
As through the soft sod the pale wind-flower creeps,
Or the frightened arbutus through brown grasses peeps,
   Stir the songs in my heart.

O hasten, brave Spring, o'er the mountains!
   Free the songs in my heart!
Call the birds from the blossoming hedges;
Rouse the flowers in the shadowy ledges.
As the larks in the rapture of azure June skies,
As the blooms in the dance with the bright butterflies,
   Sing, O Songs, in my heart!

REPRESSION

O bursting bud and leafing tree!
   O rushing stream, aflow with cool, spring rain!
Ye can not know the vague unrest
   That makes mere living, these spring days, a pain!
The green peeps through the sere, dead leaves,
   The tender seed throws off its coverings brown,
And only eager dreams and hopes
   Their restless springtime longings must keep down.
The sunshine, with its thrilling touch,
   Awakens quick ambitions in the trees,

And tender stirrings fill the nest,
   And ghosts of fragrance coquette in the breeze;
And yet, in all this fresh, new life,
   Our souls are still imprisoned, and our eyes
In vain for some dear secret look,
   In smiling fields and streams and skies.

LISTENING

   I sit on the bare, brown rocks,
         And listen, listen.
The purring waves tease the sedges gray,
The sea-weeds shine in the chilly spray,
And a white sail skims 'gainst that sunset glow,
Like the wing of an angel flying low.
All the air is full of a spell intense,
A-thrill with mysterious, subtle sense!
O waves! O sky! Let a whispered thought
From your throbbing heart to my heart be brought!

   I lean on the lichened wall,
         And listen, listen.
There's a swallow there, in that far, far blue,
And the redbud's burning the forest through;
And the dogwood bloom, on that sunny knoll,
Is as cool and white as a maiden's soul.
All the air is full of a strange, sweet sense
Of a secret hid, of a hope intense!
O rapturous bird, strike some subtle key
That will teach my soul Spring's harmony!

FATE

O pale Anemone! what treacherous breath
   Beguiled thy soul from out the heaven of flowers,
And dropped thee here, while still the wintry death
   Of last year's bloom is mourned? No April showers

Have come, as yet, to wake, with gentle tap,
  The fragile bloodroot or the violet brave;
No sun has stirred the fern-fronds in their nap,
  Or tempted e'en the snowdrop from its grave;
But thou, White Spirit, tenderer than these,
  Above the snow-bleached grass and leaves dost rise
With brave child-face. Dost wait for some kind breeze
  To waft thee back again to warmer skies?
"Alas! I know not," said the bloom. "My fate
Called me thus early and I could not wait."

REVIVAL

A sudden robin note through whirling flakes;
Half snow, half rain, for days — then sunshine breaks;
'Mong ragged leaves the vigorous lily-stalks;
A fringe of snowdrops down the garden-walks;
The bloodroots' fingers reaching towards the sun;
Perchance courageous wind-flowers, one by one;
A robin in the maple plumes his wing,
Then swells his throat with gladness,— it is Spring!

FOREBODINGS

From azure into ashes turns the sky,
  The ragged clouds sweep fast behind the hill;
The river blackens, tattered blooms blow by;
  The forest stirs expectant — then all's still,
Save startled birds a-cry from nest to nest,
And thunderous warnings in the lurid west.

AFTERWARDS

The wrinkled river smoothes its shadowed face;
  The young leaves shake their green folds to the sun;
Faint blue creeps up behind the hills apace;
  A waste of petals strews the orchard slopes;
Then pallid green turns gold; on glistening stems,
The burdened flower-cups brim with twinkling gems.

TWILIGHT

The cold sky-fires behind the trees' black bars;
　The dull gray ribbon of the frozen stream;
The hush of snow; two white, uncertain stars;
　The fading line of far-off, lonely fields;
A snowy bough beneath its load breaks shrill;
Mysterious twilight comes, and all is still.

DAWN

The pallid East aflush with doubtful rose;
　The restless stream astir in dawn-thrilled wood;
The whirr of birds, the white star's dimming glows;
　The vague, wide fields, half lost in folds of mist;
A clear-voiced thrush chants on a dew-wet spray;
A light wind whispers in the boughs,—'tis day!

WILLIAM NORMAN GUTHRIE

WILLIAM NORMAN GUTHRIE, son of William Eugene and Frances Silva (d'Arusmont) Guthrie, and grandson of the famous Frances Wright, was born in Dundee, Scotland, March 4, 1868. At an early age he came with his widowed mother to the United States. In 1889 he graduated from the University of the South, Sewanee, Tenn., and in 1889-90 he was assistant professor of modern languages in that institution. He was professor of modern languages at Kenyon College, Ohio, in 1892-3, at the close of which period, having been ordained to the Protestant Episcopal ministry, he became "missionary in charge," of Christ's Church, at Kennedy Heights, Hamilton County, Ohio, where he officiated until 1894, when he entered upon a wider field of professional service in the Church of the Advent, Cincinnati (1894-96). Mr. Guthrie was married, January 4, 1883, in Sewanee, Tenn., to Miss Anna Morton Stuart. From 1898 to 1900 he was lecturer on comparative literature at the University of Cincinnati, and from 1900 to 1903, director of the Cincinnati Conference of Arts and Literature. He also held, from 1902 to 1909, the position of professorial lecturer on general literature at the University of Chicago. In 1899 he was called to the rectorship of the Church of the Resurrection, Fern Bank, Ohio, where he resided until 1903, when, on account of his wife's failing health, he removed to Alameda, Cal., and there was rector of Christ's Church until 1908. Since 1902 he has been professor of general literature, and director of the University Extension Department (Summer Session), in the University of the South, at Sewanee, Tenn., his present place of abode.

During the ten years of his residence in or near Cincinnati, Mr. Guthrie made literature an avocation, publishing within that period a volume of critical essays, Modern Poet Prophets, and four unique and strikingly original books of verse: To Kindle the Yule Log (1899); Songs of American Destiny, or Vision of New Hellas (1900); The Old Hemlock — Symbolic Odes (1901); and The Christ of the Ages, in Words of Holy Writ (1903).

Endowed by nature with a fervid imagination and with unusual critical acumen, and equipped by extensive study and reading, with a familiar knowledge of the principal European languages, ancient and modern, Mr. Guthrie is a brilliant and incisive lecturer on various aspects of literature, especially on poetry, fiction, and the drama. The distinctive characteristics of his verse, which, like his spirited, graphic, and stimulating prose, is filled with surprises of thought and felicities of diction, are well suggested by an Ohio critic, who writes of the author of Songs of American Destiny that "he sings a subtle Orphic strain, in forms of poetic art which follow the cult of Leopardi and George Meredith."

THE LION
An Incident at the Zoölogical Gardens

There, on the floor of thy cage
Thou liest, O Lion,
Stretched out, indifferent!
Vast head, with weight of portentous mane —
A tangle as of autumn forests
Where the horror of jaws
Lurks in ambush;
Compact muscular legs,
Armed with death,
In which the lightning of the fatal leap,
The crack, the crash of the fall,
The rending of flesh yet alive,
Slumber unquietly;
Tail with suppressed lash
Involuntarily vibrant;
Through eyes half-shut

With cunning show of drowsiness,
The yellow flash, keen,
Like broken glitter in the moon-glare
Of little pools of steaming blood;
All, but betrays
Subtly a soul of terror.

What outrage to have caged thee!
Yet, in thy bars take comfort.
Proffers of freedom were insult —
Scorn of the harmless, the impotent:
Men dread thee!
But thou — carest not if they quake,
Requirest no flattery of fears,
Sure of thy formidable strength,
Indifferent,
Grand.

Ah, wherefore do we stop
In front of thy cage
Bound by an evil spell?
Why this shudder at times,
Not of dread — this sense
Of oppression, difficult breath,
Unaccountable? Whence this ache
Of self-pity intense as we look
At Thee, fierce brute,
Caged fiend of the wilderness,
At Thee: —

Terrible! magnificent!
That leap, shaking the iron bars
As reeds once by shrunk streams
Where thy tongue of fire
Lapped the cool:
The quick snakes of thy mane
Erect, rigid,
Quivering with wild might,

At the eruption of a roar,—
Like fire volcanic
From bottomless deeps of fury
Inflaming the sky,
Charring the fruitful earth.
What is it
Captive monster,
Late so majestic, composed,
Scornfully indolent?

A cub — set loose
For sport of children —
A cub astonished stares
In front of thy cage,
By neat-trimmed shrubbery —
Free?

Who shall utter, O Lion,
Thy stupor, agony, rage?
One of thy kind, a cub, free?
What! The wilderness nigh?
This fetid cage of shame — hallucination?
Dens full of half-tame skulking beasts,
Howls, whines, snarls of feeding time —
An obsession?
The day's peering merrymakers,
(Cowards who inspect with prudent insolence,) —
And the prowl that ends where it began
In the close stench of the walled night —
A hideous obstinate nightmare?
Ah, 'tis the Wilderness has roused her to battle —
Has conquered civilization,
At a bound come hither
To rescue her caged King?
Iron bars only between Him and —
Not freedom —
But Her?

The hot day's sleep, the night's fierce hunt,
The fight to the death with rivals
For the lioness, sleek, awaiting the issue
With treacherous fawn, and leers
Of savage pleasure?
Only these bars between Him, and —
Not freedom —
But life? — Life?

Magnificent captive,
Disdainer of liberty,
Do I not understand thee?
Am not I, too, caged?
Laws, customs, courtesies, proprieties!
I too — remember.

Not liberty, O not liberty now!
Why break through bars?
Prolonged despair hath cowed us both,
And the tyranny of use.
What? Wreck our cage?
Where then would our Wilderness be?
The torrid sun,
The fever?
Hunger for palpitant flesh,
Thirst for hot blood?
The icy night,
The blinding moon in the clear,
The shadows black of rock and tree?
The prey terrified,
The joy of his agony?
The antagonist's prowl, roar, ramp?
The ache, the bliss of omnipotent fierce life?

Only a minute the spell hath lasted —
Best, O Lion, we both were patient,

Spiritless, sleepy — sane!
May be, may be —
(The thought of it starts
A shudder like death's
Clotting the heart's blood)
May be, may be — (who knows?)
Only the semblance is left us
Of fire — as of sunsets
That flare in the heavens,
But singe not a stubble-straw
Of the western hills.
May be — were the Wilderness here indeed,
Thou, O Lion, and I —
Even Thou, and I
Were wanting.

EVOCATION

What weird dream have I dream'd
    hard to recall?
Ay! so meseem'd
    I stood in some vast hall
lonely and sad, a disillusioned youth
loathing the lie — fearing the face of truth.

All the life since, became
    unreal; yes She
    a myth, a name.
I yearn'd to bow the knee,
reverent to some strange Deity, my own
Creature-of-cloud, Witch-of-my-dreams unknown.

There mov'd unheard, but felt,
    a shining Thing
    whose either wing
cover'd me as I knelt: —
"Vision of perfect being, holy, sweet,
let me remain — perish, but kiss thy feet!"

WILLIAM NORMAN GUTHRIE

AN OLD NEST

Frail boughs of precious sprays,
that twine and press sweet blossoms cheek to cheek,
why, when no wayward breath essays
to tangle itself in your bright maze,
be ye tremulous? Speak, bright branches, speak.

"A nest lies hidden here —
an old year's nest through winter safely kept;
and happy boughs are we, for we're
of all the bloomy boughs most near
to where innocent birds last summer slept!

Two wayfarers are flown
back to the nest of merry months gone-by;
and nestle wing to wing, unknown
of all the world save us alone,
as they twitter in sleep, and dream they fly."

A RESPITE

Laughing I lay on a Summer's day,
bedded in blossoming grass;
and little, little did I think of Her!
Love is not all of life — alas!
'Would that it were,
'Would that it were.

Oh! that we could be but understood;
bees must their honey amass
when skies are blue and grasses lightly stir.
Love is not all of life — alas!
'Would that it were,
'Would that it were.

Selfish the soul that from love-dreams stole,
    watching the gay breeze pass
o'er ferns and flowers, but Oh! all things aver:
    Love is not all of life — alas!
    'Would that it were,
    'Would that it were.

IN VAIN

    A passer-by, a passer-by,
      only a passer-by!
And I hoped to have thee always nigh,
to hear thee bid me live or die
for thee, for thee — but what was I?
    Only a passer-by.

    An idle dream, an idle dream,
      only an idle dream!
For we meet to part, and when we seem
just near enough to kiss, the stream
will sweep us on, from dream to dream —
    Only an idle dream!

    O bitterness of bitterness,
      bitterest bitterness!
That the heart should spend its tenderness,
and bless a heart that cannot bless,
and waste away yet love no less —
    Bitterest bitterness!

WILLIAM NORMAN GUTHRIE

HIGHER MATHEMATICS

Two and two make five, say I!
The truth is as plain as day. For why?
The whole is more than the sum I take
      Of the parts;
Thoughts, feelings, passions, do not make
      Human hearts;
    Sums are not wholes
    With flowers and souls!
So two and two make five, say I!

WHENCE? WHITHER?

    Drift!
Who would care to lift
    The cast-off rose
From the stream's traitorous breast?
    No one knows
Whose it was — where it bloomed!
    Only doomed — doomed — doomed!
    It is best —
        Drift!

ALICE ARCHER SEWALL JAMES

ALICE ARCHER SEWALL JAMES, daughter of Reverend Frank Sewall, the eminent Swedenborgian author and divine, and of Thedia Redelia (Gilchrist) Sewall, was born in 1870, at Glendale, Ohio, where her father had his first charge as minister of the New Church. In the year of her birth the family removed to Urbana, Ohio, where, for the next sixteen years, her father officiated as a clergyman, and as President of Urbana University (a New Church institution), and where the subject of this sketch received her early education.

Manifesting in childhood a decided predilection for poetry and art, Alice was given every advantage of private instruction, both at home and abroad, and her rapidly developing talent soon commanded for her a national reputation. "In my father's home," writes Mrs. James, "there was always music and a love of beautiful things, made subservient to the faithful and laborious life of a pastor and his family. . . . I made my first intimate acquaintance with the Greek casts, at sixteen, in the Art School of Glasgow, Scotland, where we lived for two years. The following year was spent on the Continent, chiefly in Italy, where, under my father's instruction, I was introduced to Dante and the literature of the Renaissance, and to the galleries of Rome and Florence. From 1889 to 1899 my home was in Washington, D. C., where I became acquainted with the painter, Howard Helmick, to whose criticism and judgment, in all branches of literature, I owe more than I can say."

In 1899 Miss Sewall was married to John H. James, a prominent attorney of Urbana, Ohio, in which city she now resides.

As an artist Mrs. James is highly esteemed, her work having been chosen for exhibition in the collections of the New York Architectural League, the Philadelphia Academy of Art, the Chicago World's Fair, the Expositions of Atlanta and Nashville, and at the Salon, Paris; and she has contributed illustrative designs to the Century Magazine, to Harper's Monthly, and to the Cosmopolitan. Not less distinguished as a poet than as a painter, Mrs. James has produced many exquisite lyrics, which are invariably characterized by originality, vigor, and freshness of conception, purity and elevation of sentiment, delicacy of fancy, and grace of expression, as well as by rhythmic and melodious charm. She is the author of two volumes of verse, An Ode to Girlhood, and Other Poems (1899), and The Ballad of the Prince (1900); and lyrics from her pen have appeared from time to time in various leading periodicals. Her "Centennial Ode," written in commemoration of the settlement of Champaign County, Ohio, and read at Urbana, July 7, 1905, entwines an enduring Buckeye leaf in her crown of myrtle.

THE PASSING OF THE WILD [1]

    Now rise and go
To other grazing fields,
    Ye buffalo,
    Lordly and slow:
For here a tavern-house must be.
Whom for? The wild-grape-twisted tree?
The traveling moon and the journeymen stars?
    The snakes and the fierce wild hogs?
George Fithian knows, as he rolls the logs,
    And fastens the window bars!
'Tis true that Law and the conquering mind
Ride first in the forest, but close behind
    Come Friendship and Jollity;
    Here let their lodging be,
        Here swing the sign,

---

[1] Extract from "Champaign County Centennial Ode," read at Urbana, O., July 7, 1905, and published in the Urbana Tribune, July 20, 1905.

And through the doorway let the candles shine,
Warming the wilderness with hints of home,
    And better things to come.

    Plunging over root and brier
    Where the Indians light their fire,
    Breaking silence dark and deep
    Where the ancient forests sleep,
    Reckless of the bogs and snags,
    Scattering herds of antlered stags,—
    With band-box, whip, and coach-horn blast,
    Horse and four wheels crashing past,
Hail to the stage-coach and to him who drives!
Welcome, the social years and gentler lives.

Now do the fields grow fat, the barn grow red,
And covered bridges cross Mad River's bed;
From clustered orchards springs the village spire,
    And soon, oh soon, the crowds shall stand,
    With flags and brazen village band,
    Gazing down a road of steel:
    Ah, what tremors do they feel,
      At the first low thunder
      The distant corn-fields under,—
It comes, Steam-Engine, Horse of man's desire,
Live, with his passions snorting, belching fire,
Girdled with furious smoke and trailing steam,
Answering to his hand with hiss and scream;
Now are the days of horse-back journeys fled,
And the stage-coach sits a wreck in the tavern shed.

Now once more rise and once more slowly go
To other grazing fields, ye buffalo;
Man neither fears nor needs you,— has decreed
Here shall live only what shall fill his need.
Farewell, high-headed moose and sullen bear,

All shadow-peering things that fly the glare
    Of the great harvest-sun;
Farewell, ye deer, and pretty spotted fawns
Halting in troops to nibble ferny lawns
On your long pilgrimage,— shy graces, ye,
Of virgin soil, lost with maturity
    And soon forever gone.

And with you, mile on dusty mile,
The Indians pass in single file,
Proud and loth to recognize
Their day is gone. With haughty eyes,
And plumage splendid round their waist,
Their wampum belts with bead-work chased,
Their leggin-fringes tipped with steel
Blurring their tracks from either heel;
On their backs their quivers hung,
And bows with reindeer-sinew strung,
And onyx-headed arrows; so
Dressed for hunting do they go,
Conscious in every step they tread,
Of eagle-feathers round each head:

They took their squaws and painted braves,
They left their legends and their graves,
    The names, the songs, the mystery,
        Of our first history.

YOUTH [1]

I am the spirit that denies.
Yes, and with full-regarding eyes
Comprehending the facts of earth's sorrow and shame,
And denying the truth of it just the same;
That takes man's face in two palms soft,
And looks deep into its brow and oft,

---

[1] Copyright, 1899, by Harper & Brothers.

And finds the good it has longed to find,
And denies there is anything hidden behind.

I am the spirit that denies
This earth to be no more Paradise.
I deny that God walks not with men.
I have met Him at even and talked with Him then.
I deny that of love there is ever a lack,
For I've felt His sun-arm across my back
As I wandered at spring-time into the land,
And talked with the dogwood hand in hand.

I am the spirit that denies
Straight into your face, straight into your eyes,
Wise Age, that for all your wisdom and gain
You are nobler for noticing every stain.
I deny that one cannot race on through earth's heat
And come out healthy and clean and sweet.
I deny that God's path is so overgrown
That a child could not toddle straight to Him alone.

I am the spirit that denies
Any fear of the earth or the seas or the skies;
That fronts the Unknown with forehead calm,
And gathers Life's reins with my soft, wet palm.
I learn a verse from the Bible by heart,
And well provided with love, I start,
And deny that Heaven is so far away
That I cannot reach it at close of day.

TO A NEW-BORN BABY [1]

I

Rise, Baby, rise,
　Life is incomplete.
Heaven needs thine eyes,
　Earth thy dancing feet,

---
[1] Copyright, 1899, by Harper & Brothers.

Birds thy rapt attention,
  Moon thy mild dismay:
All earth's sweet invention
  For thy use at play;
Startling red the berries
  For thy wild delight,
Flowers full of fairies
  To shut them up at night,
And perfect every blade of grass
Where heaven-accustomed feet shall pass.

II

Earth has run before thee,
  Honey-hedged her lanes,
Sent up skylarks o'er thee,
  Feather-wet with rains:
Hung with dew the shadows,
  Broidered all the rocks,
Cowslipped all the meadows
  For thy nibbling flocks;
Voiced her exultation
  In summer-throated birds,
Smiled a salutation
  Far too sweet for words,
And laid before thy homesick eyes
Her memories of Paradise.

III

Come, Baby, come!
  Come to wrong and pain,
With thy quick tears, come,
  And wash earth clean again.
Come with sweet young fancies
  We have lost so soon:
Midnight fairy dances
  Whirled against the moon,

Madrigals unsung,
  All spirit-footed sighs
The dreaming trees among,
  Before thy dreaming eyes;
Strange presences along the green,
And tinkling flutes of gods unseen.

IV

Strange, thou dost not know
  What we daily pass!
Stars that come and go!
  Cobwebs in the grass!
Strange, that thou shalt find
  Dandelions new!
And of playful mind
  Man and nature too!
Strange, to recreate
  Eden round thy knees!
God, unfeared playmate,
  Souls in all the trees!
Strange, that Truth for us is hidden,
Yet daily walks with thee unbidden!

V

Virtue and valor's union
  Cometh sure of these:
That first drunk communion
  With the sinless trees;
Thoughts at morning, thought
  'Mid the larks and dew,
Most divinely fraught
  For thy uses true,
When thy youth's defiance
  Calls thee far away

Into self-reliance
  And the burning day,
And hands unknown, in service sweet,
Tie wingèd sandals to thy feet.

VI

Hail, Baby, hail!
  Life is worth the trying!
Worth it if we fail,
  Worth it even dying!
I am here; I know
  That no robin's song
But is worth the woe
  Of a whole life long.
Love is over-plenty
  For the famine stored,
Joy enough for twenty
  Round each head is poured;
And long before thy need begin
Goodness and truth are garnered in!

SAY NOT FAREWELL [1]

Say not farewell!
  The lovely hour goes;
Into the purple distance of the lake
  The gleaming rower rows.
  Yet see, the lovely hour
  Lets drop its jeweled power;
The sacred instant, shook with sudden breeze,
Flies; and from all the magic morning trees
  The dew slips silently.
  So let thine own tears be —

---
[1] From the Century Magazine, Sept., 1903.

Hid in the rainbow of a smiling sun;
For lo, not one
Of these the Ever-going, take
Of the sweet Now farewell!

Say not farewell!
The word that seizes on the last of bliss
Holds treachery unseen.
E'en though it hide its dagger with a kiss,
It sets a gulf between.
Into the coming hour melt away,
Obedient as the melting rose;
Or, like the unregretting Day,
Who never will return,
But radiant goes,
Drop thou thy treasure in its golden urn,
And do not say farewell!

PAUL LAURENCE DUNBAR

PAUL LAURENCE DUNBAR was born at Dayton, Ohio, June 27, 1872. His parents, Joshua and Matilda (Murphy) Dunbar, were of pure African blood, and were of lowly origin, having both been slaves in youth. His father had escaped from bondage by way of the Underground Railroad, fleeing from Kentucky to Canada, where he remained until the close of the war, when he returned to the United States and settled in Ohio. His mother, who had been emancipated in ante-bellum days, was twice married, her first husband being Wilson Murphy, to whom she was wedded in Lexington, Ky., in 1859(?), at the age of sixteen, and by whom she had two sons, Robert and William. Her marriage to Joshua Dunbar, the father of the subject of this sketch, occurred in Dayton, Ohio, in 1871. Paul was educated in the public schools of Dayton, where he showed a preference for grammar, spelling, and other studies pleasing to his literary bent. His first public appearance, as a reader of his own verse, was on the occasion of his graduation from Steele High School, in 1891, when he delivered the "class poem." After leaving the high school, he obtained employment as elevator-boy in the Callahan Building, on Main Street; and while engaged in this monotonous occupation, as well as at subsequent periods of greater freedom, his mind was inspired by ambitious thoughts, and busied with the labor of improvising songs and sketches for popular recitation. His first venture in print, a collection of fifty-six pieces, was a volume entitled Oak and Ivy, issued in 1893, from the press of the United Brethren Publishing House, Dayton, Ohio, and bearing the following dedication: "To Her who has ever been My Guide, Teacher, and Inspiration, MY MOTHER, this little volume is affectionately inscribed." He rapidly developed a talent for declamation, comic and pathetic, and appeared frequently upon the platform, at different points in Ohio and Indiana, being encouraged in his early efforts as poet and reciter by admiring friends in Dayton and by influential members of the Western Association of Writers, including John Clark Ridpath, James Newton Matthews, William Henry Venable, and James Whitcomb Riley. Soon after the publication of Oak and Ivy, the young troubadour of a neglected race received the appointment of page to Judge Dustin, of the Dayton Court of Common Pleas, where he served for some time, discharging his duties acceptably and finding leisure to continue his favorite avocation. In the same year, 1893, he obtained from Hon. Frederick Douglass an appointment as clerk in the Haytian Building, World's Fair, Chicago, Ill., and later he secured employment in the office of the Clerk of Litigation, at Chicago. It was while he was serving in this latter position, in 1895, that his second book of verse, Majors and Minors, was published, being issued in Toledo, Ohio. The decided poetical merit of this volume elicited favorable comment from various reviewers, the most prominent of these being William Dean Howells, whose generously appreciative endorsement greatly enhanced Mr. Dunbar's reputation, insuring to the young negro bard a sympathetic audience in conservative literary circles.

In the summer of 1897, Dunbar made his first visit to New York City, where he gave public readings, and where he formed the acquaintance of several prominent literary men, through whose influence the manuscript of his volume, Lyrics of Lowly Life, was advantageously placed in the hands of a leading publisher. In January of the following year, he enjoyed a short tour in England, where, according to his biographer, Lida Keck Wiggins, he gave recitations to "scores of enthusiastic audiences," and where, in London, he was banqueted by the Savage Club, and entertained by distinguished patrons at their homes.[1] Soon after his return to America he was appointed, at the solicitation of Robert G. Ingersoll, to the office of assistant in

---

[1] See Life and Works of Paul Laurence Dunbar, by Lida Keck Wiggins, with an Introduction (from "Lyrics of Lowly Life") by W. D. Howells.

PAUL LAURENCE DUNBAR

the reading-room of the Library of Congress. This position he held from October 1, 1897, to December 31, 1898.

Paul Laurence Dunbar was married, March 6, 1898, to Miss Alice Ruth Moore, of New York, a writer of some note, who had been educated in Straight University, New Orleans, a college endowed for the instruction of colored people.

Early in the year 1899 the poet's health had begun to fail. Mr. Dunbar rapidly became the victim of consumption, which compelled him to abandon the lecture-platform and necessitated his return to Dayton, where, after a lingering illness, he died, at his home, 219 North Summit Street, February 10, 1906. He was buried in Woodland Cemetery, at Dayton, Ohio. Here, on June 26, 1909, was formally dedicated to his memory a monument consisting of a large Miami Valley bowlder, to which is fixed a bronze tablet on which are inscribed the name, Paul Laurence Dunbar, and the first stanza of the author's touching elegiac entitled "A Death Song:"

> "Lay me down beneaf de willers in de grass,
> Whah de branch 'll go a-singin' as it pass.
>   An' w'en I's a-layin' low,
>   I kin hyeah it as it go
> Singin', 'Sleep, my honey, tek yo' res' at las'.' "

The phenomenal achievement of Ohio's distinguished negro bard has won for him the appreciative applause of many writers, but no critic has more truly discerned or more justly defined the intrinsic merit of the poet's work than has William Dean Howells, who, in his introduction to the volume, Lyrics of Lowly Life, records his opinion in the following words: "What struck me in reading Mr. Dunbar's poetry was what had already struck his friends in Ohio and Indiana, in Kentucky and Illinois. They had felt as I felt, that however gifted his race had proven itself in music, in oratory, in several of the other arts, here was the first instance of an American negro who had evinced innate distinction in literature. In my criticism of his book I had alleged Dumas in France, and I had forgetfully failed to allege the far greater Pushkin in Russia; but these were both mulattoes, who might have been supposed to derive their qualities from white blood vastly more artistic than ours, and who were the creatures of an environment more favorable to their literary development. So far as I could remember, Paul Dunbar was the only man of pure African blood and of American civilization to feel the negro life æsthetically and express it lyrically. It seemed to me that this had come to its most modern consciousness in him, and that his brilliant and unique achievement was to have studied the American negro objectively, and to have represented him as he found him to be, with humor, with sympathy, and yet with what the reader must instinctively feel to be entire truthfulness. I said that a race which had come to this effect in any member of it, had attained civilization in him, and I permitted myself the imaginative prophecy that the hostilities and the prejudices which had so long restrained his race were destined to vanish in the arts; that these were to be the final proofs that God had made of one blood all nations of men."

HARRIET BEECHER STOWE

She told the story, and the whole world wept
  At wrongs and cruelties it had not known
  But for this fearless woman's voice alone.
  She spoke to consciences that long had slept:
Her message, Freedom's clear reveille, swept
  From heedless hovel to complacent throne.
  Command and prophecy were in the tone
  And from its sheath the sword of justice leapt.
Around two peoples swelled a fiery wave,
  But both came forth transfigured from the flame.
Blest be the hand that dared be strong to save,
  And blest be she who in our weakness came —
  Prophet and priestess! At one stroke she gave
  A race to freedom and herself to fame.

WELTSCHMERTZ

You ask why I am sad today,
I have no cares, no griefs, you say?
Ah, yes, 'tis true, I have no grief —
But — is there not the falling leaf?

The bare tree there is mourning left
With all of autumn's gray bereft;
It is not what has happened me,
Think of the bare, dismantled tree.

The birds go South along the sky,
I hear their lingering, long good-bye.
Who goes reluctant from my breast?
And yet — the lone and wind-swept nest.

The mourning, pale-flowered hearse goes by,
Why does a tear come to my eye?
Is it the March rain blowing wild?
I have no dead, I know no child.

I am no widow by the bier
Of him I held supremely dear.
I have not seen the choicest one
Sink down as sinks the westering sun.

Faith unto faith have I beheld,
For me, few solemn notes have swelled;
Love beckoned me out to the dawn,
And happily I followed on.

And yet my heart goes out to them
Whose sorrow is their diadem;
The falling leaf, the crying bird,
The voice to be, all lost, unheard —

Not mine, not mine, and yet too much
The thrilling power of human touch;
While all the world looks on and scorns,
I wear another's crown of thorns.

Count me a priest who understands
The glorious pain of nail-pierced hands;
Count me a comrade of the thief
Hot driven into late belief.

Oh, mother's tear, oh, father's sigh,
Oh, mourning sweetheart's last good-bye,
I yet have known no mourning save
Beside some brother's brother's grave.

ANGELINA

When de fiddle gits to singin' out a ol' Vahginny reel,
An' you 'mence to feel a ticklin' in yo' toe an' in yo' heel,
Ef you t'ink you got 'uligion an' you wants to keep it, too,
You jes' bettah tek a hint an' git yo'self clean out o' view;
Case de time is mighty temptin' when de chune is in de swing,
Fu' a darky, saint or sinner man, to cut de pigeon-wing;
An' you couldn't he'p f'om dancin' ef yo' feet was boun' wif twine,
When Angelina Johnson comes a-swingin' down de line.

Don't you know Miss Angelina? She's de da'lin' of de place;
W'y, dey ain't no high-toned lady wif sich mannahs an' sich grace;
She kin move across de cabin, wif its planks all rough an' wo',
Jes' de same's ef she was dancin' on ol' mistus' ball-room flo'.
Fact is, you do' see no cabin — evaht'ing you see look gran',
An' dat one ol' squeaky fiddle soun' to you jes' lak a ban';
Cotton britches look lak broadclof, an' a linsey dress look fine,
When Angelina Johnson comes a-swingin' down de line.

Some folks say dat dancin's sinful, an' de blessed Lawd, dey say,
Gwine to purnish us fu' steppin' w'en we hyeah de music play;
But I tell you I don' b'lieve it, fu' de Lawd is wise and good,
An' he made de banjo's metal an' he made de fiddle's wood,
And he made de music in dem, so I don' quite t'ink he'll keer
Ef our feet keeps time a little to de melodies we hyeah.
W'y, dey's somep'n' downright holy in de way our faces shine,
When Angelina Johnson comes a-swingin' down de line.

Angelina steps so gentle, Angelina bows so low,
An' she lif' huh sku't so dainty dat huh shoe-top skacely show;
An' dem teef o' huh'n a-shinin', ez she tek you by de han'—
Go 'way, people, d' ain't anothah sich a lady in de lan'!
When she's movin' thoo de figgers er a-dancin' by huhse'f,
Folks jes' stan' stock-still a'sta'in', an' dey mos' nigh hol's dey
          bref;
An' de young mens, dey's a-sayin', "I's gwine mek dat damsel
          mine,"
When Angelina Johnson comes a-swingin' down de line.

LITTLE BROWN BABY

Little brown baby wif spa'klin' eyes,
    Come to yo' pappy an' set on his knee.
What you been doin', suh — makin' san' pies?
    Look at dat bib — you's ez du'ty ez me.
Look at dat mouf — dat's merlasses, I bet;
    Come hyeah, Maria, an' wipe off his han's.
Bees gwine to ketch you an' eat you up yit,
    Bein' so sticky an' sweet — goodness lan's!

Little brown baby wif spa'klin' eyes,
    Who's pappy's darlin' an' who's pappy's chile?
Who is it all de day nevah once tries
    Fu' to be cross, er once loses dat smile?

Whah did you git dem teef? My, you's a scamp!
　　Whah did dat dimple come f'om in yo' chin?
Pappy do' know yo'— I b'lieves you's a tramp;
　　Mammy, dis hyeah's some ol' straggler got in!

Let's th'ow him outen de do' in de san',
　　We do' want stragglers a-layin' 'roun' hyeah;
Let's gin him 'way to de big buggah-man;
　　I know he's hidin' erroun' hyeah right neah.
Buggah-man, buggah-man, come in de do',
　　Hyeah's a bad boy you kin have fu' to eat.
Mammy an' pappy do' want him no mo',
　　Swaller him down f'om his haid to his feet!

Dah, now, I t'ought dat you'd hug me up close.
　　Go back, ol' buggah, you shan't have dis boy.
He ain't no tramp, ner no straggler, of co'se;
　　He's pappy's pa'dner an' playmate an' joy.
Come to yo' pallet now — go to yo' res';
　　Wisht you could allus know ease an' cleah skies;
Wisht you could stay jes' a chile on my breas'—
　　Little brown baby wif spa'klin' eyes!

PARTED

De breeze is blowin' 'cross de bay.
　　My lady, my lady;
De ship hit teks me far away,
　　My lady, my lady.
Ole Mas' done sol' me down de stream;
Dey tell me 'tain't so bad's hit seem,
　　My lady, my lady.

O' co'se I knows dat you'll be true,
　　My lady, my lady;
But den I do' know whut to do,
　　My lady, my lady.

I knowed some day we'd have to pa't,
But den hit put' nigh breaks my hea't,
   My lady, my lady.

De day is long, de night is black,
   My lady, my lady;
I know you'll wait twell I come back,
   My lady, my lady.
I'll stan' de ship, I'll stan' de chain,
But I'll come back, my darlin' Jane,
   My lady, my lady.

Jes' wait, jes' b'lieve in whut I say,
   My lady, my lady;
D' ain't nothin' dat kin keep me 'way,
   My lady, my lady.
A man's a man, an' love is love;
God knows ouah hea'ts, my little dove;
He'll he'p us f'om his th'one above,
   My lady, my lady.

HYMN

O li'l' lamb out in de col',
De Mastah call you to de fol',
   O li'l' lamb!
He hyeah you bleatin' on de hill;
Come hyeah an' keep yo' mou'nin' still,
   O li'l' lamb!

De Mastah sen' de Shepud fo'f;
He wandah souf, he wandah no'f,
   O li'l' lamb!
He wandah eas', he wandah wes';
De win' a-wrenchin' at his breas',
   O li'l' lamb!

Oh, tell de Shepud whaih you hide;
He want you walkin' by his side,
　　　O li'l' lamb!
He know you weak, he know you so';
But come, don' stay away no mo',
　　　O li'l' lamb!

An' af'ah while de lamb he hyeah
De Shepud's voice a-callin' cleah —
　　　Sweet li'l' lamb!
He answah f'om de brambles thick,
"O Shepud, I's a-comin' quick"—
　　　O li'l' lamb!

OHIO
COMMEMORATION
ODES

OHIO CENTENNIAL ODE

Read in the Coliseum, Columbus, Ohio, on the Opening Day,
September 4, 1888, of the State Celebration
of the Centennial Year.

BY COATES KINNEY

In what historic thousand years of man
  Has there been builded such a State as this?
Yet, since the clamor of the axes ran
  Along the great woods, with the groan and hiss
And crash of trees, to hew thy groundsels here,
  Ohio, but a century has gone,
And thy republic's building stands the peer
  Of any that the sun and stars shine on.
Not on a fallen empire's rubbish-heap,
  Not on old quicksands wet with blood of wrong,
Do the foundations of thy structure sleep,
  But on a ground of nature, new and strong.
Men that had faced the Old World seven years
  In battle on the Old World turned their backs
And, quitting Old-World thoughts and hopes and fears,
  With only rifle, powder-horn, and axe
For tools of civilization, won their way
  Into the wilderness, against wild man and beast,
And laid the wood-glooms open to the day,
  And from the sway of savagery released
The land to nobler uses of a higher race;
  Where Labor, Knowledge, Freedom, Peace, and Law
Have wrought all miracles of dream in place
  And time — ay, more than ever dream foresaw.

A hundred years of Labor! Labor free!
  Our River ran between it and the Curse,

And freemen proved how toil can glory be.
    The heroes that Ohio took to nurse
        (As the she-wolf the founders of old Rome)—
    Their deeds of fame let history rehearse
And oratory celebrate; but see
        This paradise their hands have made our home!
Nod, plumes of wheat, wave, banderoles of corn,
    Toss, orchard-oriflammes, swing, wreaths of vine,
    Shout, happy farms, with voice of sheep and kine,
        For the old victories conquered here on these
    The fields of Labor when, ere we were born,
        The fathers fought the armies of the trees,
        And, chopping out the night, chopt in the morn!

A hundred years of Knowledge! We have mixt
    More brains with Labor in the century
Than man had done since the decree was fixt
    That labor was his doom and dignity.
All honor to those far-foreworking men
    Who, as they stooped their sickles in to fling,
    Or took the wheat upon their cradles' swing,
Thought of the boy, the little citizen
There gathering sheaves, and planned the school for him,
    Which should wind up the clockwork of his mind
To cunning moves of wheels and blades that skim
    Across the fields, and reap, and rake, and bind!
They planned the schools — the woods were full of schools!
    Our learning has not soared, but it has spread:
Ohio's intellects are sharpened tools
    To deal with daily fact and daily bread.
The starry peaks of knowledge in thin air
    Her culture has not climbed, but on the plain,
In whatsoever is to do or dare
    With mind or matter, there behold her reign.
The axemen who chopt out the clearing here
    Where stands the Capital, could they today

OHIO CENTENNIAL ODE

    Arise and see our hundred years' display —
Steam-wagons in their thundering career —
Wires that a friend's voice waft across a State,
    And wires that wink a thought across the sea,
And wires wherein imprisoned lightnings wait
    To leap forth at the turning of a key —
Could they these shows of mind in matter note,
    Machines that almost conscious souls confess,
    Seeming to will and think — the printing-press,
Not quite intelligent enough to vote —
Could they arise these marvels to behold,
    What would to them the past Republic seem —
The State historified in volumes old,
    Or prophesied in Grecian Plato's dream?

A hundred years of Freedom! Freedom such
    No other people on the earth had known
    Till our America the world had shown
What Freedom meant. No foot of slave might touch
Our earth, no master's lash outrage our heaven:
    The Declaration of the Great July,
Fired by our Ordinance of Eighty-seven,
    Flamed from the River to the northern sky; —
Ay, that flame rose against the arctic stars,
    And shone a new aurore across the land.
A Body scored with stripes of whip and scars
    Of branding-iron seemed to understand —
Soulless though reckoned by our Union's pact —
    That It was Man, for whom that heavenly sign
Lit up the North; and while the bloodhounds tracked
    Him footsore through Kentucky, stars benign
Befriended him and brought him to our shore,
    A stranger, frightened, hungry, travel-worn;
And we laid hands on him and gave him o'er
    Again to bondage, as in fealty sworn.
So rich in freedom, we had none to give!
    While we might quaff, we could not pass the cup:

No slave should touch foot on our soil and live
  Upon it slave — he must be given up!
When that first man was wrested from our State,
  Then slavery had crossed the Rubicon;
Then Freedom was the whole Republic's fate;
  Then John Brown's soul began its marching-on;
Then the 'Ohio Idea' had to go
  Where'er the banner of the Union flew,
From northmost limits in Alaskan snow
  To southmost in the Mexic waters blue.

A hundred years of Peace! Yes, less the four
  (Our little Indian squabbles were not war),
The four when we, in battle's shock and roar,
  Declared that Freedom was worth dying for.
    Ohio gave to that great fight for Man
    Her Grant, her Sherman, and her Sheridan,
And her victorious hundred thousands more.
Victorious, yes, though legions of them sleep
  In garments rolled in blood on foughten fields —
Though still the mothers and the widows weep
  For the slain heroes borne home on their shields.
Their glorious victory this day behold:
  They conquered Peace; and where their manly frays
Across the land of bondage stormed and rolled,
  Millions of grateful freedmen hymn their praise.
Ohio honors them with happy tears:
  The battles that they braved for her,
  The banner that they waved for her,
  The freedom that they saved for her,
Shall keep their laurels green a thousand years.

A hundred years of Law! The people's will,
    The might of the majority,
    The right of the minority,
    The light hand with authority

OHIO CENTENNIAL ODE

We promised, with the purpose to fulfill.
But the contagion of the border-taint
   Blackened our statutes with its shameful stain,
And left the color of our conscience faint
   Till freshened by the battle-storm's red rain.
Ay, war has legislated; it has cast
   The 'White Man's Government' out into night,
And Labor, Knowledge, Freedom, Peace, at last
   Stand color-blind in Law's resplendent light.

Now hail, my State of States! thy justice wins —
   Thy justice and thy valor now are one;
Thou hast arisen, and thy little sins
   Are spots of darkness lost upon the sun.
Thy sun is up — O, may it never set! —
   These hundred years were but thy morning-red:
It shall be forenoon for thy glory yet
   When all who this day look on thee are dead.
O, splendor of the noon awaiting thee!
O, rights of man and hights of manhood free!
Hail beautiful Ohio that shalt be!
   Hail! Ship of State! and take our parting cheers!
Ah, God! that we might gather here to see
   Thy sails loom in swoln with a thousand years!

CLEVELAND CENTENNIAL ODE

Read at Cleveland, Ohio, July 22, 1896, on the Occasion of the Celebration of the One Hundredth Anniversary of the Founding of the City of Cleveland and the Settlement of the Western Reserve.

BY JOHN JAMES PIATT

I

Praise to the sower of the seed,
    The planter of the tree!—
What though another for the harvest gold
    The ready sickle hold,
Or breathe the blossom, watch the fruit unfold?
    Enough for him, indeed,
That he should plant the tree, should sow the seed,
And earn the reaper's guerdon, even if he
    Should not the reaper be:
"Let him who after a while, when I shall pass, may dwell
In my sweet close, 'neath my dear roof instead,
Enjoy the harvest, pluck the fruit as well,
    Though I myself be dead,—
    For every other man is other me."

II

    And praise be theirs who plan
    And fix the corner-stone
Of house or fane devote to God or man,
    Not for themselves alone.
    —Not for themselves alone
The Pilgrim Fathers of the Western Wood,
Not only for themselves and for their own,
Came hither planting in heroic mood

The seeds of civil-graced society,
Repeating their New England by the sea
    In the green wilderness.
From church and school, with church and school they came
To kindle here their consecrated flame:
With the high passion for humanity,
The largest light, the amplest liberty,
(No man a slave, unless himself enthrall,)
The key of knowledge in the door of Truth
    For eager-seeking youth,
With priceless opportunity for all,
(The tree of knowledge no forbidden tree,)—
    Free speech and conscience free.
    — Honor and praise no less
Be theirs, who in the mighty forest, then
    The haunt of savage men,
And tenanted by ravening beasts of prey
    Only less fierce than they,
(The fever-chill, the hunger-pang they bore,
Dangers of day and darkness at their door)
Abode, and in the panther-startled shade
The deep foundations of an empire laid.
    The corner-stone they put
(Where he the patriot sage,[1] with foresight keen,
Its fittest site on some vague chart had seen)
    Of the fair Place we know —
Their capital of New Connecticut.

III

    In the green solitude,
    A hundred years ago,
    The founder stood.
Hark, the first axe-stroke in the clearing! Lo,

---

[1] "It appears that Dr. Benjamin Franklin, as early as 1754, had indicated the mouth of the Cuyahoga, on Lake Erie, as an eligible site for a future commercial and maritime city."—J. J. P.

The log house with its civilizing gleam
    By yonder Indian stream! —
Such was the small beginning far away
    We celebrate to-day.

IV

There were two prophecies. He the founder, he
Whose statue stands in yonder public square,
    (He only came and went:
The city itself is his best monument,)
    That lonely evening gleam,
    Reflected heavenly fair
    In the still Indian stream,
    He saw, and prophesied,
    With home-returning eyes:
A peaceful forest-shadowed town should rise,
    Here by this azure Inland Sea,
With clustered church-spires, happy roofs half seen
Through leafy avenues of ambush green,
And school-house belfry — such he erewhile knew,
And the fond picture homesick memory drew,
In far New England by the Atlantic tide,
It was not long before the prophecy
    Had grown reality:
That Forest City seemed a haven of rest —
    New Haven of the West.
Another later came, in dreamful mood,
Where the tree-shadowed early village stood,
Who saw the flitting sails, the horizon-bound
    Of the great Inland Sea before
    Its open harbor door,
With the broad wealth-abundant land around;
(What wealth above of corn and fleece and vine! —
What wealth beneath of myriad-gifted mine!)
To him another vision: prophet-wise,
    With prescient eyes,

CLEVELAND CENTENNIAL ODE

    A great commercial mart he saw arise,
With arms outstretching over land and sea,
And linking continent to continent
      With bands of gold beneficent;
The smoke of steamers, plying ceaselessly,
Bearing our harvest stores to far-off hands
      In transatlantic lands;
With interchange of goods and gifts divine
      In rivalry benign,
Lo, peaceful navies, alien with our own!
The foundry's plume of fire, a dreadful flower,
      He saw, at midnight hour.
With ears that heard, as eyes that saw, the foreknown,
He heard the hum of mighty industries,—
The vulcanic forge's echoing clang of steel,
      The whirring wheel,
With other myriad sounds akin to these;
And up and down, and everywhere, the beat
      Of busy-moving feet,—
In throngèd thoroughfares of Trade apart,
The throbbing of the Titan Labor's heart.—
He saw and heard: a transient shadow he,
      But lo, the prophecy!
The Genie's dream-built tower, in morning's ray,
In fable-world it shone — the City stands to-day!

V

    Whoever backward looks shall see
    What wonder-working strange,
    Of ever-moving change!
    Lo, everywhere around we meet,
    In every highway, every street,
  New daily miracles of the century!
The harnessed elements, with that elusive sprite,
The errand-running Slave, with world-compelling might,

Obedient to man, and hurrying to and fro,
Wherever he would send, wherever wish to go!
      In every house at night
      The enchanted lamp alight,
      In each frequented way
      Its keen celestial ray,—
New wonders of a new world, they rise from day to day;
And all repeated, all reflected show
      In the fair Place we know! . . .
      — A sigh for their sad fate,
      For those red tribes, so late
Tenants-at-will of their vast hunting-ground,
      That had nor mete nor bound
      In the deep wood around.
      Him, lord the forest knew,
On Cuyahoga's stream where glides his bark canoe?
We have not banished quite their names from stream and
          wood,
We cannot banish quite their ghosts that will intrude;
      We cannot exorcise
      Their still reproachful eyes.
      Pity we must their fate—
      The inexorable doom
      That gave our fathers room;—
      That they must fade,
      Shadow-like, into shade,
So we might celebrate the city's founding here:
      That they must disappear,
      So we might celebrate
Their mighty wilderness our mighty State,
Among the brightest of her galaxy,
(With New Connecticut her chiefest pride,)
Mother of famous soldiers, statesmen tried,
(New Mother of Presidents, her well-beloved,
      In camp and council proved.) . . .
— One time an alien fleet was hovering near,
(Let us be strong, and well protect our own!)

CLEVELAND CENTENNIAL ODE

When on yon shore the school-boy at his play
    Stooped down with hand at ear
    By the lake-side to hear
    The guns at Put-in-Bay.
War summoned then and since again her sons.
(City and State, with common sympathies,
    Unite in claiming these.)
    Her Past is bitter-sweet.
Heroic grief, heroic gladness meet,
With memories proud in monumental stone,
    In civic square and street:
Of him that hero of an earlier day;
Of those her later, now her aureoled ones,
    Her eager youth who went
To battle as to tennis tournament,
    Not for themselves alone,
Not only for themselves and for their own,—
    For all men, us and ours!
Returning but in sacred memories,
That ever green are kept and sweet with flowers;
Of him the kindly neighbor, cordial friend,
(Now far uplifted from familiar ways,
Blameless and high above the stain of praise,)
Down-stricken at the Helm of Highest Trust.
    (She keeps his honored dust.)
And many another worthy even as they,
Banded to sweep the nightmare dark and dire,
If with cyclonic broom—with earthquake, flood, and fire—
    From our great land away![1] . . .
    — Old griefs and glories blend.

---

[1] "Commodore Perry, the Union soldiers from Cleveland, President Garfield, and the anti-slavery leaders and agitators of the Western Reserve are referred to in the foregoing passage."—J. J. P.

VI

Into the Future — who shall look
Into that cloud-clasped Book?
What strong miraculous spark
Shall pierce that deep-walled dark?
Whoever forward looks shall see,
Mayhap, a vision, an enthusiast's dream,
Of this or of another century,—
The flower of each together here as one
Blossoming in the sun.
Whoever looks shall see, reflected there,
The features of her Past, oh, not less fair;
The features of her Present, even more bright:
A city that shall seem
To bear aloft and hold a steadfast light:
With ampler domes of Science, Learning, Art,
In academic groves apart:
Earth-blessing commerce at her every door,
With sails that come and go forevermore:
The earthly Titan's sweltering toil made light
By the invisible heaven-descended might,
Goodfellow or frolic sprite:
With myriad mechanisms faëry-nice,
Beneficent art and delicate artifice,—
All human goods and graces priceless wrought
In every house for nought
But a mere wish or thought:
The enchanted statue's grace
In every market-place,—
But Nature breathing ever, everywhere,
Her breath from flower and leaf, from park and pasture
fair:
Streets that are highways to green fields and woods,
With charmèd solitudes,
Whither the workman pent
Flies from his toil, content:

CLEVELAND CENTENNIAL ODE

With hanging gardens of delight
For all men's sense and sight,
Where they may see the dancing fountain's flower,
Faërily silvered, wavering in the moon,
And hear the wild bird sing his vesper hymn in June,
Through the still twilight hour. . . .
— In that bright city then,
Himself one of a myriad multitude,
Shall the Good Citizen,
Who loves his fellow-men,
Who makes self-interest work for common good,
Dwell, and make beautiful his dwelling-place,
Striving to keep his city pure and clean,
With avenues to heaven its walls between.
Gentle, but strong and just,
He holds his vote a sacred gift and trust,
And every neighbor's sacred as his own,
Not bossed, or bought, or sold
For bribe of public place or private gold.
He knows his public duty, will not shirk
His burden of public work:
Public Affairs his pleasure, study, pride
Rightly to know and not ignore but guide,
Not leaving to ignorant, faithless hands to rule
City and court and school.
He gives his hand and heart
To make a sacred shrine the voting-place,
Not a foul huckster's mart,—
Where woman, if she please, may use her right
Inalienable as man's to speak, how still!
A still small voice to execute her will,
And go with son or sire, without disgrace,
In Sabbath garments pure and dedicate
To home and child and State,
Even as at church to share their sacrament,
Guarding her world-old sphere beneficent

And share of government.
He builds for others, not for himself alone,
Not only for himself and for his own,
And gladdens with all good that comes to all,
    Wherever it befall.
So the House Beautiful the poor man's home shall be,
    In that far, better day,
    (Is it so far away?)
    The day we may not see,
    Save only in prophecy,
When, standing like that City on a Hill,
    With few or peer or mate,
She shall be seen afar and known of all,
Our City Beautiful — Forest City still,
    The seaside Capital
    Of our proud Forest State!

CINCINNATI

A CIVIC ODE

Read in McMicken Hall, University of Cincinnati, on the Evening of University Alumni Day, November 22, 1907.

BY WILLIAM HENRY VENABLE

I

O not unsung, not unrenowned,
Ere brave Saint Clair to his reward had gone,
Or yet from yond the ample bound
Of green Ohio's hunting-ground
Tecumseh faced the Anglo-Saxon dawn,
My City Beautiful was throned and crowned:
Then all Hesperia confest
With jubilant acclaim,
Her sovereign and inviolable name,
Queen of the West!

II

Upon the proud young bosom she was nursed,
Of the Republic, in the wild
Security of God's primeval wood:
Illustrious Child!
By Liberty begotten, first
Of all that august civic sisterhood
Born since the grand Ordain of Eighty-Seven
Promulged its mandatory plevin,
Which fain had reconciled
Human decretals and the voice of Heaven.

III

    Baptismal sponsors gave
Her virtuous patronymical and brave,
From hoary chronicle and legend caught,
And blazon of that laureled son of Mars,
    Whose purple heraldry of scars,
(From fields of valorous duty brought,)
      Enriched patrician Rome with dower
    Of ancient honorable power.

    The half-tradition old
    Of Cincinnatus told,
Who cast aside the victor's brand and took
In peaceful grasp the whetted pruning-hook,
And drave the plowshare through the furrowed mold,
Was golden legend unto Washington
And his compeers in patriotic arms,
    'Who flung the sword and musket down,
      (Their martial fields of glory won,)
    Shouldered the ax and spade,
    To wage a conquering crusade
Against brute forces and insensate foes:
    Besieged the stubborn shade,
    Subdued their savage farms,
      Builded the busy town,
And bade the desert blossom as the rose.

IV

    Upgrew a fair Emporium beside
Ohio's amber flood, as by the yellow tide
    Of storied Tiber, sprung, of yore,
    On lowland and acropolis,
    The elder world's metropolis,
    Along the imperial shore!

CINCINNATI: A CIVIC ODE

V

Yet not of Latian swarm were they
Who hived the early honey of the West;
They boasted Borean sires of strenuous clay:
Long-striding men of soldierly broad breast,
Of dauntless brain and all-achieving hands,
  Fetched out of British and Teutonic lands,
Schooled for command by knowing to obey,
Inured to fight and disciplined to pray,
    Columbian leaders of potential sway,
      Survivors of the European Best!

VI

  With grand desire and purpose vast,
    To purge from dross the metal true,
  And pour the seven-times-molten Past
    In perfect patterns of the New,
    They led the migratory van:
And every hero carried in his heart
The constitution and politic chart,
The code, the creed, the high-imagined plan
Of that Ideal State whereunto wend
The hopeful dreams of universal man,
    And whither all the ages tend.

VII

  Such the stock adventure brought
    Over Alleghany ranges,
  By the Revolution taught
    War and Fortune's bitter changes:
They hewed the forest jungle, broke
    The wild, reluctant plain;
With rhythmic sinews, stroke on stroke,
    They cradled in the grain;

The masted barge on gliding keel
    Rich bales of traffic bore;
The laden steamer's cataract wheel
    Befoamed the River shore;
Anon, as rolls the thunder-peal,
    As glares the lightning flame,
O'er trammeled miles of outspun steel
    The Locomotive came! —
Electron's viewless messengers, more fleet
Than herald Mercury of wingèd feet,
Far-flashing, multiplied the thrilling word,
Freedom! and Freedom! — Freedom, evermore!
Which all the Appalachian echoes heard
And broad Atlantic's rumorous billows bore
Persuasive to his utmost peopled shore,
Tempting shrewd Mammon, and with louder voice
    Bidding courageous Poverty rejoice!
Then Westward ho! the Movers found their goal,
    Ohio, thine auspicious Metropole! —
Nor landmark-trees blazed by his hatchet blade,
Nor scanty bounds by Filson's chain surveyed,
Might longer then suffice as border-line;
Not Eastern Row nor Western, could confine
Emption of homestead, or sequestered hold
Salubrious Mohawk's northward-spreading wold:
A century's growth, down crashed the 'builder Oak,'
The quarry from Silurian slumber woke,
The town, advancing, saw the farms retreat,
The turnpike rumbled, now a paven street: —
With bold and eager Emulation rode
Young Enterprise; keen Industry and Wealth
Sought new employ and prosperous abode
With blithe Success and robust Hope and Health,
In verdant vale wherethrough Dameta flowed,
Or high upon the crofts and bowery hills,
Above the gardens and the rural mills

CINCINNATI: A CIVIC ODE

Of Mahketewa's brook and affluent rills:
Their palaces adorned each rampart green,
Their cottages in every dell were seen,
  O'er which the well-belovèd Queen
      Holds chartered reign
      And eminent domain!

VIII

     Today wouldst thou behold
What ensigns of magnificence and might
Her spacious realms of urban grandeur show?
Choose for thy belvedere some foreland bold,
  Auburn, or Echo, or aërial height
    Of sun-clad Eden's blossomy plateau: —
      There bid thy wildered gaze
      Explore the chequered maze,
Unending street, innumerable square,
Park, courtyard, terrace, fountain, esplanade,
Gay boulevard and thronging thoroughfare,
Far villas peering out from bosky shade,
Cliff-clambering roads and shimmering waterways:
Lo, Architecture here and Sculpture vie
With rival works of carven wonder shown
In sumptuous granite and marmorean stone;
Behold stupendous where proud citadels
  Of legionary Trade aspire the sky;
And where Religion's sanctuaries raise
Their domed and steepled votive splendors high:
  (Upon the hush of Sabbath morning swells
  How sweet, their chime of tolerant bells!)

IX

Seen dimly over many a roofy mile,
  Where hills obscure environ vales remote,
Rise colonnaded stacks of chimney pile,
  Above whose dusky summits float

Pennons of smoke, like signal flags unfurled
  Atop their truce-proclaiming towers,
  By the allied triumphal powers
Of Science, Labor, and mechanic Skill,
Subduing nature to man's godlike will:
Forth yonder myriad factories are whirled,
    By steam-and-lightning's aid,
Invention's yield perpetual, conveyed
Beyond strange seas to buy the bartered world! —
Hark, the hoarse whistle, and dull, distant roar
Of rumbling freight-trains, ponderous and slow,
Monsters of iron joint, which come and go
Obedient to the watchful semaphore
That curbs their guided course along the shore
  Edged by the margin of the southering River:
Now golden gleam, now silvern flash and quiver
The molten mirrors of its burnished tide
Whereover costly argosies of Commerce ride!

X

Thrice-happy City, dearest to my heart,
Who, showering benison upon her own,
Endows her opulent material mart
With lavish purchase from each ransacked zone,
Yet ne'er forgot exchange of rarer kind,
By trade-winds from all ports of Wisdom blown —
  Imperishable merchandise of Mind:
Man may not live by bread alone,
But every word of God shall be made known! —
    Thy voyagers of Argonaut,
Enriched with dazzling ransom of their toil
In ravaged Colchis, costlier guerdon brought
As trophy home than prize of golden spoil:
Gems from the trove of Truth, for ages sought,
  Precious beyond appraise in sordid fee;

CINCINNATI: A CIVIC ODE

Audit of Culture, treasury of Art:
Whate'er the Daughters of Mnemosyne
In templed grove of Academe impart:
Heroic Song, Philosophy divine,
Precept oracular, Narration old,
Or aught by sage Antiquity extolled,
   Or murmured at Apollo's lucent shrine.
Here Education rounds a cosmic plan,
Enough omnipotent aye to create
From nebulous childhood, ordered worlds of man,
   Evolving Scholar, Citizen, and State.
Each liberal science, every craft austere,
All sedulous joys of book and pen are here,
Delights that charm the reason or engage
   Imagination's quickened eye or ear:
Pencil of limner, sculptor's cunning steel,
   And whirling marvel of Palissy's wheel; —
Drama, in pomp of gorgeous equipage,
Ostends upon the applauded stage
   Phantasmagoria of the living Age;
And, by celestial votaries attended,
Impassioned Music, from the spheres descended,
   Abiding here in tutelar control,
Commands orchestral diapasons pour
Exalted fugue and symphony along
Resounding aisle and bannered corridor;
Or, while the organ's mellow thunders roll,
She bids enraptured voices thrill the soul
With heaven-born harmony of choral song!

XI

O Cincinnati! whom the Pioneers,
   How many weary lustrums long ago,
With orisons and dedicated tears,
Blest, kneeling, when the pure December snow

Melted for pity into drops of spring.
My heart renews their throbbing fervor now,
   Their toil, their love, their hope, remembering,
I breathe their patriot ardor and their vow,
Their exultation and prophetic faith I sing!—
For they were Freedom's vanguard, and they bore
   Her starry flag and led her empire West,
Ere yet the wounds of sacrificial war
   Had healed upon their Mother-Country's breast:
Courageous they and loyal! evermore
Bold for The People! valorous and strong
Against embattled Myrmidons of Wrong:
   Forever honorable, true, and just!
Historial years, above their crumbling dust,
   On wings of peace and wings of war have flown.
Returning Aprils green the grateful sod
There where with hands that knew the ax to wield
They pledged a log-hewn temple unto God
Or ere they thrice had husked the ripened field
   Or promised harvest o'er the tilth had sown:
Seers, Legislators, Politicians, these,
   From ancestors indomitable, sprung!
Who, as with brawn of sinewy grip they swung
Their polished helves and launcht the steely edge,
   Invading so the monarchy of trees,
Or smote with ponderous maul the iron wedge,—
Labored meanwhile within the spacious Mind,
Planning and building, for their fellow-kind,
   Futurity colossal, on the vast
   Foundations of the immemorial Past!

APPENDIX

APPENDIX

REFERENCE-LISTS
BIBLIOGRAPHIC AND CRITICAL

BENNETT, HENRY HOLCOMB. Editor: A History of Ross County, Ohio (1903). Author: The Animal Paint Book (1906). No volume of verse from the pen of Henry H. Bennett has yet been published. (See biographical sketch, page 276.)

BENNETT, JOHN. John Bennett is the author of three romantic novels: Master Skylark (1897); The Story of Barnaby Lee (1900); and The Treasure of Peyre Gaillard (1906). He is also the illustrator of Miscellany and Silhouette Tales. No collection of poems by John Bennett has yet been published, though choice specimens of his verse are presented in the pages of Master Skylark. Selections from his work are to be found in Stedman's American Anthology and in Warner's Library of the World's Best Literature. The author's delicacy of sentiment, vivid fancy, and melodious charm are most strikingly illustrated in the lyrics entitled: "Song of the Hunt," "The Merry Springtime," "Song of the Dutch Cannoneers," "To the Robin That Sings at My Window, "'Tis Done," "God Bless You, Dear, Today," "Her Answer," "The Hills of Ross," "In a Rose-Garden," "The Love of a Summer Day."

BIRD, HELEN LOUISA BOSTWICK. Helen L. B. Bird is the author of two small volumes, one in prose and the other in verse: the former being a booklet of stories written for children, entitled "Buds, Blossoms, and Berries," published in 1861, by Follett, Foster & Co., Columbus, O.; the latter, a collection of forty-eight lyrics, entitled "Four O'Clocks," issued by Claxton & Co., Philadelphia, in 1888.

The poems named in the following list, most of which may be found in the volume, Four O'Clocks, are in the author's best vein: "My Mountain," "My River," "My Lake," "My Island," "So Many Times," "Too Fine for Mortal Ear," "Drafted," "The Origin of Dimples," "The Lost Image," "In Her Sleep," "How the Gates Came Ajar," "Peace," "The Little Coffin," "An Eastern Tale," "At the Wood's Edge," "One Week After," "In the Fisher's Hut," "My Little Saint," "Far-Sight," "Found in an Urn," "Counterparts," "On the Mountain," "Noon-of-June."

POETS OF OHIO

BRANNAN, WILLIAM PENN. Author: Vagaries of Vandyke Browne, an Autobiography in Verse. R. W. Carroll & Co., Cincinnati, 1865. (See biographical sketch, page 102.)

BROTHERTON, ALICE WILLIAMS. Mrs. Brotherton is the author of three published volumes: Beyond the Veil (poems, 1886); (The Sailing of King Olaf, and Other Poems (1887); and What the Wind Told the Tree-Tops (prose and verse, 1888). Selections from her poems are to be found in Stedman's Library of American Literature; in Stedman's American Anthology; in Piatt's Union of American Poetry and Art; in Crandall's Representative Sonnets; in Poets and Poetry of Indiana (compiled by Benjamin S. Parker and Enos B. Heiney. Silver, Burdett & Co., New York, 1900); and in Days and Deeds, compiled by Burton Egbert Stevenson.

A list of Mrs. Brotherton's best poems would include the following titles: "The Blazing Heart," "My Enemy," "The Poison Flask," "Rosenlied I," "Rosenlied II," "The Spinner," "Campion," "Shakespeare," "Ballad of the Master," "Woman and Artist," "The Song of Fleeting Love," "The Legend of the Snowdrop," "Repression," "Under the Beeches," "A Song in Summer," "The Day of the Dead," "An Old-Time Garden," "How Fear Turneth Aside Favor," "A Persian Fable."

CARY, ALICE. Eighty-nine of Alice Cary's early lyrics appear in the volume, Poems of Alice and Phoebe Cary, issued in 1850, by Moss & Brother, Philadelphia. The first independent publication by Alice Cary, a collection of thirty-five of her short stories and sketches of country life in Ohio, was issued in 1851, under the title, "Clovernook; or Recollections of Our Home in the West." Then appeared, Hagar, a Story of Today (1852), followed by Lyra, and Other Poems (1852). A second series of Clovernook sketches was published in 1853, after which were issued: Clovernook Children (1854); Poems (1855); Hollywood (a novel, 1855); Married; Not Mated (1856); Pictures of Country Life (1859); Ballads, Lyrics, and Hymns (1866); Snowberries, a Book for Young Folks (1867); The Bishop's Son (1867); and A Lover's Diary (1868). The last product of Alice Cary's prolific pen, a story which she did not live to finish, was a reform novel entitled "The Born Thrall," the opening chapters of which appeared in The Revolution, a journal conducted by Susan B. Anthony, and devoted to the cause of woman's rights.

To the student wishing to familiarize himself with the best poetical work of Alice Cary, the lyrics named in the following list are recommended for critical reading: "Balder's Wife," "The Gray Swan," "The Bridal Veil," "Thanksgiving," "Now, and Then," "Idle," "Tricksey's

APPENDIX

Ring," "Little Cyrus," "An Order for a Picture," "Pictures of Memory," "The Field Sweet-Briar," "No Ring," "Open Secrets," "Life's Mysteries," "Sixteen," "Idle Fears," "One of Many," "To the Spirit of Song," "Sometimes," "A Dream," "Be Still," "One Dust," "Forgiveness," "Life of Life," "Dying Hymn," "Jessie Carrol."

CARY, PHOEBE. Phoebe Cary's writings consist almost entirely of verse. Forty-five of the author's early lyrics appear in the joint collection, Poems of Alice and Phoebe Cary, published by Moss & Brother, Philadelphia, in 1850. Two independent volumes of verse from her pen are: Poems and Parodies (1854) and Poems of Faith, Hope, and Love (1868). Her best lyrics are contained in a memorial volume entitled "The Poetical Works of Alice and Phoebe Cary," edited by Mary Clemmer (Ames), and issued by Hurd & Houghton, Boston, 1874.

List of select poems: "The Only Ornament," "True Love," "The Harmless Luxury," "A Woman's Answer," "I Cannot Tell," "A Weary Heart," "Our Homestead," "Equality," "Favored," "Song" ("I see him part the careless throng"), "Tried and True," "Jealousy," "Hymn" ("How dare I in Thy courts appear"), "Hymn" ("Come down, O Lord, and with us live"), "Vain Repentance," "Cowper's Consolation," "A Prayer," "Living by Faith," "A Monkish Legend."

CURRY, OTWAY. No complete collection of the poems of Otway Curry has ever been published, though fair samples of his work are to be found in Coggeshall's The Poets and Poetry of the West (1860). Several of Curry's productions were very popular in their day, often "going the rounds" of the newspaper press, and not infrequently being reproduced in school-readers. Among those of his lyrics best worthy of preservation and remembrance are: "The Lost Pleiad," "Aaven," "The Goings Forth of God," "To a Midnight Phantom," "Kingdom Come," "Chasidine," and "Adjuration."

DUMONT, JULIA L. Julia L. Dumont is the author of a volume entitled "Life Sketches from Common Paths," issued by Appleton & Company, New York, in 1856. Though Mrs. Dumont wrote much in verse, her poems were never collected into a volume. Of the ten lyrical selections which represent her work in Coggeshall's pioneer anthology, none is more deserving of commendation than "The Future Life," an extract from which is given in this volume.

DUNBAR, PAUL LAURENCE. Paul Laurence Dunbar's writings, in prose and in verse, number some twenty publications, the chief among which are: Oak and Ivy (Dayton, 1893); Majors and Minors (Toledo, 1895); Lyrics of Lowly Life (1896); Folks from Dixie

(1898); The Uncalled (a novel, 1898); Lyrics of the Hearthside (1899); Poems of Cabin and Field (1899); The Strength of Gideon (a novel, 1900); The Love of Landry (a novel, 1900); The Sport of the Gods (a novel, 1901); The Fanatics (a novel, 1901); Candle-Lightin' Time (1902); Lyrics of Love and Laughter (1903); Heart of Happy Hollow (1904); Li'l' Gal (verse, 1904); Lyrics of Sunshine and Shadow (1905); and Howdy, Honey, Howdy (1905).

A profusely illustrated subscription volume of four hundred and thirty pages, entitled "The Life and Works of Paul Laurence Dunbar," containing "his complete poetical works, his best short stories, numerous anecdotes, and a biography of the poet," compiled and edited by Lida Keck Wiggins, was published in 1907, under the imprint of J. L. Nichols & Co.

List of select poems: "Little Brown Baby," "Angelina," "Parted," "Weltschmertz," "Life's Tragedy," "Harriet Beecher Stowe," "Hymn," "The News," "The End of the Chapter," "Love and Grief," "Love's Chastening," "Mortality," "She Told Her Beads," "Mare Rubrum," "The Crisis," "The Sum," "Prometheus," "Love Despoiled," "Protest," "Retort," "Jealous," "Despair," "Crismus on the Plantation."

EMMETT, DANIEL DECATUR. The entertaining story of "Uncle Dan Emmett's" long life is fully told in a biography written and published in Columbus, O., in 1904, by the librarian of the Ohio State Library, Hon. C. B. Galbreath, who discusses thoroughly the question of the authorship of "Dixie."

GALLAGHER, WILLIAM DAVIS. Three small volumes of verse, by W. D. Gallagher, were issued in the years 1835-6, under the titles, "Erato No. I," "Erato No. II," "Erato No. III." In 1841 Mr. Gallagher compiled and published a volume entitled "Selections from Western Poetry," the first of our local anthologies. His latest and most important book, Miami Woods, A Golden Wedding, and Other Poems, (a volume of 264 pages,) was published by The Robert Clarke Co., Cincinnati, in 1881. The title-poem, "Miami Woods," a lengthy pastoral, the composition of which was begun in 1839 and completed in 1856, is unique in character and diversified in its interest, and exhibits the author's mastery of sustained and musical blank verse. In addition to this elaborate work, a list of Gallagher's best poems would include the lyrics entitled: "On the Banks of the Tennessee," "Song of the Pioneers," "The Mothers of the West," "The Cardinal Bird," "The Spotted Fawn," "The Mountain Paths." "August," "The Brown Thrush," "Dandelions," "The Happy Valleys," "Happiness — A Picture," "Truth and Freedom," "Conservatism."

APPENDIX

GUTHRIE, WILLIAM NORMAN. The published writings of W. N. Guthrie comprise: Love Conquereth (1890); Modern Poet Prophets, Essays Critical and Interpretative (1897, 1899); To Kindle the Yule Log, a Booklet of Verse (1899); Songs of American Destiny, or Vision of New Hellas (1900); The Old Hemlock — Symbolic Odes (1901); The Christ of the Ages in Words of Holy Writ (1903); The Dewdrops, and Other Pieces Written for Music (1905); Orpheus Today, St. Francis of the Trees, and Other Verse (1907); and The City of St. Francis (1907).

List of select poems: "The Lion — An Incident in the Zoölogical Gardens," "Revocation," "A Respite," "An Old Nest," "Dirge," "In Vain," "To a Latterday Prophet," "Sympathetic Music," "Higher Mathematics," "Whence? Whither?" "Lullaby," "The Cloud in the Valley."

HANBY, BENJAMIN RUSSEL. For an extended biography of Benjamin Russel Hanby see article by Hon. C. B. Galbreath, in the Ohio Archæological and Historical Quarterly, April, 1905.

HOWELLS, WILLIAM DEAN. The wide-ranging list of books by W. D. Howells, comprises the following titles: Venetian Life; Italian Journeys; Suburban Sketches; No Love Lost; Their Wedding Journey; A Chance Acquaintance; A Foregone Conclusion; Out of the Question; A Counterfeit Presentment; The Lady of Aroostook; The Undiscovered Country; A Fearful Responsibility, and Other Tales; Dr. Breen's Practice; A Modern Instance; A Woman's Reason; Three Villages; The Rise of Silas Lapham; Tuscan Cities; A Little Girl among the Old Masters; The Minister's Charge; Indian Summer; Modern Italian Poets; April Hopes; Annie Kilburn; A Hazard of New Fortunes; The Sleeping-Car, and Other Farces; The Mouse-Trap, and Other Farces; The Shadow of a Dream; An Imperative Duty; The Albany Depot; Criticism and Fiction; The Quality of Mercy; The Letter of Introduction; A Little Swiss Sojourn; Christmas Every Day; The Unexpected Guests; The World of Chance; The Coast of Bohemia; A Traveler from Altruria; My Literary Passions; The Day of Their Wedding; A Parting and a Meeting; Impressions and Experiences; The Landlord of the Lion's Head; An Open-Eyed Conspiracy; The Story of a Play; Ragged Lady; Their Silver Wedding Journey; Literary Friends and Acquaintance; A Pair of Patient Lovers; Heroines of Fiction; The Kentons; Literature and Life; The Flight of Pony Baker; Questionable Shapes; Miss Ballard's Inspiration; The Son of Royal Langbrith; London Films; Certain Delightful English Towns; Between the Dark and the Daylight; Choice

Autobiographies, with essays (8 vols., edited); Library of Universal Adventure (edited); and Harper's Novelettes (edited, with H. M. Alden); to which are to be added the titles of five volumes of verse: Poems (1867); No Love Lost, a Poem of Travel (1868); Poems (1886); Stops of Various Quills (1895); and The Mother and the Father (a poetic drama, 1909).

List of select poems: "Forlorn," "In Earliest Spring," "Dead," "Clement," "The Captain's Story," "The Movers," "The Burning Tree," "From Generation to Generation," "The Bewildered Guest," "In the Dark," "If," "Solitude," "Respite," "Question," "The Burden," "Calvary," "Society," "Friends and Foes," "Judgment Day," "Someone Else," "Life," "Temperament," "What Shall It Profit?"

JAMES, ALICE ARCHER SEWALL. Author: An Ode to Girlhood, and Other Poems (1899); The Ballad of the Prince (1900). Also, poems and illustrations in Christmas numbers of Harper's, 1893, 1894, 1897, and in the Century, the Cosmopolitan, and other magazines. List of select poems: "Champaign County Centennial Ode," "Sinfonia Eroica," "Youth," "The Inexpressible," "To a New-Born Baby," "The Wedding Gown," "As They Walk in the Pleasant Country," "Say Not Farewell."

JONES, CHARLES A. A small volume by Charles A. Jones, entitled "The Outlaw, and Other Poems," and dedicated to Morgan Neville, was published by Josiah Drake, Cincinnati, in 1835. A few of the author's poems have survived, partly on account of their historical significance, and of these, "Tecumseh," "The Pioneers," and "To an Old Mound," possess considerable literary merit.

KINNEY, COATES. Coates Kinney is the author of three published volumes: Keeuka, and Other Poems (1855); Lyrics of the Ideal and Real (1887); and Mists of Fire, a Trilogy; and Some Eclogs (1899). Chief among his unpublished works are: a novel entitled "A Drama of Doubles;" a philosophical essay, "Unthinkable Data of Human Thought;" and an elaborate speculative poem entitled "Apparitions." Of the author's lyrical productions, those named in the following list are recommended for critical study: "Ships Coming In," "To an Old Appletree," "Our Only Day," "Mars," "Child Lost," "Alone," "Madonna," "Egypt," "Singing Flame," "The Shibboleth," "Emma Stuart," "Rain on the Roof," "Vesuvius," "Aspiration and Inspiration," "The Haunting Voice," "Consummation," "The Last Meeting," "Sea-Sonnets Toward Italy," "The American Citizen," "The Land Redeemed," "My Lord," "Isle of Willows," "A Bird's Autumn Lyric," "Victrice," "Innervale."

APPENDIX

LITTLE, HARVEY D. No complete collection of Harvey D. Little's poems has ever been published. Four lyrics from his pen appear in Coggeshall's The Poets and Poetry of the West (1860).

LYTLE, WILLIAM HAINES. A collection of the poems of William Haines Lytle, edited, with memoir, by W. H. Venable, was published in 1894, by The Robert Clarke Co., under the auspices of Mr. Lytle's sister, Mrs. Josephine R. Foster. Of the many noble lyrics contained in this volume, we would recommend for special study: "Popocatapetl," "Antony and Cleopatra," "Macdonald's Drummer," "Brigand's Song," "Anacreontic," "Jacqueline," "The Volunteers," "In Camp," " 'Tis not the Time," "When the Long Shadows," "The Siege of Chapultepec."

McLAUGHLIN, EDWARD A. Author: The Lovers of the Deep. (Edward Lucas, Cincinnati, 1841.)

MOORE, THOMAS EMMETT. Author: My Lord Farquhar, a Romance. (The Abbey Press, New York, 1902). No collection of poems by Thomas Emmett Moore has yet been published. (See biographical sketch, page 273.)

PIATT, JOHN JAMES. The published works of John James Piatt comprise: Poems of Two Friends (with W. D. Howells, 1860); The Nests at Washington, and Other Poems (with Mrs. Piatt, 1864); Poems in Sunshine and Firelight (1866); Western Windows (1869); Landmarks, and Other Poems (1871); Poems of House and Home (1879); Idyls and Lyrics of the Ohio Valley (1884, 1888, 1893); The Children Out of Doors (with Mrs. Piatt, 1885); At the Holy Well (1887); A Book of Gold, and Other Sonnets (1889); Little New World Idyls, and Other Poems (1893); The Ghost's Entry, and Other Poems (1895); Odes in Ohio, and Other Poems (1897). Two volumes of prose from his pen are: A Return to Paradise (1870), and Pencilled Fly-Leaves (1880). He has edited: The Union of American Poetry and Art (1880), and The Hesperian Tree, An Annual of the Ohio Valley (2 vols., 1900, 1903).

List of select poems: "Cleveland Centennial Ode" (1896), "Honors of War," "The Golden Hand," "The Morning Street," "King's Tavern," "Sonnet to Lincoln," "The Open Slave-Pen," "A Voice in Ohio," "Use and Beauty," "The Three Work-Days," "Taking the Night Train," "Reading the Mile-Stone," "New Grass," "The Pioneer's Chimney," "The Book of Gold," "Anniversary," "Mirage," "The Child in the Street," "At Home," "Sundown," "Farther," "Home

Longing," "A Flower in a Book," "Carpe Diem," "Keeping a Rose's Company," "The Guerdon," "Lost Kingdom of Gods," "Torch-light in Fall-time," "Ode" (written for the occasion of the opening of the Cincinnati Music Hall, in 1878).

PIATT, SARAH MORGAN BRYAN. No one is more appreciative of Mrs. Piatt's genius than her poet-husband, to whom the reading world is indebted for the publication of her verse. A few of her poems appeared in the volume, The Nests at Washington, and Other Poems, issued in Cincinnati, in 1864. Her first independent volume, A Woman's Poems, was published in Boston, in 1871, without the author's name. Then were issued: A Voyage to the Fortunate Isles, and Other Poems (1874); That New World and Other Poems (1876); Poems in Company with Children (1877); Dramatic Persons and Moods (1880); The Children Out of Doors, and Other Poems (with Mr. Piatt, in 1885); An Irish Garland (1885); Selected Poems (1885); In Primrose Time (1886); Child's-World Ballads (1887); The Witch in the Glass (1889); An Irish Wild-Flower (1891); An Enchanted Castle (1893); Complete Poems (2 vols., 1894); and Child's-World Ballads (second series, 1896).

List of select poems: "Transfigured," "Fallen Angels," "A Doubt," "The House below the Hill," "Sometime," "The Thought of Astyanax beside Iulus," "My Wedding Ring," "A Masked Ball," "Leaving Love," "Life and Death," "A Pique at Parting," "Her Word of Reproach," "A Lesson in a Picture," "After the Quarrel," "Caprice at Home," "Comfort — by a Coffin," "Giving up the World," "No Help," "Asking for Tears," "Sad Wisdom — Four Years Old," "Calling the Dead," "Folded Hands," "Reproof to a Rose," "Good-by — A Woman's Song," "The Highest Mountain," "Her Last Gift," "A Sister of Mercy," "Jealous of a Statue," "At the Play," "We Women," "There was a Rose," "Love-Stories," "To be Dead," "In Doubt," "A Look into the Grave," "Little Christian's Trouble," "Say the Sweet Words," "I Want It Yesterday," "The End of the Rainbow," "Last Words," "Marble or Dust," "Stone for a Statue," "Sweet World, if you will hear me now."

PLIMPTON, FLORUS BEARDSLEY. A sumptuous and beautiful memorial volume of F. B. Plimpton's poems, compiled and edited by his widow, with an introduction by Murat Halstead, was published in Cincinnati, in 1886. This collection, to which is prefixed a dedicatory tribute in verse, by Edith M. Thomas, comprises seventy lyrics, all of which possess the vitality and charm of genuine literature. List of select poems: "Morning on Maryland Hights,"

APPENDIX

"Summer Days," "The Reformer," "Pittsburg," "In Remembrance," "Waiting to Die," "Return," "Louis Wetzel," "The Oak," "Souvenirs," "Prayer of Old Age," "Sonnet" ("So delicate and fair"), "The Cricket," "The Universal Robber," "Fort Du Quesne," "A Poor Man's Thanksgiving," "Love's Heralds," "Make It Four, Yer Honor," "The Emigrant's Invitation," "The Morning Prayer," "Her Record," "Sleigh-Ride Song," "Waiting," "In Memory."

READ, THOMAS BUCHANAN. A volume of "Poems" by T. B. Read was published in Boston, in 1847. This was followed by Lays and Ballads, which was issued in Philadelphia, in 1848; and in the same year appeared Read's volume, The Female Poets of America, also issued in Philadelphia. Another volume of "Poems" was published in London, in 1852; and a new edition in Philadelphia in 1853. Then appeared, successively: The New Pastoral (1855); The House by the Sea (1856); Sylvia; or, The Lost Shepherd: an Eclogue, and Other Poems (1857); Rural Poems (1857); The Wagoner of the Alleghanies (1862); A Summer Story, Sheridan's Ride, and Other Poems (1865); Good Samaritans, a Poem (Cincinnati, 1867). A complete edition of Read's poetical works, in two volumes, was issued in Philadelphia, in 1860-62; and, in three volumes, in 1865-67.

A prolific and versatile writer, Thomas Buchanan Read produced many poems of exceptional merit. Perhaps the consensus of criticism would pronounce "Drifting," "The Closing Scene," and "Sheridan's Ride," to be, on the whole, his best lyrics.

SNIDER, DENTON JAQUES. The published prose writings of Denton Jaques Snider comprise: Commentaries on the Literary Bibles (9 vols., 1877-93); A Walk in Hellas (1882); The Freeburgers (a novel, 1889); World's Fair Studies (1895); Commentaries on Froebel's Play-Songs (1895); Psychology and the Psychosis (1896); The Will and Its World (1899); The Psychology of Froebel's Play-Gifts (1900); The Life of Frederick Froebel (1901); The Father of History (1901); Herodotus (1901); Social Institutions (1901); The State (1902); Ancient European Philosophy (1903); Modern European Philosophy (1904); Architecture (1905); and A Tour in Europe (1907). The author's poetical works are comprised in five volumes: Delphic Days (1878); Agamemnon's Daughter (1885); Prorsus Retrorsus (1890); Homer in Chios (1891); and Johnny Appleseed's Rhymes (1894).

SPERRY, WILLIAM JAMES. (See biographical sketch, page 99.)

SYMMES, FRANCES NEWTON. The only collection of poems from the pen of Frances Newton Symmes, thus far published, is a brochure of verse entitled "Brier Bloom," issued from the press of Cranston & Curts, Cincinnati, in 1893. Of the thirty-five poems contained in this collection, those named in the following list are deserving of special mention: "Listening," "Repression," "Heart Stirrings," "Fate," "Moonrise," "March Winds," "Two Thoughts," "In Winter Times," "Ennui," "Too Late," "A Little Lesson," "Roses at Gethsemane," "In the Rain," "To Live," "Wait," "Wishing Weather."

THOMAS, EDITH MATILDA. The published work of Edith M. Thomas, in prose and verse, comprises: A New Year's Masque, and Other Poems (1885); The Round Year (prose, 1886); Lyrics and Sonnets (1887); Children of the Season (prose, 1888); Babes of the Year (prose, 1888); Babes of the Nation (prose, 1889); Heaven and Earth (prose, 1889); The Inverted Torch (1890); Fair Shadow Land (1893); In Sunshine Land (1894); In the Young World (1895); A Winter Swallow, and Other Verse (1896); The Dancers (1903); Cassia, and Other Verse (1905); Children of Christmas (juvenile verse, 1908); The Guest at the Gate (1909).

List of select poems: "At Lethe's Brink," "Dead Low Tide," "Thefts of the Morning," "Syrinx," "Wild Honey," "Vertumnus," "Spirit to Spirit," "A Nocturn," "The Domino," "Avalon — Fair Avalon," "The Bronzes of Epirus," "Delay," "Insulation," "The End of the World," "Migration," "Mother England," "Old World Bells," "The Wind of Spring," "The Tide of the Past," "The Blessèd Present," "When, Muse?" "Revival of Romance," "Reproof from the Muse," "The Breath of Hamstead Heath," "The Grave of Keats," "Over the Brink," "Far Otherwhere," numbers: VI, XVIII, XXVIII, XXIX, XXXIII, LXIV, LXIX (from The Inverted Torch), "Forbearance," "Humility," "A Rainbow," "Insomnia," "A Little Boy's Vain Regret," "Constancy in Change," "To Imagination," "The Old Soul" (Scribner's Mag., Sept., 1907).

THOMAS, FREDERICK WILLIAM. Author: The Emigrant, or Reflections While Descending the Ohio (1833); Clinton Bradshaw (a novel, 1835); East and West (a novel, 1836); Howard Pinkney, (a novel, 1840); The Beechen Tree, a Tale in Rhyme; and Other Poems (1844); Sketches of Character (1849); and John Randolph of Roanoke (1853).

THOMAS, LEWIS FOULKE. Author: Osceola (a drama, 1838); Inda, and Other Poems (1842); and Rhymes of the Routes (1847).

APPENDIX

VENABLE, WILLIAM HENRY. The published writings of W. H. Venable, in prose and verse, comprise: A School History of the United States (1872); June on the Miami, and Other Poems (1872); The School Stage (1873); The Amateur Actor (1874); Dramas and Dramatic Scenes (1874); The Teacher's Dream (illustrated by Farny, 1881); Melodies of the Heart, Songs of Freedom and Faith, and Other Poems (1885); Footprints of the Pioneers (1888); The Teacher's Dream and Other Songs of School-Days (1889); Beginnings of Literary Culture in the Ohio Valley (1891); John Hancock, Educator (1892); Let Him First Be a Man, and Other Essays (1894); Poems of William Haines Lytle (edited, with memoir, 1894); The Last Flight (1894); Tales from Ohio History (1896); Selections from the Poems of Wordsworth (1898); Selections from the Poems of Byron (1898); Selections from the Poems of Burns (1898); Santa Claus and the Black Cat, or Who is Your Master, a Christmas Story (1898); A Dream of Empire, or the House of Blennerhassett (an historical romance, 1901); Tom Tad (a novel of boy-life, 1902); Ohio Literary Men and Women (a centennial sketch, 1903); Saga of the Oak, and Other Poems (1904); Cincinnati: a Civic Ode (1907); and Floridian Sonnets (1909).

List of select poems: "Saga of the Oak," "My Catbird," "We, the People," "The Founders of Ohio," "The Last Flight," "Immortal Birdsong," "Inviolate," "A Gentle Man," "Unreconciled," "Anniversary," "The Teacher's Dream," "The School-Girl," "Johnny Appleseed," "John Filson," "A Ballad of Old Kentucky," "De Foe in the Pillory," "Wagner's Kaiser-March," "National Song," "Viva la Guerra," "El Emplazado," "Coffea Arabica," "A Welcome to Boz," "Hinchman's Mill," "Summer Love," "A Diamond," "The Tunes Dan Harrison Used to Play," "Forest Song," "Wag," "Donatello," "Fairyland," "Amaurote."

WOOLSEY, SARAH CHAUNCEY. The published writings of Sarah Chauncey Woolsey ("Susan Coolidge") comprise: The New Year's Bargain (1871); What Katy Did (a series begun in 1872); Mischief's Thanksgiving, and Other Stories (1874); Nine Little Goslings (1875); For Summer Afternoons (1876); Autobiography and Correspondence of Mrs. Delancey (edited, 1879); Eyebright (1879); The Diary and Letters of Frances Burney (edited, 1880); Verses (1880); A Guernsey Lily (1881); Cross Patch (1881); My Household Pets (translated from Gautier, 1882); A Round Dozen (1883); A Little Country Girl (1885); One Day in a Baby's Life (translated from Arnaud, 1886); A Short History of Philadelphia (1887); Ballads of Romance and History (with others, 1887); Clover

(1888); Just Sixteen (1889); In the High Valley (1891); A Few More Verses (1892); The Barberry Bush, and Other Stories about Girls (1893); Not Quite Eighteen (1894); Old Convent School in Paris (1895); and Last Poems (1906). Fairly representative of Miss Woolsey's poetical work are the lyrics entitled: "Gulf Stream," "Bereaved," "Ashes," "Good-bye," "Bindweed," and "Thorns."